RESEARCH IN GEORGIA

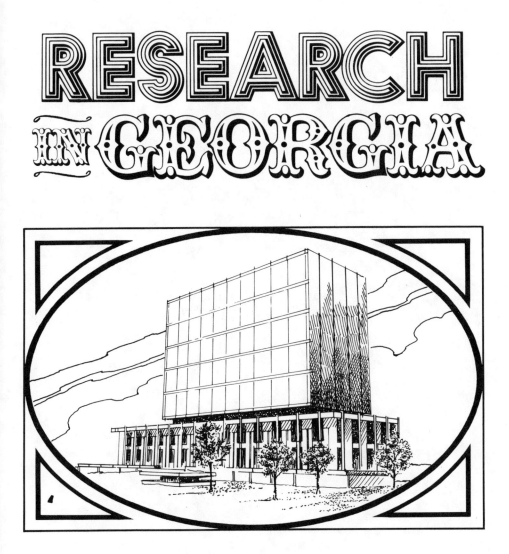

Compiled by
Robert Scott Davis, Jr.

Cover Design by Briane Myers

SOUTHERN HISTORICAL PRESS
c/o The Rev. S. Emmett Lucas, Jr.
P.O. Box 738
Easley, South Carolina 29640

ISBN 0-89308-199-X

Library of Congress Card Catalog Number: 81-50452

DEDICATED TO THE MEMORY OF

BEN W. FORTSON, JR.
Georgia Secretary of State, 1946-1979

and

DR. LEN G. CLEVELAND
Historical Research Advisor,
Georgia Department of Archives and History

In their passing, the Georgia Department of Archives and History lost two of its greatest strengths and I, two friends.

The author would like to express his deep-felt thanks to Kenneth H. Thomas, Jr., of the Georgia Department of Natural Resources for his help in editing this material.

I am not an alarmist, but I come to sound an alarm. If the perishing records of Georgia are to be saved from destruction, the most vital need of our state at this time is a Department of Archives, not a temporary makeshift, but a permanent bureau of history, to constitute within itself a separate and distinct sphere of work and to correlate with other departments of state government. The value of such a bureau will be infinite — its costs infinitesimal. To say that we possess a history worthy of preservation is not an extravagant boast. So rich indeed is the history of our state that in preserving it we should be second to no state in the American Union.

Lucian Lamar Knight (1917), Founder
Georgia Department of Archives and History

BEN W. FORTSON, JR.
State Archives and Records Building
330 Capitol Avenue, SE; Atlanta, Georgia 30334
(Photograph courtesy of the Georgia Department of Archives and History)

ABOUT THE AUTHOR

Robert Scott Davis, Jr., "Bob," was born in Shirley, Massachusetts, on February 14, 1954; the son of Robert Scott Davis, Sr., of Atlanta, Georgia, and Elizabeth Kathleen Holbert Davis, of Jasper, Georgia. Bob received his Bachelor of Arts degree from Piedmont College in 1978 and his Master of Education degree from North Georgia College in 1980. In 1974, he was a history intern with the Historic Preservation Section, Georgia Department of Natural Resources; in 1976, one of the Jaycees' Outstanding Young Men of America; and he has recently been nominated for the "Who's Who" of American Genealogy. He has contributed articles to *Georgia Social Science Journal, South Carolina Historical Magazine, Atlanta Historical Journal, Georgia Baptist Viewpoints, Richmond County History, Georgia Archive,* and for several genealogical periodicals. Among his books are **The Wilkes County Papers, 1773-1833; The Families of Burke County, 1755-1855, a Census; Georgia Citizens and Soldiers of the American Revolution; The Georgia Land Lottery Papers, 1805-1914;** and **Kettle Creek Battle and Battlefield.**

Bob Davis currently resides with his grandmother and brother in Jasper and works as a private researcher.

DEDICATION

For Anita, Tommy, Richard and Susan.
Special appreciation goes to Susan
for her expert help on the manuscript.

CONTENTS

PREFACE

Georgia's records are enormous in volume and complex in nature. Time, geography, politics, and patriotism have all contributed in various ways to the creation and preservation of these documents. So much has survived, and so much that has survived is so out of the ordinary and confusing to the average person that many researchers suffer from "Georgia Shock" — a feeling of being overwhelmed when trying to grasp the basics of research in Georgia.

Georgia, "the Unfinished State" and "Empire State of the South," is the largest of the original thirteen colonies, the largest state east of the Mississippi, and second only to Texas in the number of counties. In fact, some Georgia counties were creating records for a century or more before some states even existed. Because of Georgia's location, this state was one of the major areas where American settlement and migration turned from moving south to west. As a result, many of the famous people and families of the American West had ancestral ties to Georgia. As the settlement of Georgia took place, many records were maintained that were similar to those of other areas, but other forms of official documentation that are unique to Georgia were also created to deal with this state's own particular needs.

Georgia researchers bemoan the fact that certain state records and some records of some counties (notably Burke, Gwinnett, Heard, Twiggs, Washington, and Wilkinson) have been destroyed. However, some substitutes for most of the lost records exist; and when compared with some other southern states, Georgia's losses appear minor. Some state and county records have been discarded — and unfortunately some counties are still throwing out old records — but private individuals often recognized the value of the discarded documents and rescued the records. Today, such papers as those salvaged by Dr. Joseph Toomey and Telamon Cuyler are turning up intact in private hands and in research libraries across the country.

Because Georgia has had so many records to survive, such a long and varied past, and so many counties to inspire local histories, the amount of Georgia genealogical and historical material in print is also immense. Indeed, coming to grips with this mountain of histories, genealogies, compilations of biographical sketches, periodicals, and other publications can be as difficult as trying to understand the state's original records!

The state government of Georgia has spent as much, and probably more, as any other southern state for preserving and making the state's historical and genealogical resources publicly available. However, because so much was created and so much has survived in Georgia, the amount of funding needed for Georgia records is much greater than the amount needed by other states. As a result, some neighboring states appear to have spent more to make their resources available to the genealogist and the historian. However, some have actually done and spent less, but with the dubious advantage of having far fewer surviving research resources. Hence, their expenses were less because they had fewer records to make available.

For all of these reasons, a book like this one — to outline what is available in Georgia and how it can be used in family research — has been needed for a long time. I make no pretense that this work is everything to every researcher or that it is the final word in Georgia research. Hopefully, however, this work will be a beginning for other guides and bibliographies that will answer whatever questions that are not dealt with here. Perhaps this book will also inspire the research public to put greater pressure on the Georgia legislature to do better by the Archives than they have done in the past and on the Archives to expend a greater proportion of its resources on its most important public — the researcher interested in Georgia.

In a sense, I have been working on this book for eight years — since the first time I visited the Georgia Department of Archives and History in 1972 to seek, and obtain, help with a high school time capsule project from the director and the secretary of state. Over the years, a number of people have given me ideas and information that have gone into what you now hold. Thanking them here is too small a token of appreciation for their kind help; particularly Jane Adams, Marilyn Adams, Frances Beckemeyer, Dr. Ed Bridges, Ted O. Brooke, Rod Browning, Pat Bryant, Emily Calhoun, Ruth Corry, Roy Lamar Ector, Elizabeth Fitzpatrick, Mae Ruth Green, Sandy Groover, Marion Hemperley, Eugenia Howard, Margaret Johnsen, Dr. D'Arcy Jones, Audrey Kinney, Frances C. Lane, Silas Emmett Lucas, Jr., Daryl Maroney, Gail Miller, Sally Moseley, Charlotte Ray, Merita Rozier, Peter Schinkel, Leoda Sherry, JoAnne Smalley, Harmon Smith, Gladys Tavenner, Kenneth M. Thomas, Jr., Brigit Townsend, and Mary Bondurant Warren.

A person could spend a lifetime getting to know Georgia through the state's records. I can think of no happier way to spend a lifetime.

Robert S. Davis, Jr.
Jasper, Ga.
November 6, 1980

HISTORY OF THE GEORGIA DEPARTMENT
OF ARCHIVES AND HISTORY

Today the Georgia Department of Archives and History maintains four buildings, employs a full-time staff of over eighty members and houses more than 1500 tons of governmental and historic records in controlled environments. These achievements were unimaginable on July 29, 1918, the day the Georgia House of Representatives defeated a bill to create a department of archives. Lucian Lamar Knight, who wrote the bill, had lost again.

The previous year a similar bill had not made it out of committee, despite the support which Knight had solicited from past, present and future governors, judges of state courts, patriotic societies, and the 500 members of an organization that Knight had recently founded. The Georgia Historical Association had agreed with the speech he gave at their first meeting, "Georgia's Most Vital Need: A Department of Archives."

In that address Knight described offices in the state capitol, so crowded with current paperwork that old records were moved to dark corners or to the basement, exposed to humidity and insects. And he reminded his listeners that the functions of a state archives could not be undertaken by the Office of the Compiler of State Records, which he directed.

Shortly before Knight's speech rare papers had been found in the basement of the capitol, where the janitor had been using them to light the furnace. The need for a central depository of records was obvious; but the Office of Compiler could only publish copies of the records and sell these publications at the State Library.

Yet books for sale are not original records preserved for public use. Knight emphasizes access to the past as a strong argument for a state archives: "Our history ought not to be commercialized, but placed within the reach of all."

Unfortunately neither Knight's speech to the Georgia Historical Association nor the support he organized could sway the legislature. Knight did not quit trying, however. He continued to lobby, perhaps with too much zeal.

"No Brains and No Sense"

The morning after the bill's defeat he tried to convince an antagonistic representative from Spalding County that, at a time when Georgia boys were fighting international battles, the value of preserving historic records should be obvious. Both men grew agitated. The representative said he would never support such nonsense as a state archives. Knight's frustration exploded: he said the representative had "no brains and no sense," then walked away.

Knight was not to escape so lightly. That afternoon, the representative from Spalding told the House that Knight had attempted to coerce his vote and had then insulted him. Speaking of the Compiler, the representative said he would have "dealt with him physically" if Knight had not run away.

"You're a liar!" someone said twice from the gallery. When Knight was discovered, he was placed under house arrest on a charge of disturbance and ordered to appear before the House the next day to explain his outburst.

On the afternoon of August 1, Knight might have given elaborate defenses of his conduct. Instead he apologized to the representative for their misunderstanding and to the House for his intemperence, then espoused his love for Georgia, a love which would ever prevent him from deliberately dishonoring her legislature. He spoke only three minutes, but that proved to be enough.

He was absolved from the charge of disturbance. Then on August 14, 1918, the legislature passed the bill to create a department of archives under guidance of a State Historical Commission. Six days later Governor Dorsey signed the bill into law. On September 10, the State Historical Commission elected the head of the new agency. January 1, 1919, Knight assumed duties as the first State Historian and Director of the Georgia Department of Archives and History, and with one assistant began operations on the third floor of the capitol with a budget of $7200.

Still Scrapping

If Knight thought then that he had secured the new department, he learned otherwise during the next three years. At the next session of the legislature the House held up the appropriations bill to examine the budget of the Archives, and Knight had to defend his work to the general appropriations committee before they continued his funding. In 1921 and 1922 Governor Hardwick, who bore an old political grudge against Knight, supported bills to abolish the Archives. Both years Knight spoke before the judiciary committee and preserved his agency.

Meanwhile the department began tasks which would rapidly expand. Knight and his assistant worked to assemble old records from state agencies, gathered records of Georgia's efforts in the World War and began the department's artifact collection with a Confederate uniform and flag. They published the first state *Statistical Record* and each month, by 1924, answered 150 letters from historians and other researchers.

On January 1, 1925, Knight retired as director, leaving behind a secure department and two recommendations that would ensure the growth of the Archives. Ruth Blair, his assistant since 1919, would succeed him as director, and she would oversee the department's move from crowded offices to the capitol's spacious balconies near the State Library rooms.

New Directions

Blair remained at the new location for five years and continued to compile and catalog state records, as well as expand the department's services. She published early tax digests, recovered a rare signature of Button Gwinnet and began contributing articles to the *Georgia Historical Quarterly*. By 1929 she could review the accomplishments of ten years and announce that the Archives had won the return of valuable state papers, accepted hundreds of private donations and a large group of county records, and built an artifact collection of 200 items. Most importantly, the department had made great progress in compiling and cataloging state records and now possessed 10,000 volumes and 400,000 loose papers. It was ready for the next expansion.

The descendants of A.G. Rhodes, a wealthy Atlanta businessman, offered his large residence as a permanent home for the Archives in early 1929. On May 1, the State Historical Commission unanimously accepted the offer.

The R.G. Rhodes House, home of the Georgia Department of Archives and History from 1930 to 1965, is still maintained by the Archives and is currently being restored.

Changing Times

It began like a fairy tale: in 1930 the Georgia Archives — a tiny Cinderella department among state agencies — moved its books and manuscripts from the crowded balconies of the Capitol to a four-story castle.

It ended as a dreary reality: by the middle '50s squirrels and insects were at the records, and common hazards were water in the basement and falling plaster.

But residence in Rhodes Hall brought growth to the department, and in 1930 Director Ruth Blair was pleased to have suddenly so much space. After a year of making repairs to the building, installing shelving and moving, the department returned to its work on the records of Georgia, yet it never regained the methodical pace that characterized its growth in the late '20s. New responsibilities, budget changes and voluminous additions to its records effected a lurching development for the Archives during the next twenty years.

"Greatly Handicapped"

Blair faced the worst period, as the Depression hit at the peak of the Archives' first large-scale public service project — helping to compile 132 county histories, which were to be deposited in the Archives on Georgia Day, 1933, the 200th birthday of Oglethorpe's colony. Blair wrote that year, however, that service was "greatly handicapped by the loss of four assistants," and the next year the Archives operated with less funds than it had begun with in 1918. Political changes came with the hard times, for under a reorganization act of 1931 the Archives was made a division of the office of secretary of state. On top of these developments appeared a "records explosion" when in three years the department received 320,000 papers from the Executive Department, 84 large drawers of Pardon and Parole Board records and 3000 bulky tax digests.

Through this difficult period, Blair had established the department at a conspicuous location and brought it to the threshhold of large challenges. Following Blair's retirement in 1936, Louise Frederick Hays led a resurgence of work on the records and responded to opportunities during and after World War II. For six years until 1942, the federal Works Progress Administration paid as many as twenty-five workers a year to compile and index the backlog of records. As the WPA project ended another began, when the department started using a Barrow laminator — the most advanced machine for sealing documents in a protective coat of plastic. A second technical service came in 1947, with a reading machine and some microfilm copies of genealogical records. In this period Hays also expanded public education programs. She helped assemble materials for the Georgia Heritage train, which brought documents and artifacts to people throughout the state. And she used radio and newspapers to publicize the value of Georgia's records.

By 1950, twenty years in Rhodes Hall had matured the department, bringing new public and technical services. But perhaps the most significant changes of these years came in the appointment of a new secretary of state and in the hiring of a clerk.

Archival Dreams

In 1933 a young woman had accepted a clerical position, and over the next seventeen years, Mary Givens Bryan worked hard, studied the practices of archives and rose to secretary, assistant director, acting director when Hays fell ill in 1950, and finally director upon the death of Hays the following year.

During this period of training, Bryan developed dreams of what the Archives could be.

She fortunately worked for a secretary of state who was willing to fight for those dreams. Appointed to office after serving in both houses of the state legislature, Ben W. Fortson, Jr., had the influence and determination to work with Bryan on developing a truly great archives program.

Fortson and Bryan began by expanding technical services. They added a large press, a paper cutter and microfilm facilities in Rhodes Hall, then with a program using portable equipment began to microfilm records in county courthouses. At first they had difficulty winning the permission of county clerks, who saw little reason for the Archives to keep microfilmed "security copies." But six months after fire destroyed many Wilkes County courthouse papers, Bryan wrote, "New counties can hardly wait for us to get to their records."

Squirrels and Insects

While increasing technical services, Fortson and Bryan did not neglect their duty to properly house Georgia's records. Yet after the 1,330 volumes and 1,000,000 papers of the state land office were moved into Rhodes Hall in 1951, the department nearly ceased to add to its holdings due to limited space. The castle, so large in 1930, was no longer adequate. Worse, Rhodes Hall was deteriorating. Rain leaked through the roof and walls, and Bryan could not control the squirrels and insects that found Georgia's records much to their taste.

In 1955 Bryan and Fortson went to the public. For three years they used radio, television and newspapers to broadcast their plight, until the legislature approved a new building. Governor Griffin, however, left office without granting construction funds, and new Governor Vandiver set tight budgets. When Bryan had to cut staff members, it seemed unlikely that the governor would spend millions for a new building.

Yet Bryan kept up her publicity campaign. Patriotic women's societies joined the effort, as did others who understood the value of historic records. Veterans' organizations, the Georgia National Guard, lawyers, county commissioners, education and press associations, museum and university groups, the Lions, the Optimists, the League of Women Voters, the Georgia Federation of Women's Clubs, and church groups throughout the state, all realized the need for a new Archives' building. When in addition the Governor's Commission on Economy and Reorganization recommended construction, Bryan finally won $300,000 for architectural plans after five years of pushing.

Her patient work since her days as a clerk was beginning to earn rewards. As the whirlwind of publicity was winning a new building, Bryan was gaining a professional reputation with memberships and offices in historical, genealogical and archival groups, including the presidency of the Society of American Archivists, 1959-60.

In her presidential address she spoke on "Changing Times," on the need for archives to enter a modern phase, with computers and other technologies, while maintaining a broad historic perspective.

For her, it was a familiar topic, and following her speech she renewed efforts to escort the Archives into the technological era. At last in 1961 the legislature gave $6,000,000 for a new building, with adequate space, controlled environments, a modern laboratory for restoring documents and a records management program.

Delays and Burdens

It seemed that Bryan would realize her dreams. Yet overseeing construction of the building meant consultation on building plans with the national and many state archives, it meant a swarm of furniture and office equipment salesmen, it meant publicity which brought more research requests and visitors, while Bryan struggled to manage, by 1963, the department's 90,000 volumes and 4,000,000 papers.

Construction delays mounted and Bryan's health suffered. In June, 1963, a crane crashed into an elevator shaft, further slowing the work. In July Bryan had to enter a hospital, yet she returned to such long hours that by October she complained of being "nearly dead with all the demands." Over the next year she saw progress on construction but also felt her burdens, until she wrote in May, 1964, that "the new building is nearing completion, and I am so weary . . . I wonder if I will live to see it dedicated."

Her fears were justified. In early July she again entered a hospital, where she died two weeks later.

But the dream lived on, with Bryan's assistant named to head the Archives in August. The next year Carroll Hart would move the department into the Archives and Records Building for which Mary Bryan had given her time and health.

Active Service

From occupying a new building to applying current technologies, the Archives during the last decade and a half has pursued its central mission of preserving Georgia's records. As the state has changed, with social tumult and the growth of science and government, so has the Archives. Today's responsibility to safeguard records includes a duty to offer many active services.

A Photogenic Building

But before expanding services, the department first underwent a lengthy adjustment to its new home, officially dedicated in October, 1965. That ceremony inaugurated a period of increased public visibility, the number of visitors to the department doubling in one year. Photographers used the Archives and Records Building as a backdrop for women's fashions. An advertising agency distributed a display on the Archives to Atlanta shopping malls. *Radio Free Europe* broadcast an interview with Director Carroll Hart.

While the department's headquarters attracted the public eye, its reputation rippled through professional circles. The Archives hosted the first meeting of what became the South Atlantic Archives and Records Conference. Shortly after came a joint meeting of the Society of American Archivists and the American Association for State and Local History, with 500 archivists and historians from across the nation in attendance. And in 1967 the department held its first annual Archives Institute, offering four weeks of professional training to its own staff and to beginning archivists from other institutions.

A solid reputation in its own field and public exposure helped to identify the Archives with its new building, yet truly capping this period of adjustment were achievements in collecting and referencing the records of Georgia. The Archives' Civil War Section completed a three-year project of arranging Pension Office and Roster Commission Papers. Mobile camera operators finished the enormous task of microfilming county courthouse records created before 1900. Revolutionary War records were inventories, and the original acts of the state general assembly from 1750 to 1799 were given restoration treatment. In addition, the Archives again demonstrated the practical value of its work by supplying records of the state-owned W & A Railroad depot in Chattanooga, Tennessee, that in 1970 helped to settle a legal dispute in Georgia's favor.

Exploding Records

Yet even as the department was proving itself in its new location, demands for more services rose. One problem was dramatically symbolized when Civil War cannonballs donated in 1931 were discovered to be still live, and demolition experts from Fort McPherson were called in to remove and detonate the charges. That left the Archives facing the other type of records explosion, as a preliminary records survey in state agencies brought the department seventeen tons of paper in two years. And in startling fashion, the number of patrons more than tripled from 1965 to 1970, while requests for photocopies of records shot from 10,000 to over 200,000.

More troubling to Carroll Hart and her staff, however, was the task of salvaging historically valuable documents from burgeoning state records. The need for efficient control over state paperwork had multiplied since the mid '50s, when former Archives' Director Mary Bryan and the late Secretary of State Ben Fortson had planned for a records management program. By the late '60s, state and county agencies were calling the Archives for assistance. In response, the department held records management workshops in 1968. But that same year the Archives' first attempt to win legal authority for a full program failed; some state officials, unaware of how responsibilities of archivists and records managers dovetail, saw the program as one that might be administered separately. Only after two years of gaining authority in small increments did the Archives win funding for a records management program and the right to advise highly populated counties on the needed procedures.

From Act to Reaction

During the program's initial years, staff conducted volume inventories of records in state and Fulton County administrative offices; assisted twenty divisions of government with paperwork management; began issuing monthly *Records Management Bulletins;* and worked on a records center in the Archives' first basement vault. Yet more could be done to encourage economical records keeping among state agencies, and in 1972 Governor Carter's reorganization of state government produced the Georgia Records Act, which clarified the right of agencies to use new techniques, such as conversion of paper records to microfilm, and which added clout to the whole management program.

The effects of this law were quickly registered: between 1971 and 1974, the Archives' total holdings went from 25,000 to 77,000 cubic feet, while reference requests, as agencies now called the records center when they needed files from previous years, rose from 21,000 to 124,000. The program developed new facets as well, from regularly training state and county personnel to microfilming state superior court records. Today the Archives manages an efficient warehousing operation at the new records center, boasts specialists in economical record keeping procedures, and offers training, storage and financial savings to government agencies throughout the state.

Bursts and Sprouts

Even as the records management program has expanded, the department has undertaken new efforts in other areas. Responding to 1975 federal legislation that required tighter protection of confidential and vital records, the

xvii

department revamped its building security system. As the Bicentennial burst over Georgia, the Archives contributed to workshops on local history, sent exhibitions across the state, and hosted both the Georgia Studies Symposium of state historians and a display of Currier and Ives' works on "The Story of the Revolution." That same year the department served reporters and political researchers who combed through presidential candidate Jimmy Carter's gubernatorial papers. When Alex Haley's *Roots* sprouted a bumper crop of genealogical interest, the Archives offered a series of workshops on black family history. With the spread of county microfilming programs, the department has fulfilled ever more requests for technical assistance. Responding to other technological developments, the Archives annually invites public discussion of such topics as tape-recorded oral history or the computer's role in archives, these workshops in "20th Century Documentation" a part of the Archives Institute.

As a state archives, the department appreciates the recognition it has received both from the people of Georgia and from professional organizations. In 1973 the state celebrated May 12 as "Archives Day." In 1977 the Society of American Archivists bestowed its Distinguished Service Award. Both honors measure, in a manner statistics alone cannot gauge, the Archives' growing responsibilities as an administrative arm of state government and the evolution of its mission to preserve state records, be they parchments inscribed 200 years ago or electromagnetic signals registered tomorrow.

1

PREPARING FOR YOUR RESEARCH

SAVING GEORGIA RECORDS

You can help save valuable Georgia records — all it takes is a letter. The Georgia Department of Archives & History is considering the merits of finding space, money, and personnel to bring in Georgia's pre-1900 loose county records, pre-1900 bound volumes that have not previously been microfilmed, and pre-1940 newspapers from the state's courthouses and having these papers microfilmed before returning them to their respective counties. These microfilm copies would be available to the general public at the Georgia Archives. This project will require resources that the Archives is short on, particularly money, but these problems can be overcome by starting with what the Archives can provide and later seeking an appropriation from the legislature, the governor's emergency fund, or private and government grants. The Georgia Department of Archives & History must be persuaded, however, that this effort is worthwhile. All persons interested in saving the old records of Georgia's counties are encouraged to write to the addresses given below, asking that this project be started as soon as possible.

Among the kinds of records being found in these loose papers are many which do not have surviving copies anywhere else; such as county copies of state and federal census records, tax digests, records of students of poor schools, and lists of Revolutionary War soldiers and other persons who participated in the land lotteries but whose names do not appear on the published lists of winners. Marriage bonds and estate records that were missed in compiling the bound books of public record or were copied into books of record that have not survived have also been discovered in these papers. Many original deeds have also survived in this way, to be used for comparison against the often garbled or incomplete copies in the copied (and recopied, as they wore out) books of record. The plaintiffs' petitions, evidence books, and interrogatories (written testimony from distant witnesses) that would be included in this project are a valuable source of personal and historical data.

Unfortunately, such records, together with county copies of local newspapers, are the papers most often destroyed by county officials to conserve space. They are also the ones to which the public is most often denied access because officials do not like to take the time to allow researchers the opportunity of using the areas where these materials are stored. The records are often kept in old buildings that have, in the last two decades, been lost in fires

2 / *Research In Georgia*

at an alarming rate. Only by having such material microfilmed by the Department of Archives can the information they contain be protected and the public guaranteed access.

Please encourage your friends to join you in writing to any or all of the following officials to push for having the pre-1900 loose county records, the pre-1900 bound volumes that have not been microfilmed, and the pre-1940 newspapers in Georgia's courthouses microfilmed.

Additionally, the Georgia Archives has microfilm of county records of Georgia counties created after 1900 that they have not made available in the Microfilm Library. The Archives mistakenly believes that the demand for this microfilm is not great enough to merit the cost of processing it. Actually, the demand has not been greater only because the researchers have been unaware that the Archives had microfilmed the records of the post-1900 counties. The Georgia Archives should be encouraged to make this microfilm as available as the microfilm of the records of the counties created before 1900.

> David B. Poythress
> Secretary of State
> State Capitol
> Atlanta, Georgia 30334
>
> Carroll Hart, Director
> Ga. Dept. of Archives & History
> 330 Capitol Avenue, SE
> Atlanta, Georgia 30334
>
> Governor George Busbee
> State Capitol
> Atlanta, Georgia 30334

And your state senator and house member.

Saving YOUR Georgia Records Forever. The Georgia Department of Archives & History accepts donations of Georgia-related manuscripts, church records, newspapers, and genealogical and historical books. The Department is also happy to receive contributions of family records and typed family histories, which they place in their genealogical folders collection. In this way, some individuals who never publish family histories may preserve their research for the use of others.

The Department of Archives will borrow original records for microfilming. The microfilm copies are placed in their Microfilm Library for use by the public, and the original records are returned to their owner. There is no charge for this service.

Persons interested in loaning or donating material to the Archives should write to the Director, Georgia Department of Archives & History, 330 Capitol Avenue, SE, Atlanta, Georgia 30334.

WHAT TO KNOW BEFORE STARTING YOUR RESEARCH

Contacting Family Members. Before you begin digging into Georgia records for your family tree, get as much information on your family's past as you can from relatives, Bible records, and family papers. When seeking information, in person or by mail, ask not only for basic data such as names, dates, relationships, and places; but also try to get "family stories" or background data on occupations, religion, politics, military service, wealth, status, or nationality of your ancestors **and their kin** (brothers, sisters, uncles, aunts, cousins, etc.). This information will not only add some color to your family history, but can also be used to find valuable genealogical data in Georgia records. For example, the Georgia Archives has records that can be used for finding data on your family if you have an ancestor or relative who was an Indian, a minister, a slave owner, a Loyalist, a goldminer, a murder victim, a convict, an asylum inmate, a carpetbagger, a legislator, or in any of several other categories. As you obtain data on family members, you can also check these same records for interesting facts or new avenues of research.

Before visiting Georgia libraries and archives or using this book extensively, write down all you know about your family tree and keep this information with you for quick reference when doing research. The "how to" booklets listed elsewhere in this book suggest the better ways of conducting interviews or writing inquiries and some of the best methods for easy record and note keeping. It is a good idea to write or call prior to your planned visit to make sure the facility will be open. Specific days that archives and libraries (particularly college libraries) are closed vary from institution to institution, year to year, and sometimes even from month to month.

Before beginning your Georgia research or using this book to answer specific questions that you may already have, sit down with this book and carefully read it from cover to cover, making notes about specific records and avenues of research of which you are interested. Every "rule" in Georgia research has exceptions, and being aware of all of these "buts" and "maybes" from the beginning can save time, trouble, and expense.

Surrogate Researching. The Georgia Archives and other research libraries **do not conduct research by telephone** and generally will answer only very simple, specific, and basic questions by mail. For best results, include a self-addressed stamped envelope at least 4 x 9½ inches before folding (this is the standard size for mailing pamphlets, handouts, etc.).

Libraries and archives that issue lists of persons who do research for a fee (professional researchers) usually do not guarantee the qualifications and the quality of the researchers' work. The client must decide which researcher to hire and if the work was satisfactory.

What Is Not Available. The Georgia Archives and other libraries do not have a giant, all-inclusive index to Georgia records. Such an index does not exist here, in Washington D.C., or in Utah. Most facilities have only very broad and general catalogues to their holdings. These finding aids vary considerably in detail, completeness, and quality.

Because of budget, the book collection at the Archives is grossly incomplete, even on Georgia works. The Department also does not have copies of all family histories, cemetery records, newspapers, church records, or any other type of Georgia records. Concentrating its public holdings on pre-1900 records, many of the Archives' later records are not open and available to the public.

Obtaining the birth certificate of anyone but yourself, your children, or wards is all but legally impossible in Georgia. Death certificates, however, often contain much of the same information and are generally available through the Vital Records Unit, Georgia Department of Human Resources. These are discussed in detail later.

Exceptions. All records, no matter how official, old, or original, can have errors. Particularly notorious for mistakes are federal census records.

When applied to most original records, and some books as well, the word "index" usually means that the names are merely grouped according to the first letter of the surname. This is an example of how some names might appear under the letter "A" in an index to a deed book:

— A —

Ansley, Thomas
Abbott, John
Allen, Robt.
Anthony, Frederick
Allen, Robert
Abot, John S.

Note that "Abbott, John" and "Abot, John S." may or may not be the same person.

By law and by tradition, marriage records in Georgia are filed in the **bride's county of residence**. The most common exceptions to this rule are mail-order brides and elopements. However, it is still common to find that the couple filed their marriage license in the bride's county even when they eloped. When checking other counties for marriage records, be sure not to overlook counties in adjoining, nearby states.

In some wills, some or all of the children of the testator (the person who made the will) are not named. In fact, sometimes even the existence of children is not mentioned. The latter is particularly true when the unmentioned children are adults and/or are the children of a previous marriage.

Even though there seems to be no logical reason for this, sometimes information on a family can be found in records and histories of counties adjoining the family's county of residence. When checking the data of neighboring counties, remember those in adjoining states.

Abstracts of records published in books or genealogical magazines sometimes only include information on persons or families the compiler was interested in, and references in these same records to other families or persons are omitted. Such editing (commonly called "selective genealogy"), is almost never indicated by the compiler. Some compilers also "correct" spellings of names because they **believe or want to believe** that the correct spelling is different from what the actual record states. Such "corrections" are sometimes wrong, and usually no indication is given in the book or article that the name appears differently on the original record. Abstracts of cemetery and deed records are particularly notorious for all of these problems.

Other Aids. Many researchers find that having a Georgia state highway map with them is useful when doing research in Georgia records. Such maps are indexed for easy reference and can be useful in locating communities and learning the names of neighboring towns and counties near where a family lived and where useful records might be found. The maps are free from Georgia

Welcome Centers and are also available at the Georgia Department of Archives and History. They can be ordered by mail from the Georgia Department of Transportation, 2 Capitol Square, Atlanta, Georgia 30334. The Ga. DOT also **sells** road maps for individual counties. These are particularly useful because they show the present locations of existing churches and cemeteries.

After a county loses records in a natural disaster, personal copies of wills and deeds are often used to re-record some lost documents. Researchers should always check the oldest surviving deed and will books and/or the first will and deed books after the loss of the records in such a county for re-recorded deeds and wills regardless of the dates shown for these books of record. In some counties, re-recorded records date as early as sixty years before the destruction of the original recorded copies.

Despite the pitfalls, research in Georgia is possible and is often exciting — not to mention a good deal of fun. Luck is always with you and can even be a valuable research tool. You meet some most interesting people — both inside and outside of the records.

DEPARTMENT GUIDE — Archives & History

Address — 330 Capitol Avenue, SE, Atlanta, Georgia 30334. Phone 404/656-2393.

Hours — 8 a.m. to 4:30 p.m. Monday through Friday; 9:30 a.m. to 3:30 p.m. Saturday.

Days Closed — All Sundays; most federal holidays; and Georgia's state holidays except when the legislature is in session. Researchers should write or call the Archives before making a visit as the days it is closed vary from year to year.

Directions — The Archives building is on Capitol Avenue, near the corner of Capitol Avenue and Memorial Drive.

When arriving in Atlanta from the East on Interstate 20, take Exit 24 — **Capitol Avenue and Memorial Drive** — and you will be right at the Archives building.

When arriving in Atlanta from the West on Interstate 20, drive under Capitol Avenue and take Exit 25 — **Hill Street-Stadium.** Turn left onto Hill Street and drive back onto Interstate 20. You will now be driving west instead of east. Immediately take Exit 24 — **Capitol Avenue and Memorial Drive.** You will then be right at the Archives.

When arriving in Atlanta from the South on Interstates 75 & 85, take Exit 91 — **Capitol Avenue** — and turn left. The Archives building will be one block north on the right.

When arriving in Atlanta from the North on Interstates 75 & 85, take Exit 93 — and turn right onto Martin Luther King Jr. Drive and then drive two blocks to Washington Street (in front of the State Capitol building) and turn left. Drive one block south and turn left onto Mitchell Street. Immediately turn right onto Capitol Avenue. The Archives will be two blocks south on the left; but because no left turns are allowed at the Archives building, you must pass the building and drive two blocks further south to the Atlanta stadium parking, turn left into their parking lot, and turn

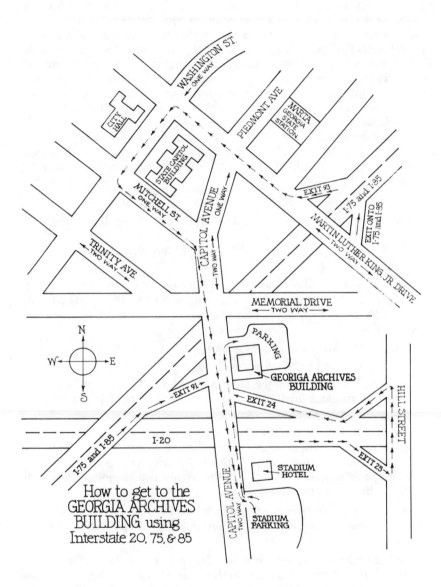

How to get to the
GEORGIA ARCHIVES
BUILDING using
Interstate 20, 75, & 85

around. Returning north on Capitol Avenue, you can make a right turn into the Archives' parking lot.

Parking — Available at the Archives building until 6:00 p.m. except on Sunday. Fee is $1.00 per day.

Facilities for the Handicapped — Access to the Archives building for persons in wheelchairs is possible through the lower entrance on weekdays (elevator service), but they must be assisted in entering the building through the front entrance on weekends. Special restroom facilities for the handicapped do not presently exist anywhere in the building, and there are no special facilities for the blind or sight impaired.

Lodging — The Stadium Hotel, currently operated by Best Western, has the nearest accommodations. It is on Capitol Avenue, one block south of the Archives. For hotel/motel information in the Atlanta area contact:

> Tourist Information
> Atlanta Convention and Business Bureau
> 233 Peachtree Street, NE, Suite 200
> Atlanta, Georgia 30043   Phone: 404/659-4270

Public Transportation — Metropolitan Atlanta Rapid Transit Authority (MARTA) buses arrive regularly just outside the Archives building at the corner of Capitol Avenue and Memorial Drive. Visitors should contact MARTA for bus information, explaining where they will be staying and that they would like to go to the Capitol/Memorial stop.

> MARTA Schedule Information
> 401 W. Peachtree Street, 2200 Peachtree Summit
> Atlanta, Georgia 30365   Phone 404/522-4711

The Georgia State Station of the East-West line of MARTA's rapid rail system is only two blocks north of the Archives building. Walk south from the station on Piedmont Avenue, cross Martin Luther King Jr. Drive, and continue south on what is then Capitol Avenue. The Archives building is two blocks south on the left.

Copying Costs — Photostatic copies range in cost from 10¢ per copy on the self-service copier in the Central Research Library to a maximum of $3 per page in the Microfilm Library. Photostatic copies of some federal and private records are prohibited.

Interlibrary Loan — The Georgia Department of Archives & History does not participate in any form of interlibrary loan.

DEPARTMENT GUIDE — Surveyor General

Address — Same as for the Department of Archives & History.
Phone — 404/656-2367
Hours — 8 a.m. to 4:30 p.m. Monday through Friday
Days Closed — All Saturdays and Sundays; all holidays that the Department

of Archives and History is closed.

Directions — On floor 2V of the same building that houses the Archives.

RESEARCH CHECKLIST

The following list was prepared to itemize the major genealogical sources at the Georgia Archives. Researchers may want to copy this checklist and make notations on the copy before making a trip to the facility.

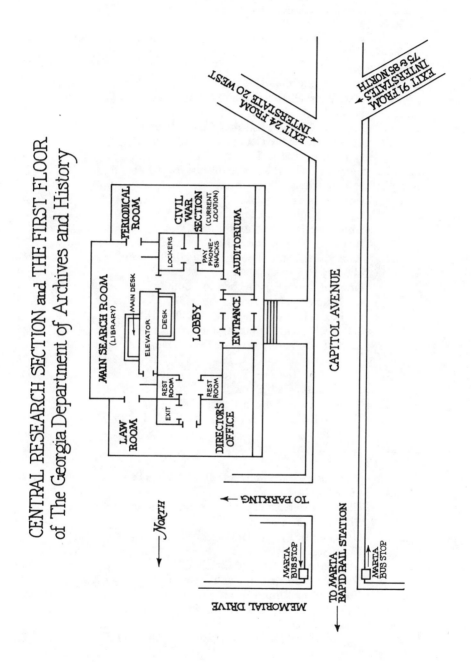

CENTRAL RESEARCH SECTION and THE FIRST FLOOR
of The Georgia Department of Archives and History

2

CENTRAL RESEARCH LIBRARY

LIMITATIONS

Because the Archives has a very limited budget for buying books and has, consequently, had to rely heavily on donations from patrons for much of its book collection, the Central Research Library does not have many of the published works on Georgia. Their collection of family histories is particularly "hit or miss." In fact, the Archives does not have some works found at almost any large local library in Georgia. Additionally, the Archives does not have complete sets of some series of books. They have some series of books with volumes from two or more different editions. However, they also have some very unique volumes that can be found nowhere else in Georgia. Researchers should be aware that the library's card catalogue is very incomplete. Also, books shown in the card catalogue as being on the shelf may be somewhere else. Patrons having trouble locating a particular book should ask the library staff for assistance.

Researchers should consider writing to local or regional libraries in Georgia, visiting the University of Georgia libraries in Athens, or consulting the bibliographies listed elsewhere in this book for specific works in their areas of interest in Georgia research.

The Georgia Department of Archives and History welcomes additions to their collection of books of interest to Georgia researchers. Contributions of books or money for buying books for the Archives through the Georgia Genealogical Society, P.O. Box 38066, Atlanta, Ga. 30334, are tax deductible.

FREE PAMPHLETS AND PUBLICATIONS FOR SALE

The Department of Archives & History offers several free pamphlets and handouts on Georgia research which can be obtained in person or by mail. Researchers should be aware that these materials are often out of date or inaccurate. The booklet on their Civil War Records Section is complete and accurate (barring any major changes in that section in the near future), although it does not describe the Civil War collections in other parts of the Archives. A guide to researching Revolutionary War ancestors in Georgia (including at the Georgia Archives) is in Part 1 of **Georgia Citizens and Soldiers of the American Revolution** by this author and published in 1979 in Easley, South Carolina, by the Southern Historical Press.

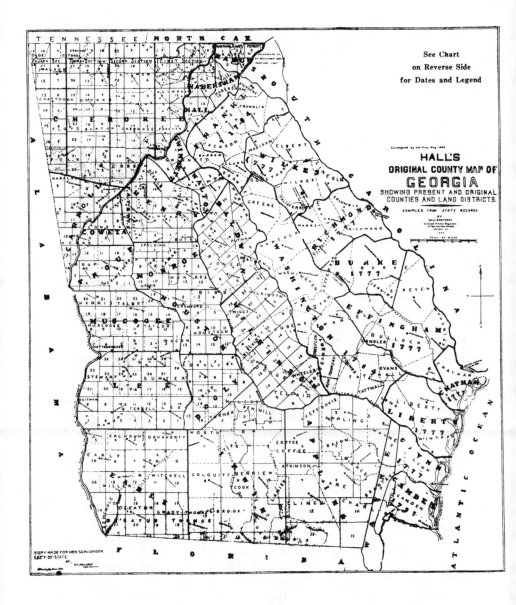

The Archives offers for sale some catalogues to their manuscript collections. In late 1981, they will have such a catalogue to their Indian records. Listed below are the publications they currently sell. **Prices are subject to change.**

Colonial Records of the State of Georgia. Comp. by Allen D. Candler. 1904-1916, vols. 1-14, 16-17, 21, 23, 25-26. Hard cover, $50.00 per volume.

Revolutionary Records of the State of Georgia. Comp. by Allen D. Candler. 1908, 3 vols. Hard cover, $50.00 per volume.

Roster of the Confederate Soldiers of Georgia, 1861-1865. Comp. by Lillian Henderson. 59-64-CW-1, 6 vols. Hard cover, $7.50 per volume.

Georgia's Official and Statistical Register, 1923-(present). Since 1952 issued biennially; some back volumes available. 1977-1978 volume, hard cover, $43.00.

Microfilm Records: Black History. 73-ML-1, 27 pp. Paper, $1.00.

Hall's Original County Map of Georgia Showing Present and Original Counties and Land Districts; Compiled from State Records. 1895. Available in two sizes: 8½" x 11", $1.00; 25" x 28", $2.00.

Women's Records: A Preliminary Guide. 1978, 84 pp. Paper, $2.00.

BOOKS

For several years, the library has been organized, right to left around the room from the front entrance, as follows:

† Books of patriotic societies and DAR typescripts of family, church, Bible, cemetery, census, and county records. These books are arranged by society, county, and subject. The typescripts (not the notebooks) of the DAR's McCall Genealogical Collection has a family name index (vol. 30A by Dr. Jessie Mize). The Archives has a card catalogue to some of the DAR typescripts and has Mary G. Bryan, **Catalogue of Georgia Society, DAR Library in the Georgia Department of Archives and History** (Atlanta: Georgia Department of Archives and History, 1956). An index to the DAR typescripts is currently being prepared.

† Family histories and genealogies, arranged alphabetically by the major family name in each book. The archives does not have every printed Georgia Genealogy.

† Books on Georgia counties and towns, including published and unpublished county, town, and church histories; abstracts of county and cemetery records; and census records by county. These books are arranged generally by county. Those on Atlanta are kept on the shelf separately.

† Books on Georgia in general, including published abstracts of the records of land lotteries, land grants, colonial Georgia, newspapers, church minutes, and compilations of biographical sketches.

† Books on other states, arranged by state.

† Biographies and typescripts of diaries, including many Georgians.

† Books on research in foreign countries.

† Guides and catalogues of other libraries and archives in America and abroad.

• **Note:** Published general indexes to Georgia census records and other important books are kept at the main desk and may be requested there. Some new books are not kept at their proper place on the shelf but on a special shelf by the windows. Volumes cited in the card catalogue but which cannot be found on the shelves or any of the above may be on the desks of staff members or stolen. Ask for assistance in locating any book you cannot find on the shelves. The general indexes to census records of other states are kept at a small table near the center of the room. The Archives' Library has the following published statewide census indexes:

> Alabama — 1820, 1830, 1840, 1850
> Arkansas — 1830, 1840
> Connecticut — 1790
> Delaware — Reconstructed 1790
> Florida — 1830, 1850
> Georgia — Substitute for 1790, 1820, 1830, 1840 (2), 1850
> Kentucky — Substitute for 1790, 1800, 1810
> Louisiana — 1810, 1820
> Maine — 1790
> Maryland — 1790
> Massachusetts — 1790
> Michigan — 1850
> Mississippi — 1820, 1830, 1850
> Missouri — 1830
> New Hampshire — 1790
> New York — 1790, 1800
> North Carolina — 1784-87, 1790, 1800, 1810, 1820, 1830
> Pennsylvania — 1790, 1800
> Rhode Island — 1774, 1790
> South Carolina — 1790, 1800, 1810, 1820, 1830, 1840, 1850
> Tennessee — 1820, 1830
> Texas — 1810, 1829-36, 1840, 1850
> Vermont — 1790, 1800
> Virginia — 1790, 1810, Supplement to 1810, 1820

The Microfilm Library has a copy of **Virginia Tax Payers, 1782-87, Other Than Those Published by the United States Census Bureau,** by Augusta B. Fothergill and John Mack Naugle (n.p., 1940).

The Central Research Library has a number of bound typescripts of private and county records; published books that have additional information or corrections written in the margin, or related newspaper clippings pasted inside the covers; and typescripts of Georgia state records prepared by the WPA. These special books and typescripts are intermixed with the other books in the library, with no separate catalogue or guide and usually no indication on their covers of their special contents. The typescripts prepared by the WPA include:

† Comprehensive indexes to the **Colonial Records** and the **Revolutionary Records of the State of Georgia**. This index does **not** cover the unpublished volumes of the **Colonial Records** which are, however, indexed separately.

† Unpublished volumes of the **Colonial Records of the State of Georgia** series. Indexed. These volumes are being published by Dr. Kenneth Coleman and Dr. Milton Ready through the University of Georgia Press.

† "Georgia Military Affairs," 9 volumes of early, loose Georgia military rosters and related records from 1775 through 1842. Indexed.

† "Georgia Military Record Book," vol. 1, 1779-1839. Similar to "Georgia Military Affairs," but based on a handwritten manuscript rather than loose papers. Later volumes of this series are available on microfilm in the Microfilm Library under "Georgia Official Records." Indexed.

† "Passports Issued by Georgia Governors, 1785-1820," by Louise F. Hays, but later published by Mary G. Bryan through the National Genealogical Society. These are passports issued to Georgians wishing to settle in other areas of **America**. Indexed.

† "Indian Depredations," 5 volumes, in 8 typescript books, of property losses sustained by Georgians, usually as a result of Creek Indian raids. Some of these records include lengthy depositions about battles with the Creeks during the American Revolution and later. Indexed.

† "Cherokee Indian Letters," "Creek Indian Letters," and related volumes of usually executive correspondence dealing with the Indians and Georgia. These typescripts include some information on white men with Indian families. Indexed.

† "Typescripts of early legislative minutes and governors letterbooks." These typescripts include personal information in petitions to the legislature and requests for payment for services and property losses during the American Revolution. Indexed.

Many of the original loose papers (up to 60% in some instances) used in compiling the above typescripts cannot now be located. It is believed that most of them are filed in various record groups still in the Archives.

MANUSCRIPT COLLECTION

People File or Vertical File. The Central Research Library, or Main Search Room, has an alphabetical card file containing hundreds of thousands of names of individuals and families. These cards serve as a rough index to:

† Genealogical and family history folders at the Archives. (The Archives accepts donations of copies of family records and typed manuscripts of family histories for these folders.)

† Correspondence with early Georgia governors and directors of the Georgia Department of Archives and History.

† Some of the personal data in early Georgia laws and legislative minutes.

† Some of the military records.

† Some of the early loose civil and military commissions.

To see a document described on one of these cards, a request must be made at the main desk in the library. These cards also contain some genealogical data, which is not always accurate, and individual public service records.

• **Note**: If the staff is unable to find a petition or letter dated in the 1700s or early 1800s to which you find a citation in this card catalogue, the document may be on microfilm in the Microfilm Library under Georgia Official Records, Executive Department, Pre-1800 Correspondence. This microfilm includes most of the pre-1800 documents, other than military records, sent to the Georgia government (not just governors). **Microfilmed with these records were any other loose papers sent to the Georgia government by the same persons during and after 1800**. All of these records were taken out of their folders and placed in storage since patrons could now see them on microfilm.

County and Subject Files, File II. The Archives also has file folders on Georgia counties and on certain general topics, such as Negro history. No catalogue or list of these files is available to the public. To check for these files, researchers should submit a list of counties and/or topics they are interested in to the main desk in the library; the Archives staff will then check to see if they have files on any of the requested topics. Some files on individuals not mentioned in the People File or Vertical File must be sought in the same way, such as the files of loose papers relating to Elijah Clarke.

Contained within these files are miscellaneous assortments of original loose papers, correspondence with the Archives, pamphlets, newspaper and magazine clippings, transcripts of-private and county records, church records (usually filed by county), and much more.

The Kenneth H. Thomas, Jr., file in this collection contains a complete set of his newspaper columns on genealogy from **The Atlanta Journal-Constitution** (which started in 1977).

Private Manuscripts. The library also has a separate card catalogue to private manuscript collections. These records consist of letters, diaries, genealogical collections, legal papers, and much more from almost every period of Georgia history, but particularly the 1800s. This card catalogue is poorly cross referenced, when cross referenced at all. Also, it **does not** include private collections in the Civil War Records Section and the Microfilm Library. Manuscript collections in this catalogue must be requested through the Archives staff.

Genealogical Exchange Cards. The library also has a separate card file for their genealogical exchange program. Researchers fill out cards that are provided free by the Archives (up to five cards will be provided per request by mail) requesting information on specific persons or families. These cards are then filed alphabetically in a card catalogue that is open to the public in the Archives library. See the example on the next page.

The obverse of this card may be filled out with information on the family you are researching.

This card will be placed in the Archives card catalog for the convenience of those researching the same families.

If you wish to complete this card and give it to the librarian in the Search Room, it will be placed in the file for you.

PLEASE USE INK

AR 78-25

Name of family being researched

Ancestor:

Who settled in, State:
County:
Time period:

Contact:

Name _____

Street _____

City, State, Zip _____

Telephone: Date:

GA. DEPT. OF ARCHIVES AND HISTORY

LAW ROOM

Published copies of Georgia state laws, digests, codes, supreme court cases, and legislative minutes can be found in a small room adjoining the Main Search Room. These books contain a great deal of personal information, such as early divorces and name changes. For a bibliography of published records from these books, see Chapter 11. The People File or Vertical File in the Central Research Library serves as an index to some of the personal data in the laws and legislative minutes.

This small room also contains the two volumes of **Georgia Decisions**, abstracts of some early Georgia superior court cases (1805-1843); and the multi-volume **Georgia Reports**, abstracts of state supreme court cases beginning in 1846. The originals of the supreme court case papers are at the

Archives and are available through the Historical Research Advisor, as is the docket listing the cases. The original court case papers include documents not published in **Georgia Reports**. Most of these supreme court cases are not of great research value; however, others contain detailed personal data, information on counties or states of previous residence, and copies of wills and other legal documents from counties that have lost the original records in fires.

• **Note**: The Archives does not have copies of all Georgia's published digests, laws, and legislative minutes. For missing volumes, researchers should contact the University of Georgia libraries. The Archives' collection of published laws and digests should not be confused with the State (Law) Library of Georgia in the Judicial Building across the street from the State Capitol.

The Cobb Digest (1851) of Georgia laws uses a system of abbreviations for indicating where additional information on a law can be found in an earlier digest. These abbreviations (I, II, III, IV) represent the following respective digests, as described on page 723 of Cobb's Digest. "An Act Prescribing the Form of a Digest or Manual of the Laws of Georgia": I — Marbury and Crawford, II — Clayton's Digest, III — Lamar's Digest, IV — Dawson's Digest.

PERIODICAL ROOM

Adjoining the Main Search Room is the Periodical Room where bound and unbound copies of journals, magazines, quarterlies, and newsletters are kept. The Periodical Room has back issues of **most** Georgia historical and genealogical periodicals and their available indexes. Particularly valuable to researchers are the bibliographies/indexes of **Family Puzzlers** (Georgia's weekly genealogical magazine), **Georgia Genealogical Magazine**, and **Georgia Genealogist**. Issues of **Georgia Life** included articles on Georgia families.

Newsletters are not kept on the shelves in the Periodical Room, but in a filing cabinet not open to the public. Back issues can be requested from the staff. The Archives also has bound back issues of **The Atlanta Journal-Constitution** magazine. These, too, must be requested from the Archives staff.

The Periodical Room has several publications from other states and some that cover the entire country. However, their holdings of these materials are incomplete, as is the case for most libraries and archives. For example, they only have some back issues of the **New England Historical and Genealogical Register**.

The Periodical Room also has a typescript index to the **Georgia Historical Quarterly** to 1932. A complete card index to the **Quarterly** is available in the Georgia Room of the University of Georgia Library, and a comprehensive index is being prepared for publication by the Georgia Historical Society.

Also in the Periodical Room is a typescript comprehensive index to the **Collections of the Georgia Historical Society** to 1932. Later volumes of this series are individually indexed. The collections deal largely with colonial and Revolutionary War records.

A typescript index to the surviving Savannah newspapers, Georgia's only newspapers until the 1780s and which covered a much greater area than just Chatham County in news and legal notices for many years afterward, is available in the Periodical Room for the years 1763 through 1830. A continuation of this index for the period 1836 through 1845 is available in the Microfilm

Library. More of this index is available at the University of Georgia libraries and all of the index that has survived, which covers up to the 1930s, is at the Georgia Historical Society Library in Savannah. Although the index to Savannah newspapers has errors and omissions, it is certainly easier to use in research than trying to scan each issue.

- **Note**: A large collection of periodicals for other states, 3,600 issues of 250 periodicals for 1974-1977, can be found at the Genealogical Center Library, 15 Dunwoody Park Road, Suite 130, Atlanta, Ga. 30338.

HISTORICAL RESEARCH ADVISOR

The Research Advisor, whose office is in the Periodical Room, has special guides, catalogues, and indexes to state records and private collections. Although the advisor's primary responsibility is to aid in scholarly research, the collections and records available through the advisor also have great genealogical value. However, these guides, catalogues, etc., are too broad and general to list specific individuals or families.

- **Note**: The Historical Research Advisor is not at the Archives on Saturdays, and these materials must be requested on weekdays for use on Saturdays.
  Among the more genealogically important records available are:

† **Governor's Letterbooks, 1786-1897**. These 41 volumes are of far more historical importance than genealogical, but they can be useful when a researcher has found a letter from an ancestor in the loose Georgia papers at the Archives; in the Telamon Cuyler Collection, Special Collections, University of Georgia libraries; or in the collection of the William R. Perkins Library (particularly the Georgia Papers), Duke University. Also, if an ancestor was a prominent state official, some information on his career may be found in these volumes. The earliest governors letterbooks are compiled into typescripts in the Central Research Library. Most of the original volumes and the typescripts are indexed.

† **Central Register of Convicts, 1817-1897** (Record Group 21-1-5), provides the name, age, place of birth, physical description, residence, crime, and other information on every individual imprisoned by the state of Georgia. These records are contained in three (formerly four) volumes. Volume one contains the earliest records but has pages missing. Volume two contains the same information as volume one, including information from the lost pages in volume one. For more information, see **Descriptive Inventory Number 1: Records of the Georgia Prison Commission, 1817-1936** (Atlanta: Georgia Department of Archives and History, 1969).

† **Governors Proclamations, 1823-1869** (Record Group 1-1-23), provides the names and physical descriptions of murderers who fled justice plus the name and usually the date of death of each victim. Earlier proclamations are available on microfilm in the Microfilm Library. After 1869, these proclamations were recorded in the executive minutes (available from the Historical Research Advisor). See Robert S. Davis, Jr., "Georgia Murders, Murderers, and Murder Victims, 1823-1840," **Georgia Genealogical Society Quarterly** vol. 15 (1979), pp. 103-15.

† **Board of Physicians Records, 1826-1881** (Record Group 6-10-11), includes the minutes of the board and the book of applications for certification. The latter includes personal information on individuals who applied for permits as Georgia doctors and related medical fields. The Central Research Library has photostatic copies of these records that are indexed.

† **Records of Confiscations of Loyalist Property, 1780s** (Record Groups 1-6 and 37-8). The material in RG 1-6 is a manuscript volume of county-level records of confiscation of Loyalist property. The material in RG 37-8 is a manuscript volume "Commissioners to Examine Claims Against Confiscated Estates." Contrary to a recent notation on this volume, this material is only a similar document and not the record published by Allen D. Candler in **The Revolutionary Records of the State of Georgia** (1908). This record and the one used by Candler each had names not found in the other. An index to all these Loyalist confiscation records and those found in Georgia Colonial Conveyance Book BBB is currently being prepared for publication by the R.J. Taylor, Jr., Foundation. See Marilyn Adams, **A Preliminary Guide to Eighteenth Century Records Held by the Georgia Department of Archives and History** (Atlanta: Georgia Department of Archives and History, 1976).

• Georgia Loyalists were persons who remained loyal to the king during the American Revolution. As a result of their loyalty, they suffered confiscation of property and banishment from Georgia when royal authority was overthrown.

† **Military Records Collection, 1776-1860?** Also known as the county military records, these are loose rosters and related records **not** used in the "Georgia Military Affairs." Some of these records are filed by county and some by time period. Others are in an oversize file. They are not indexed. These loose records may be the "10,000" items donated to the Georgia Department of Archives and History by Telamon Cuyler in 1935 (see the annual report of the director of the Georgia Department of Archives and History, January 1, 1936).

† **Original Loose Papers Used to Compile the Typescripts in the Main Search Room, 1733-1860?** These loose records were used to compile the "Georgia Military Affairs," "Indian Depredations," "Passports Issued by Georgia Governors," and other typescripts now in the Central Research Library. For information on the genealogical value of these records, see the description of these typescripts on page 17.

† **Medical Case Histories, State Asylum, March 20, 1853-1905.** Records of persons confined in the state insane asylum, filed alphabetically by names of patients. Records of inmates held during the last seventy-five years are restricted and must be requested from the Director, Central State Hospital, Milledgeville, Georgia 30161; but they are extremely difficult to get, because of privacy restrictions. Records of burials of inmates at the asylum, 1880-1951, are in the Microfilm Library on reel 223-24.

† **Loose Civil and Military Commissions, 1789-1868** (Record Group 1-2-32). These papers are original commissions for county officials and militia officers, chiefly filed by county. The commissions provide little information

beyond the fact that an individual lived in a certain place at a certain time while holding a particular office or rank. However, these records are useful for obtaining a photocopy of an ancestor's autograph on an interesting-looking document. Most of these records are indexed in the People File or Vertical File in the Central Research Library. Bound copies of commissions or commission books are in the Microfilm Library, described in the card file under "Georgia Official Records." Special Collections, University of Georgia libraries, has loose commissions in their Telamon Cuyler and Keith Read Collection that are not available at the Georgia Archives.

† **Loose State Supreme Court Case Papers, 1846-1900s?** Most of these loose court case papers are of little interest to researchers, but some contain detailed personal information; wills and other records from counties that have lost their records in courthouse fires, and information on migrations. These papers are abstracted in **Georgia Reports**, although many of the loose papers that accompanied the court case papers were not abstracted or even mentioned. The Archives also has the state supreme court docket which, although not an index, is a fast means of checking the court case papers for records relating to ancestors.

† **Tax Records, 1780s to Present.** The Archives has a large collection of Georgia tax digests, including all of them after 1872. Most of the pre-1873 digests are on microfilm in the Microfilm Library and can be requested there. However, most of the tax digests after 1872 are not on microfilm and must be requested either from the Historical Research Advisor or any staff member in the Central Research Library. This collection is not catalogued or inventoried, and individual digests can be extremely difficult for the staff to find.

† **Returns of Qualified Voters, 1867** (Record Group 1-1-108). Records of over 95,000 whites and 93,000 blacks who took amnesty oaths after the Civil War and registered to vote for delegates to a constitutional convention for bringing Georgia back into the Union. These returns are arranged by county and then by militia district but are not indexed. Each return provides the name, race, number of amnesty oath, date of registration, and other information on each person who registered. The "other information" varies considerably from county to county. In some, the number of years each person lived in the state, district, and county is provided; and in others the state or county of birth is given. Detailed naturalization information is provided in some returns, such as those for the city of Augusta, Richmond County. However, some registers provide little more than each person's name. Some county copies of these returns are reported to provide additional personal information. For background on these records, see Mary Warren's article in **Family Puzzlers, no. 671**, August 28, 1980; and **Reconstruction Sources in the Georgia Department of Archives and History** (Atlanta: Georgia Department of Archives and History, 1969).

† **Registration Oath Book, 1867** (Record Group 1-1-107), contains records related to the returns of qualified voters, giving names of persons registered, county and date of registration, and sometimes race. These books are arranged by county; not indexed.

† **Spanish-American War Records, 1898** (Record Groups 22-3-12 and 22-3-18). These records provide the name, age, residence, occupation, place of birth, date of enlistment, and ranks held for every man who served in the 1st, 2nd, and 3rd Georgia infantry regiments and batteries A and B of the Georgia Artillery. They are not indexed, unfortunately, but are arranged by company. Researchers should write to Military Service Records (NNCC), Washington, D.C. 20408, for their ancestor's specific unit before consulting these records.

The Archives does not have state-level records for later wars that are open to the public. However, some county-level service records for World War I and later are on microfilm in the Microfilm Library, filed by county. The Central Research Library also has a few books of compiled World War I service records. For service records of wars **after** the Spanish-American War, write the National Personnel Records Center, GSA (Military Records), 9700 Page Boulevard, St. Louis, Mo. 63132. For military records **before** World War I that are kept by the federal government, write to Military Service Records (NNCC), Washington, D.C. 20408.

† **Official Register of National Guard Officers of Georgia, 1916-1917** (Record Group 22-3-19), gives published registers of officers of the Georgia National Guard on the eve of America's entry into World War I; including name, rank, personal data, record of military service, and other information on each officer. Also included are lists of retired officers and historical information on past and present units.

† **Loose County Records, 1760s-1900s?** The Archives has begun to bring in loose county records from across the state. Most of these have never been microfilmed, and they may never be because of their sheer volume. The Hancock County loose papers, for example, fill fifty-two boxes. Among these papers are being found poor school children records, lists of persons who qualified for the Georgia land lotteries (whether they won or not), tax records, unrecorded marriages, original deeds (including information that was garbled or omitted when the deeds were recorded), original wills (including names that were crossed out before the wills were recorded), and much more from almost every period of Georgia state history.

New collections of these loose papers are being brought into the Archives constantly. Researchers may contact the Government Records Office of the Archives to learn if the counties they are interested in have had their loose records brought in. According to Elizabeth Fitzpatrick of the Government Records Office, the loose papers of the following counties are now in the Archives: Baldwin (a few papers), Bartow, Bulloch, Chatham (loose marriages and naturalizations), Chattooga, Chattahoochee, Cobb (loose estate records), Columbia, Crawford, Franklin, Forsyth (marriage records), Gilmer, Hancock, Henry, Jasper, Montgomery, Morgan, Oglethorpe, Walton, Wilcox, and Wilkes.

These records are seldom organized in any manner, and searching these papers for a specific family or person can mean digging through thousands of documents, one by one. Other collections of loose county papers are on microfilm in the Microfilm Library. The Joseph M. Toomey Collection of Loose Wilkes County Records is in the Manuscripts Section and must be requested from the Archives staff.

PRINTS AND PHOTOGRAPHS

A Print Archivist, or specialist in ordering copies of the historical photographs in the Archives' print collection and from the photographs copied from various Georgia counties by the Vanishing Georgia Project, currently has an office in the Periodical Room. A card catalogue of these two photograph collections is currently being prepared. If the archivist should be moved in the near future, researchers may inquire about the collections in the Central Research Library.

CIVIL WAR RECORDS SECTION (First Floor)

This section currently adjoins the Periodical Room, but it may soon be moved. The Archives provides a very useful, free pamphlet on the Civil War Records Section. This pamphlet does not mention the Civil War manuscript collections available in the Microfilm Library and the Central Research Section. Among the more genealogically significant records in the Civil War Records Section are:

† **Compiled Service Records of Georgia Confederate Soldiers.** These are indexed. Compiled service records for Georgians who served in the Union Army during the Civil War must be ordered from Military Service Records (NNCC), Washington, D.C. 20408.

† **Civil War Pension Records** for Georgians who served in the Confederate Army or state troops. These pensions were given to veterans and widows of veterans who were living in Georgia after the war, regardless of the state in which service was performed. The Civil War Records Section has an index to these pensions although the pension papers are also arranged alphabetically, by county. Civil War service pensions for Georgians who served in Union forces must be requested from Military Service Records (NNCC), Washington, D.C. 20408.

† **Supplement One** — or **Georgia State Civil War Pension Papers** not included in the microfilm copy of pension records. These papers include legitimate pension claims that were, for a variety of reasons, not previously microfilmed; plus fraudulent and rejected pension claims. Although not indexed, these papers are arranged by county and then alphabetically. Like the regular pension claims, they are on microfilm in the Civil War Records Section. Supplement Two, composed of similar records, also exists; but it has not been organized well enough to be made available to researchers.

† **Rosters of Georgia Confederate and State Troops,** arranged by unit and by county. Many of these rosters were compiled from interviews with veterans. The rosters of the Georgia volunteer infantry regiments have been published.

† **Private Manuscript Collections.** A catalogue to these collections is available. This catalogue does not include the UDC typescripts (see below) and the Civil War collections in the Central Research Section and the Microfilm Library.

† **United Daughters of the Confederacy** typescripts of private papers and diaries from the Civil War. These have a cumulative index.

† **Miscellaneous Records Index.** Serves as an index to miscellaneous state service documents such as enlistment papers in the state troops, typed or photocopied private material, and other records available in the Civil War Records Section.

† **List of Men Between the Ages of 16 and 60 who had not volunteered by January 1, 1864.** These records give the name, age, place of birth, occupation, and reason for not having enlisted. These records that have survived are arranged by county and indexed in the miscellaneous records index (see above).

† **Salt Books,** providing lists of heads of families, widows, and wives entitled to special allotments of salt during the war. These records are arranged by county but are not indexed.

† The 128-volume **War of the Rebellion** series. Includes correspondence and reports of military officers during the war. These books are useful for tracing the movements of a particular unit. The series has a cumulative index.

† **Register of inmates at the Georgia Confederate Soldiers Home, 1901-1941.** Includes some biographical information on each inmate. Widows who were in the home in later years are not included.

The Civil War Section also has some books, published memoirs, and military histories on the Civil War including some pension indexes for other states. They also have a few records of Georgia soldiers' graves.

• **Note**: In addition to having a large collection of private manuscript collections relating to the Civil War, the Microfilm Library has county copies of rosters and pension records plus tax digests from the early 1900s that list Confederate pensioners and widows. These are filed by county.

3

MICROFILM LIBRARY (SECOND FLOOR)

CATALOGUES AND GUIDES

The Microfilm Library has two card catalogue cabinets — one for county records and tax digests; and the other for all other microfilm. Guides and indexes to some of these holdings are at the main desk. They also have some of the published indexes to census records and other books that are useful in working with over 27,000 reels of microfilm. These volumes are extra copies of books from the Central Research Library downstairs. Central Research also has other volumes that relate to records in the Microfilm Library, including census indexes for Georgia and other states.

Magnifying glasses are available for use by researchers having trouble reading microfilm.

FEDERAL CENSUS RECORDS

Georgia. The Microfilm Library has copies of all surviving, available federal census records for Georgia, including the extra schedules and the soundex indexes for the 1880 and 1900 censuses. The 1790, 1800, and 1810 censuses are missing for Georgia, but a county copy of the 1800 census for Oglethorpe County has survived and is available in the Microfilm Library. The 1820 census for Franklin, Rabun, Twiggs, and a part of Columbia County are also missing. For published substitutes for these lost Georgia census records, see Chapter 8. The 1890 federal census for Georgia, except for some fragments for Columbus, Georgia, was lost in a fire on January 10, 1921, as was most of this census for the rest of the country. However, some of the information from the 1890 Washington County, Georgia, census was copied into county records and has survived. The most recent Georgia census currently available to the general public, and found in the Microfilm Library, is the 1900 census, with its soundex index. Information from later census records is available, under certain restrictions, from the U.S. Department of Commerce, Bureau of the Census, Pittsburg, Kansas 66762.

GENERAL

The federal censuses were taken every ten years, beginning in 1790, and were intended to provide information on the population of the United States for the following census days:

Census	Census Day
1790-1820	1st Mon. in Aug., Census Yr.
1830-1900	June 1 of Census Year
1910	April 15, 1910
1920	January 1, 1920
1930-1980	April 1 of Census Year

However, some census takers erroneously recorded their information on each family as the families appeared on the days the census taker made his visits and not on the "census days" shown above.

Federal population schedules for the 1790, 1800, 1810, 1820, 1830, and 1840 censuses provide the names of the heads of each household; a statistical breakdown of the members of each household by race, sex, and age group; and other information. Beginning with the 1850 census, the name of **every** member of the household is recorded; giving race, sex, age, place of birth, and other information. Beginning with the 1870 census, Indians are recorded as a separate race. Starting with the 1880 federal census, the birth states or countries of the **parents** of each person in the census is also recorded. A more detailed description of this information found in the population schedules follows this section. Researchers should be aware that federal census information is not always reliable because of human error by both the enumerator and the information provider.

EXTRA SCHEDULES

The Microfilm Library also has copies of the surviving extra schedules of the federal censuses for Georgia. These include the mortality schedules, providing the names and information on persons **who died** during the census years of 1850, 1860, 1870, and 1880; the agriculture schedules, providing the name of every farm owner/renter and information on the products produced and the value of every farm visited during those same years (however, for the 1850 census, this schedule is missing for the counties of Quitman through Wilkinson); the slave schedules for the 1850 and 1860 censuses, providing the names of each slave owner (including those who were dead but whose slaves had not been divided or sold) and statistical descriptions of the slaves; the schedule of manufacturers for the 1820 and 1880 censuses; and the dependent, defective, and delinquent class schedule of the 1880 census, providing information on the insane or idiotic, homeless children, convicts, indigents, poor house inmates, and anyone else boarded at public expense. The Microfilm Library also has copies of the schedule of mines, agriculture, commerce, and manufacturing for the 1840 census and the social schedules for the 1850 and 1860 federal censuses. However, these particular schedules are only county-by-county, statistical summaries and do not list names. The 1870 social schedule for Georgia is among the collections of the William R. Perkins Library, Duke University. The Georgia Archives does not currently have a copy of this schedule.

The Microfilm Library has **most** of the published statewide indexes to Georgia census records (1820 through 1850, conclusive). Others for Georgia and other states are downstairs in the Central Research Library.

• **Note:** Some census records, particularly for the mountain counties of north Georgia; have families, settlements, and sometimes entire militia districts recorded in the wrong counties by census takers who were uncertain about county boundaries. Statewide census indexes are useful for learning the correct county in which a family has been erroneously recorded.

Federal census records for **some** Georgia counties for the 1850 federal census not only provide the state or country of birth, but also the **county** of birth. Among these are the 1850 censuses of Tattnall, Jefferson, and parts of Muskogee and Cobb counties.

The 1900 federal census of McIntosh County provides the complete date of birth of every person listed.

• The following is adopted from a Census Bureau publication:

National Archives & Records Service

CENSUS DATA, 1790-1890

Census of 1790

Name of head of family; address; number of free white males of 16 years and up, including heads; free white males under 16; free white females, including heads; all other free persons; number of slaves.

Census of 1800

Name of head of family; address; number of free white males and females under 10 years of age, 10 and under 16, 16 and under 26, 26 and under 45, and 45 years and upward; all other free persons, except Indians not taxed; number of slaves.

Census of 1810

Same as Census of 1800

Census of 1820

Name of head of family; address; number of free white males and females under 10 years of age, 10 and under 16, 16 and under 26, 26 and under 45, and 45 years and upward; number of free white males between 16 and 18 years; foreigners not naturalized; male and female slaves and free colored persons under 14 years, 14 and under 26, 26 and under 45, and 45 and upward; all other free persons, except Indians not taxed; number of persons (including slaves) engaged in agriculture, commerce, and manufactures.

Census of 1830

Name of head of family; address; number of free white males and females in 5-year age groups to 20, 10-year age groups from 20 to 100 years old and over; number of slaves and free colored persons in six broad age groups; number of deaf and dumb under 14, 14 to 24, and 25 years and upward; number of blind; foreigners not naturalized.

Census of 1840

Name of head of family; address, number of free white males and females in 5-year age groups to 20, 10-year age groups from 20 to 100, and 100 years old and over; number of slaves and free colored persons in six broad age groups; number of deaf and dumb; number of blind; number of insane and idiotic in public or private charge; number of persons in each family employed in each of seven classes of occupations; number of schools and number of scholars; number of white persons over 20 who could not read and write; names of pensioners for Revolutionary or military service.

Census of 1850

Name; address; age; sex; color (white, black, or mulatto) for each person; whether deaf and dumb, blind, insane or idiotic; all free persons required to give value of real estate owned; profession, occupation, or trade for each male person over 15; place of birth; whether married within the year; whether attended school within the year; whether unable to read or write for persons over 20; whether a pauper or convict.

Census of 1860

Name; address; age; sex; color (white, black, or mulatto) for each person; whether deaf and dumb, blind, insane, or idiotic; all free persons required to give value of real estate and of personal estate owned; profession, occupation, or trade for each male and female over 15; place of birth (state, territory, or country); whether married within the year; whether attended school within the year; whether unable to read and write for persons over 20; whether a pauper or convict.

Census of 1870

Address; name; age; sex; color (including Chinese and Indian); citizenship for males over 21; profession, occupation, or trade; value of real estate; value of personal estate; place of birth; whether father and mother were foreign born; born within the year; married within the year; attended school within the year; for persons 10 years old and over whether able to read and write; whether deaf and dumb, blind, or idiotic.

Census of 1880

Address; name; relationship to head of family; sex; race; age; marital status; born within the year; married within the year; profession, occupation, or trade; number of months unemployed during census year; whether person is sick or temporarily disabled so as to be unable to attend to ordinary business or duties; if so, what is the sickness or disability; whether blind, deaf and dumb, idiotic, insane, maimed, crippled or bedridden; attended school within the year; ability to read and write; place of birth of person, father, and mother.

Census of 1890

99% of the schedules were destroyed by fire in 1921. Content was similar to that for the 1900 census.

Census of 1900

Address (street and house no. in large cities); relationship to head of family; color or race (W-white, B-black [negro or negro descent], Ch-Chinese, Jp-Japanese, and In-Indian); month and year of birth; age at last birthday; marital status (single, married, divorced, widowed); number of years married to present husband; number of children of wife; number of children living; place of birth of person and parents (state or county only); citizenship; if foreign born, year of immigration, and number of years in U.S.; citizenship status if over 21 (Al-alien, Pa-declaration of intent has been filed, Na-naturalized); occupation; education — can read, write, and speak English; ownership of home (O-owned, R-rented); whether a home (H) or a farm (F); and whether free (F) or mortgage (M). Separate schedules were prepared for institutions, military establishments, and Indian reservations.

• The originals of the 1900 Federal census were destroyed years ago with the consent of Congress. Only the microfilm copies survive.

• **Note:** The Federal Records Center at 1557 St. Joseph Avenue, East Point, Georgia 30344 has all the surviving population schedules for the entire U.S. that are currently available, 1790 through 1900, inclusive. They also have the published general indexes to these census records. The Genealogical Center Library at 15 Dunwoody Park Road, Suite 130, Atlanta, Georgia 30308, has copies of all the general census indexes published by Accelerated Indexing Systems (more than 200 volumes covering all federal censuses up to and including the 1850 census). The Mormon Branch Genealogical Library at 1155 Mt. Vernon Road, Dunwoody, Georgia 30338, has the census for the entire U.S. for 1840. The Microfilm Library, University of Georgia libraries, has copies of the federal census records of the entire South. Many local and regional libraries in Georgia have federal census records for their regions and some for the entire state.

Other States. The Microfilm Library also has many federal census records for other states, including all the population schedules (free and black) for the entire U.S. for 1860, with the exception of some counties in Alabama and South Carolina. Most of these 1860 census records, however, are kept separate from the other census records. The reels are available to the public but must be requested from the Microfilm Library staff. Below is a list of the out-of-state census records available in the Microfilm Library.

Alabama

1830 — Blount, Franklin, Jefferson, Jackson, Lauderdale, Lawrence, Limestone, Madison, Marion, Morgan, St. Clair, Walker, Mobile, Baldwin, Monroe, Dallas, Pickens, Bibb, Montgomery, Clarke, Shelby, Butler, Henry, Marengo, Greene, Pike, Perry, Conecuh, Autauga, Wilcox, Fayette, Dale, Covington, Washington, Lowndes, Tuscaloosa, City of Mobile.

1840 — Autauga, Barbour, Baldwin, Bibb, Butler, Chambers, Clarke, Conecuh, Coosa, Covington, Benton, Blount, Cherokee, DeKalb, Fayette, Franklin, Dale, Dallas, Greene, Henry, Jefferson, Lowndes, Jackson, Lauderdale, Limestone, Lawrence, Macon, Marengo, Mobile, Montgomery, Monroe, Perry, Pickens, Pike, Morgan, Marion, Marshall, Madison, Randolph,

St. Clair, Talladega, Russell, Shelby, Sumter, Tallapoosa, Washington, Walker, Wilcox.

1850 – Autauga, Baldwin, Barbour, Benton, Bibb, Blount, Butler, Chambers, Cherokee, Choctaw, Clarke, Coffee, Conecuh, Coosa, Covington, Dale, Dallas, DeKalb, Fayette, Franklin, Greene, Hancock, Henry, Jackson, Jefferson, Lauderdale, Lawrence, Limestone, Lowndes, Macon, Madison, Marengo, Marion, Marshall, Mobile, Monroe, Montgomery, Morgan, Perry, Pickens, Pike, Randolph, Russell, St. Clair, Shelby, Sumter, Talladega, Tallapoosa, Tuscaloosa, Walker, Washington, Wilcox.

1860 – Autauga, Baldwin, Barbour, Bibb, Blount, Butler, Calhoun, Chambers, Cherokee, Choctaw, Clarke, Coffee, Conecuh, Coosa, Covington, Dallas, Dale, DeKalb, Fayette, Franklin, Greene, Henry, Jackson, Jefferson, Lawrence, Limestone, Lowndes, Macon, Monroe, Marion, Marshall, Mobile, Marengo, Montgomery, Morgan, Perry, Pickens, Pike, Talladega, Sumter, Randolph, Russell, St. Clair, Shelby, Tallapoosa, Walker, Washington, Wilcox, Winston.

Slave Schedule, 1860 – Autauga, Baldwin, Barbour, Bibb, Blount, Butler, Calhoun, Chambers, Cherokee, Choctaw, Clarke, Coffee, Conecuh, Coosa, Covington, Dale, Dallas, DeKalb, Fayette, Franklin, Greene, Henry, Jackson, Jefferson, Madison, Marengo, Lawrence, Lauderdale, Limestone, Lowndes, Marion, Marshall, Macon, Mobile, Monroe, Montgomery, Morgan, Pickens, Perry, Pike, Randolph, Russell, Shelby, St. Clair, Sumter, Tallapoosa, Talladega, Walker, Washington, Wilcox, Winston.

1870 – Barbour, Bibb, Chambers, Coffee, Colbert, Conecuh, Coosa, Covington, Crenshaw, Dale, Dallas, DeKalb, Elmore, Escambia, Etowah, Fayette, Franklin, Geneva, Greene, Hale (part), Jackson, Jefferson, Lauderdale, Montgomery (excluding city of Montgomery), Monroe (part), Morgan, Perry, Montgomery, Pickens, Pike, Randolph, Russell, Sanford, Shelby, Tallapoosa, Tuscaloosa (part), Talladega, Lee.

† **1880** Dallas (part), DeKalb, Elmore, Escambia, Henry (part), Jackson, Jefferson, Lamar, Lauderdale, Montgomery, Morgan, Perry, Pickens (part), Pike, Randolph (part).

Arkansas

† **1840** – Arkansas, Benton, Carroll, Chicot, Clarke, Conway, Crawford, Crittenden, Desha, Franklin, Greene, Hempstead, Hot Springs, Independence, Izard, Jackson, Jefferson, Johnson, Lafayette, Lawrence, Madison, Marion, Mississippi, Monroe, Phillips, Pike, Poinsett, Pope, Pulaski, Randolph, St. Francis, Saline, Scott, Searcy, Sevier, Union, Van Buren, Washington, White.

† **1860** – All Counties

† **1870** – Greene, Hempstead, Hot Springs, Johnson, Lafayette.

† **1880** – Marion, Miller, Mississippi, Monroe.

California

† **1850** – Butte, Calaveras, Colusa, El Dorado, Los Angeles, Marin, Mariposa, Mendocino, Monterey, Napa, Sacramento, Santa Cruz, San Diego, San

Jaoquin, San Luis Obispo, Shasta, Solano, Sonoma, Sutter, Trinity, Tuolumne, Yolo, Yuba.

† 1852 — Butte, Calaveras, Colusa, Contra Costa, San Francisco, San Joaquin, San Luis Obispo, Santa Barbara, Santa Clara, Santa Cruz, Shasta, Sierra, Siskiyou, Solano, Sonamo, Sutter, Trinity, Tulare, Tuolumne, Yolo, Yuba (part 1).

† 1860 — All Counties

Connecticut

† 1860 — All Counties

Delaware

† 1860 — All Counties

District of Columbia

† 1860 — All Counties

Florida

† 1850 — Alachua, Benton, Calhoun, Columbia, Dade, Duval, Escambia, Franklin, Gadsden, Hamilton, Hillsborough, Holmes, Jackson, Jefferson, Leon, Levy, Madison, Marion, Monroe, Nassau, Orange, Putnam, St. Johns, St. Lucie, Santa Rosa, Wakulla, Walton, Washington.

† 1860 — All Counties

† 1880 — Gadsden (part), Hamilton, Hernando, Hillsborough, Holmes, Jackson.

Illinois

† 1850 — Monroe, Montgomery, Perry, Piatt, Pike.

† 1860 — All Counties

† 1890 — McDonough.

Indiana

† 1860 — All Counties

Iowa

† 1850 — Allamakee, Appanoose, Benton, Black Hawk, Boone, Buchanan, Cedar, Clarke, Clayton, Clinton, Dallas, Davis.

† 1860 — All Counties

† 1870 — Dubuque (part), Emmet, Fayette, Floyd, Franklin, Fremont, Greene, Grundy, Guthrie, Hamilton

Kansas

† 1860 — All Counties

Kentucky

† **1810** – Estill, Fayette, Fleming, Floyd, Franklin, Gallatir, Garrard, Greenup, Green, Grayson, Hardin, Harrison, Henderson, Henry, Hopkins.

† **1820** – Barren, Estill, Fayette, Gallatin, Grant, Hart, Henderson, Jefferson, Jessamine, Owen, Shelby, Campbell, Christian, Green, Lewis, Nicholas, Muhlenberg, Union.

† **1850** – Adair, Allen, Anderson, Ballard.

† **1860** – All Counties

Louisiana

† **1810** – Ascension, Assumption, Attakapus, Avoyelles, Baton Rouge, Catahoula, Concordia, Iberville, Lafourche, Natchitoches, Orleans, Opelousas, Orrachita, Plaquamines, Ponte Coupee, Rapids, St. Bernard, St. Charles, St. James, St. John the Baptist.

† **1830** – Lafourche, Ascension, St. Helena, St. Tammany, Washington, Assumption, Terrebonne, Iberville, Concordia, Jefferson, Plaquemines, East Feliciana, West Feliciana, East Baton Rouge, West Baton Rouge, St. James (county of Arcadia), St. John the Baptist, St. Bernard, St. Charles.

† **1840** – Lafourche, Terrebonne, Iberville, East Baton Rouge, West Baton Rouge, Washington, Madison, Carroll, St. Tammany.

† **1850** – Ascension, Assumption, Avoyelles, East Baton Rouge, West Baton Rouge, Bienville, Bossier, Caddo, Calcasieu, Caldwell, Carroll, Catahoula, Claiborne, Concordia, De Soto, East Feliciana, West Feliciana, Franklin, Iberville, Jackson, Jefferson, LaFayette, Lafourche, Livingston, Madison, Morehouse, Natchitoches, Pointe Coupee, Rapides, Sabine, St. Bernard, St. Charles, St. Helena, St. James, St. John the Baptist, St. Landry, St. Martin, St. Mary, St. Tammany, Tensas, Terrebonne, Union, Vermillion, Washington.

† **1860** – All Parishes

† **1870** – East Baton Rouge, East Feliciana.

† **1880** – Concordia (part), DeSoto, East Baton Rouge, East Carroll, Soundex H-630 thru J-250.

Maine

† **1860** – All Counties

Maryland

† **1800** – St. Marys, Worcester.

† **1850** – Frederick.

† **1860** – All Counties

Massachusetts

† **1860** – All Counties

Michigan
† 1860 – All Counties

Minnesota
† 1860 – All Counties
† 1890 – Wright.

Mississippi
† 1840 – Adams, Amite, Claiborne, Copiah, Clarke, Covington, Greene, Franklin, Jasper, Hinds, Hancock, Holmes, Jackson, Jefferson, Jones, Attala, Bolivar, Carroll, Chickasaw, Choctaw, Coahoma, De Soto, Itawamba, Lafayette, Lowndes, Kemper, Leake, Lauderdale, Lawrence, Madison, Marion, Neshaba, Newton, Pike, Perry, Rankin, Scott, Simpson, Smith, Wayne, Washington, Warren, Wilkinson, Yazoo, Marshall, Monroe, Noxubee, Oktibbeha, Panola, Pontotoc, Tallahatchie, Tippah, Tishomingo, Tunica, Winston, Yalobusha.

† 1850 – Adams, Amite, Attala, Bolivar, Carroll, Chickasaw, Choctaw, Claiborne, Clarke, Coahoma, Copiah, Covington, De Soto, Franklin, Greene, Hancock, Harrison, Hinds, Holmes, Issaquena, Itawamba, Jackson, Jasper, Jefferson, Jones, Kemper, La Fayette, Lauderdale, Lawrence, Leake, Lowndes, Madison, Marion, Marshall, Monroe, Neshoba, Newton, Noxubee, Oktibbeha, Panola, Perry, Pike, Pontotoc, Rankin, Scott, Simpson, Smith, Sunflower, Tallahatchie, Tippah, Tishominto, Tunica, Warren, Washington, Wayne, Wilkinson, Winston, Yalobusha, Yazoo.

† 1860 – All Counties
† 1870 – Attala, Bolivar, Calhoun.
† 1880 – Carroll, Claiborne (part).

Missouri
† 1830 – Lincoln, Marion, Clariton, Washington, Jefferson, Franklin, Gasconade, Crawford, Cole, Montgomery, Pike, St. Charles, St. Louis, Ste. Genevieve, Perry, St. Francois, Cape Girardeau.

† 1840 – Howard, Jackson, Jefferson, Johnson, La Fayette, St. Charles, St. Francois, Ste. Genevieve.

† 1850 – Jackson, Jasper, Jefferson, St. Charles, St. Clair, St. Francois, Ste. Genevieve.

† 1860 – All Counties
† 1870 – Jasper, Jefferson.
† 1880 – Jasper (part), Jefferson, Johnson, Knox (part).
Soundex H-200 (M)-H-251, H-325-H-400K.

Nebraska
† 1860 – All Counties

New Hampshire

† 1860 — All Counties

New Jersey

† 1860 — All Counties.

† 1890 — Hudson.

New Mexico

† 1860 — All Counties

New York

† 1860 — All Counties

† 1890 — Westchester, Suffolk.

North Carolina

† 1800 — Anson, Ashe, Brunswick, Buncombe, Burke, Cabarrus, Iredell, Lincoln, Beaufort, Bertie, Camden, Chowan, Currituck, Edgecombe, Gates, Halifax, Bladen, Carteret, Caswell, Chatham, Craven, Cumberland, Dupllin, Franklin, Granville, Greene, Guilford, Hertford, Johnston, Jones, Hyde, Martin, Northampton, Orange, Pasquotank, Perquimans, Tyrrell, Washington, Lenoir, Moore, Nash, Onslow, Person, Pitt, Randolph, Robeson, Rockingham, Sampson, Stokes, Surry, Wake, Warren, Wayne, Mecklenburg, Montgomery, New Hanover, Richmond, Rowan, Rutherford, Wilkes.

† 1810 — Ashe, Beaufort, Bertie, Buncombe, Burke, Cabarrus, Camden, Carteret, Chatham, Chowan, Cumberland, Anson, Brunswick, Caswell, Currituck, Halifax, Person, Randolph, Richmond, Robeson, Bladen, Columbus, Mecklenburg, Northampton, Rutherford, Sampson, Warren, Rockingham, Rowan, Stokes, Surry, Tyrrell, Washington, Wayne, Wilkes, Duplin, Edgecombe, Franklin, Gates, Granville, Guilford, Haywood, Hertford, Hyde, Iredell, Johnston, Jones, Lenoir, Lincoln, Martin, Montgomery, Moore, Nash, Onslow, Orange, Pasquotank, Perquimans, Pitt.

† 1820 — Ashe, Caswell, Chowan, Perquimans, Richmond, Rowan, Tyrrell, Burke, Carteret, Cumberland, Hyde, Jones, Lincoln, Nash, Wayne, Wilkes, Brunswick, Camden, Columbus, Craven, Edgecombe, Gates, Mecklenburg, New Hanover, Pasquotank, Robeson, Stokes, Granville, Guilford, Halifax, Hertford, Northampton, Sampson, Anson, Buncombe, Cabarris, Dupllin, Haywood, Iredell, Johnston, Lenoir, Moore, Onslow, Rutherford, Washington, Beaufort, Bertie, Bladen, Chatham, Greene, Orange, Person, Pitt, Rockingham, Surry, Warren.

† 1830 — Macon, Montgomery, Northampton, New Hanover, Nash, Onslow, Orange, Randolph, Surry, Sampson, Stokes, Tyrrell, Wilkes, Wake, Wayne, Washington, Warren.

† 1850 — Alamance, Alexander, Anson, Stanly, Stokes, Bertie, Bladen, Brunswick, Buncombe, Burke, Cabarrus, Caldwell, Camden, Carteret, Caswell, Catawba, Chatham, Cherokee, Chowan, Cleveland, Columbus, Craven (part).

† **1860** — All Counties

† **1870** — Anson, Ashe, Chatham (part), Cherokee, Chowan, Clay, Cleveland, Columbus, Craven, Cumberland, Currituck, Dare, Davidson (part), Madison, Martin, McDowell, Person (part), Pitt, Polk, Randolph, Richmond, Robeson, Rowan.

† **1880** — Chatham (part), Cherokee, Chowan, Clay, Cleveland, Columbus, Craven, Randolph, Richmond, Robeson, Pitt, Polk, Randolph, Richmond. Soundex 11-610 thru H-635, S-310 thru P-412, S-315 thru S-353.

† **1890** — Gaston, Cleveland.

Ohio

† **1820** — Ashtabula, Warren.

† **1850** — Adams, Allen, Highland.

† **1860** — All Counties

† **1890** — Hamilton, Clinton.

Pennsylvania

† **1850** — Wayne.

† **1860** — All Counties

Rhode Island

† **1860** — All Counties

South Carolina

† **1800** — Abbeville, Barnwell, Chester, Chesterfield, Darlington, Edgefield, Fairfield, Greenville, Beaufort, Charleston, Colleton, Georgetown, Kershaw, Marion, Orangeburg, Sumter, York, Lancaster, Laurens, Marlboro, Newberry, Pendleton, Spartanburg, Union, Lancaster, Laurens.

† **1810** — Abbeville, Barnwell, Beaufort, Charleston, Chester, Chesterfield, Colleton, Lancaster, Laurens, Lexington, Marion, Marlboro, Newberry, Orangeburg, Pendleton, Richland, Spartanburg, Sumter, Union, Williamsburg, York, Darlington, Edgefield, Greenville, Horry, Kershaw, Fairfield, Georgetown.

† **1820** — Barnwell, Charleston, Chesterfield, Horry, Kershaw, Beaufort, Chester, Georgetown, Greenville, Newberry, Pendleton, Spartanburg, Williamsburg, Laurens, Lexington, Marion, Marlboro, Richland, Sumter, Union, York, Abbeville, Colleton, Darlington, Edgefield, Lancaster, Orangeburg.

† **1830** — Abbeville, Barnwell, Laurens, Chester, Fairfield, Kershaw, Marlboro, Newberry, Union, Spartanburg, Lexington, Columbia, Richland, Colleton, Orangeburg, Lancaster, Anderson, Darlington, Pickens, York, Beaufort, Charleston, Georgetown, Horry, Williamsburg, Chesterfield, Edgefield, Greenville, Marion, Sumter.

† **1840** — Abbeville, Anderson, Barnwell, Beaufort, Charleston, Colleton, Chester, Chesterfield, Darlington, Edgefield, Fairfield, Georgetown, Greenville, Horry, Kershaw, Lancaster, Laurens, Lexington, Marion, Marlboro, Newberry, Orangeburg, Pickens, Richlands, Sumter, Spartanburg, Union, Williamsburg, York.

† **1850** — Abbeville, Anderson, Barnwell, Beaufort, Charleston, Chester, Chesterfield, Colleton, Darlington, Edgefield, Fairfield, Georgetown, Greenville, Horry, Kershaw, Lancaster, Laurens, Lexington, Marion, Marlboro, Newberry, Orangeburg, Pickens, Richland, Spartanburg, Sumter, Union, Williamsburg, York.

† **1860** — Abbeville, Anderson, Barnwell, Beaufort, Charleston, Chester, Chesterfield, Clarendon, Colleton, Darlington, Edgefield, Fairfield, Georgetown, Greenville, Horry, Kershaw, Lancaster, Laurens, Lexington, Marion, Marlboro, Newberry, Orangeburg, Pickens, Richland, Spartanburg, Sumter, Union, Williamsburg, York.

† **Slave Schedule, 1860** — Abbeville, Anderson, Barnwell, Darlington, Edgefield, Beaufort, Greenville, Charleston, Chester, Chesterfield, Kershaw, Lancaster, Laurens, Clarendon, Colleton, Fairfield, Georgetown, Horry, Lexington, Marion, Marlboro, Orangeburg, Pickens, Newberry, Richland, Spartanburg, Sumter, Union, Williamsburg, York.

† **1870** — Abbeville, Anderson, Edgefield, Kershaw (part), Lancaster, Laurens, Lexington, Marion, Marlboro, Newberry, Oconee, Pickens, Richmond, Spartanburg.

† **1880** — Abbeville, Aiken, Anderson, Georgetown (part), Greenville (part), Marion (part), Marlboro, Newberry (part), Pickens, Richland, Kershaw (part), Horry (part), Lancaster, Laurens, Lexington (part), Spartanburg.

Tennessee

† **1810** — Rutherford.

† **1820** — Bedford, Davidson, Hardin, Hickman, Humphreys, Montgomery, Overton, Perry, Warren, Wayne, White, Wilson, Dickson, Franklin, Jackson, Lawrence, Lincoln, Giles, Maury, Rutherford, Shelby, Stewart, Sumner, Robertson, Smith, Williamson.

† **1830** — Carter, Marion, Monroe, Anderson, Washington, Bledsoe, Sullivan, Rhea, White, Wilson, Williamson, Wayne, Weakley.

† **1840** — Greene, Grainger, Hamilton.

† **1850** — Haywood, Henderson, Grundy, Hamillton, Hardeman, Hancock, Warren, Washington.

† **1860** — All Counties

† **1870** — Davidson (districts 17-25), Grundy, Hamilton.

† **1880** — Bledsoe, Blount, Bradley, Hamilton, Hancock, Hardeman (part), Polk, Putnam, Rhea, Roane.

Texas

† **1850** — Anderson, Angelina, Austin, Bastrop, Bexar, Bowie, Brazoria, Brazos, Burleson, Caldwell, Calhoun, Cameron, Starr, Webb, Cass, Cherokee, Collin, Colorado, Comal, Cooke, Dallas, Denton, De Witt, Ellis, Tarrant, Fannin, Fayette, Fort Bend, Galveston, Guadalupe, Gillespie, Goliad, Gonzales, Grayson, Grimes, Harris, Harrison, Hays, Henderson, Hopkins, Houston, Hunt, Jackson, Jasper, Jefferson, Kaufman, Lamar, Lavaca, Leon, Liberty, Limestone, Matagorda, Medina, Milam, Montgomery, Nacogdoches, Navarro, Newton, Nueces, Panola, Polk, Red River, Refugio, Robertson, Rusk, Sabine, San Augustine, San Patricio, Shelby, Smith, Titus, Travis, Tyler, Upshur, Van Zandt, Victoria, Williamson, Walker, Washington, Wharton.

† **Slave Schedule, 1850** — Anderson, Angelina, Austin, Bastrop, Bexar, Bowie, Brazoria, Brazos, Burleson, Caldwell, Calhoun, Cameron, Webb, Cass, Cherokee, Collin, Colorado, Comal, Cooke, Dallas, Denton, Dewitt, Fannin, Fayette, Fort Bend, Galveston, Guadalupe, Gillespie, Goliad, Gonzales, Grayson, Grimes, Harrison, Hays, Henderson, Hopkins, Houston, Hunt, Jackson, Jasper, Jefferson, Kaufman, Lamar, Lavaca, Leon, Liberty, Limestone, Matagorda, Medina, Milam, Montgomery, Nacogdoches, Navarro, Newton, Nueces, Panola, Polk, Red River, Refugio, Robertson, Rusk, Sabine, San Augustine, Shelby, Smith, Ellis, Tarrant, Titus, Travis, Tyler, Upshur, Van Zandt, Victoria, Walker, Washington, Wharton, Williamson.

† **1860** — All Counties

† **1870** — Brazos, Brown, Burlson, Burnet, Caldwell, Calhoun, Davis (now Cass), Denton, DeWitt.

† **1880** — Bowie, Brazoria, Brazos, Brown, Camp, Cass, Chambers, Cherokee, Clay (part), Childress, Gonzales, Gray, Hutchinson, Roberts, Grayson, Gregg, Grimes (part).
Soundex P-350 thru P-456, S-531 thru 626, W-341 thru W420.

Utah

† **1860** — All Counties

Vermont

† **1860** — All Counties

Virginia

† **1790** — All Counties

† **1810** — Accomack, Albermarle, Amelia, Amhurst, Augusta, Bath, Berkeley, Botetourt, Brooke, Brunswick, Buckingham, Bedford, Caroline, Chesterfield, Dinwiddie, Norfolk (Borough of), Petersburg (Town of), Rockingham, Campbell, Charles City, Charlotte, Culpepper, Cumberland, Elizabeth City, Essex, Fairfax, Fauquier, Fluvanna, Franklin, Frederick, Giles, Gloucester, Goochland, Greensville, Hampshire, Hanover, Harrison, Henrico (excluding Richmond), Isle of Wight, Jefferson, Kanawha, King and Queen, King

George, Lancaster, Lee (recapitulation only), Loudoun, Lunenburg, Madison, Mason, Mathews, Middlesex, Monongalia, Monroe, Montgomery, Nelson, New Kent, Norfolk (excluding Norfolk Borough), Northumberland, Nottoway, Ohio, Pendleton, Powhatan, Prince Edward, Prince George, Prince William, Princess Anne, Randolph, Richmond (city), Rockbridge, Shenandoah, Southhampton, Spotsylvania, Stafford, Surry, Sussex, Warwick, Washington, Westmoreland, Wood, Wythe, York.

† 1820 – Accomack, Bath, Berkeley, Campbell, Caroline, Chesterfield, Albermarle, Botetourt, Cabell, Cumberland, Giles, Lee, Mecklenburg, Montgomery, Nelson, Nicholas, Northampton, Preston, Prince William, Randolph, Rockbridge, Amelia, Amherst, Grayson, Halifax, Madison, Norfolk (excluding Norfolk Borough), Prince Edward, Richmond (City of), Augusta, Brooke, Buckingham, Greenbrier, Henrico (excluding Richmond), Isle of Wight, Bedford, Culpepper, Elizabeth City, Lancaster, Lewis, Monroe, New Kent, Richmond, Tazewell, Brunswick, Fluvanna, Jefferson, King George, Princess Anne, Charles City, Powhatan, Prince George, Spotsylvania, Sussex, Westmoreland, Williamsburg (City of), York, Charlotte, Fauquier, Franklin, Gloucester, Hampshire, King William, Dinwiddie (excluding Petersburg), Essex, Fairfax, Hardy, James City (excluding Williamsburg), Loundoun, Lunenburg, Frederick, Hanover, Harrison, Mason, Shenandoah, Warwick, Wood, Goochland, Henry, Louisa, Nansemond, Petersburg (Town of), Rockingham, Scott, Wythe, Greensville, Ohio, Pendleton, Pittsylvania, Tyler, Morgan, Northumberland, Nottoway, Orange, Patrick, Russell, Stafford, Washington, Kanawha, King and Queen, Matthews, Monongalia, Norfolk (Borough of), Southampton, Surry.

† 1830 – Augusta, Alleghany, Brooke, Bath, Berkeley, Botetourt, Cabell, Frederick, Greenbrier, Giles, Grayson, Harrison, Hampshire, Hardy, Jefferson, Kanawha, Lewis, Logan, Lee, Monongalia, Loudoun, Essex, Gloucester, Nansemond, Powhatan, Buckingham, James City, New Kent, Franklin, Westmoreland, Halifax, Goochland, Cumberland, Isle of Wight, Accomack, Louisa, King George, Richmond, Charles City, Bedford, Hanover, Princess Anne, Lancaster, Campbell, Lynchburg (City of), Fauquier, Amherst, Lunenburg, Stafford, Spotsylvania, Northampton, Patrick, Henry, Nottoway, Brunswick, Henrico, Fluvanna, Richmond (City of), Madison, Greensville, Prince William, Nelson, Matthews, Middlesex, Elizabeth City, Charlotte, Southampton, Orange, Dinwiddie, Chesterfield, Mecklenburg, Culpepper, Warwick, Caroline, Albermarle, Norfolk, Monroe, Montgomery, Morgan, Mason, Nicholas, Ohio, Preston, Pendleton, Pocahontas, Randolph, Russell, Rockingham, Rockbridge, Scott, Shenandoah, Tyler, Tazewell, Washington, Wythe, Wood, Sussex, Prince George, King William, Prince Edward, Amelia, Surry, Northumberland, Fairfax, King and Queen, Pittsylvania, York.

† 1840 – Accomack, Albermarle, Amelia, Amherst, Bedford, Brunswick, Buckingham, Augusta, Alleghany, Bath, Berkeley, Brooke, Braxton, Botetourt, Campbell, Caroline, Charles City, Charlotte, Chesterfield, Culpepper, Cumberland, Clarke, Cabell, Frederick, Fayette, Floyd, Giles, Greenbrier, Grayson, Dinwiddie, Elizabeth City, Essex, Fairfax, Fauquier, Fluvanna.

Franklin, Gloucester, Goochland, Greene, Halifax, Hanover, Henrico, Henry, Harrison, Hardy, Hampshire, Jackson, Jefferson, Isle of Wight, James City, King George, King William, King and Queen, Loudoun, Lancaster, Louisa, Lunenburg, Madison, Mathews, Mecklenburg, Middlesex, Kanawha, Logan, Lee, Lewis, Montgomery, Monogalia, Monroe, Morgan, Mason, Mercer, Marshall, Nansemond, Nelson, New Kent, Norfolk, Northampton, Northumberland, Nottoway, Nicholas, Ohio, Pocahontas, Pendleton, Page, Pulaski, Preston, Orange, Pittsylvania, Patrick, Powhatan, Princess Anne, Prince Edward, Prince George, Prince William, Rappahannock, Richmond, Southampton, Spotsylvania, Stafford, Surry, Sussex, Warwick, Westmoreland, York, Russell, Rockingham, Rockbridge, Roanoke, Randolph, Scott, Shenandoah, Smyth, Tyler, Tazewell, Warren, Washington, Wood, Wythe.

† **1850** — Accomack, Albermarle, Alexandria, Culpepper, Cumberland, Dinwiddie, Lunenburg, Madison, Marion, Mathews, Mecklenburg, Mercer.

† **1860** — All Counties

† **1870** — Cumberland, Lunenburg, Mecklenburg, Middlesex.

Washington

† **1860** — All Counties

West Virginia

† **1880** — Soundex H-1200-H-400 (1)

Wisconsin

† **1860** — All Counties

COUNTY RECORDS

The Microfilm Library has copies of most county books of record for most pre-1900 Georgia counties, including marriage books, estate record books, deed books, etc. Microfilm of records from counties created after 1900 are not available to researchers although the Archives does have security copies of many of them. Cobb County officials have denied the Archives permission to make the microfilm copies of their county's records available to researchers. Officials in Hart and Lowndes Counties have refused the Archives permission to microfilm some of their records. Early Habersham County marriage records were not microfilmed because they were bound too tight. The pre-1860 Union County deeds were missed by the Georgia Archives because they were out of the courthouse on the day the deeds were microfilmed. Contrary to rumors, pre-1900 records have survived in Wilkinson and Coffee Counties, but these have not been microfilmed. Some books of record have been overlooked by the Archives microfilming project, while other books that were judged at the time to be of limited research value, such as evidence books, were also not microfilmed. Researchers should be aware that some Georgia counties have lost some of their records to courthouse fires, Indian attack, explosions, tornadoes, hurricanes, political troubles, "the Scurge of Sherman," indifference (i.e., one county clerk used pages of old deed books to light his stove in the early 1930s), as well as neglect before they could be microfilmed. Also, some were lost in house and office fires after being borrowed from the courthouse. However, other books were saved by the fortunate accident of not being in the courthouse when other records were destroyed.

County records microfilmed by the Archives are stamped as such in their first few pages. Researchers who believe they have found genealogically significant county books of record (or even loose papers) that have been missed by the microfilming project, should write to the Government Records Office, Georgia Department of Archives and History, 330 Capitol Avenue, S.E., Atlanta, Georgia 30334.

It should be noted that some of the county records on microfilm at the Archives are no longer in their respective county courthouses. Some have been deposited at the Archives and others have been destroyed. Courthouse fires and neglect are, unfortunately, still common. Researchers should call or write to a courthouse about the records before making a visit.

The card catalogue to the microfilm of county records is arranged by county, with a separate drawer for tax digests (see Chapter 7 for county records and Chapter 9 for tax records on microfilm). This catalogue has been compiled over many years by a number of people with varying degrees of knowledge of Georgia county records. As a result, many records are incorrectly identified. In some instances more than one title is used for the same type of record. For example, what is "Year's Support" in some instances is "Twelve Months Support" in others, and in some counties the records are split up between both designations. Records that should be under the sub-heading "Ordinary" are sometimes catalogued under "Superior Court," and vice versa. For example, in one county, the Inferior Court Minutes for 1790-1829 might be filed under "Ordinary" (which is the proper heading for Inferior Court Minutes), but the county's other Inferior Court Minutes, 1830-1868, might be incorrectly catalogued under "Superior Court." Also, some types of county records are catalogued on two or more cards in such a way that a researcher might read the first card or cards, presume that this is all that has survived of that record, and not see the succeeding cards showing earlier and/or later records of the same type. **If you find a gap in a county's records, using the microfilm library's card catalogue, do not presume that such a gap actually exists until you have read every card in the catalogue for that county to make sure that the rest of the records were not misfiled or incorrectly identified.**

In some instances, the Microfilm Library's card catalogue does not indicate all or some of the official designations of certain books of record. For example, what is Mixed Estate Book AA, 1822-1845, may be only identified in the card catalogue as Mixed Estates, 1833-1845. However, a researcher using the microfilm copy of that county's estate index might find a citation to "Book AA, p. 355" and then would not be able to readily identify the record book to which the researcher is being referred.

Some of the dates indicated in the card catalogue for certain records are in error. Will books are sometimes dated by the earliest and latest dates the wills were written but for other counties by the earliest and latest dates the wills were probated.

Some records not indicated in the card catalogue as indexed actually are indexed. Researchers should check both the beginning and end of a record for the index.

STATE RECORDS

State records in the Microfilm Library are catalogued (about 2,000 cards) in the drawer marked "Georgia Official Records." Among the more genealogically important are:

† **Colonial and State Land Grants and Plats** (surveys) under the sub-heading of "Surveyor General Department." Land memorials, or quit rents, and land court minutes are under the sub-heading "Colony," **except** when they deal with only one county; then they are filed in their respective counties in the county records drawers. Records such as these provide clues to when a family moved to Georgia, their wealth, where they lived within Georgia, and the names of neighbors and other persons who could be relatives.

† **Colonial Conveyance** and other colonial Georgia books of record are under the sub-heading "Colony." These volumes are Georgia's early deed, mortgage, and estate records. For a specific listing of these books of record, see the section of this book entitled Colonial Conveyance and Other Books of Record.

† **Poor School** (early public schools) and academy lists (reels 60-62, 63) under the sub-heading "Executive Department." These fragments are state-level records that often provide the names of pupils, their ages, and the names of their parents. On these two reels, fragments for the following counties are found: Baker − 1859; Baldwin − 1831, 1841; Bibb − 1830, 1836, 1837, 1847; Bryan − 1831, 1842, 1847, 1859, 1860; Bulloch − 1834; Burke − 1829, 1835; Butts − 1835, 1837, 1838; Calhoun − 1859; Chattahoochee − 1860; Cobb − 1859; Dawson − 1859; Decatur − 1860; DeKalb − 1851, 1859, 1860; Dooly − 1859; Early − 1859; Emanuel − 1859, 1860; Gilmer − 1837, 1850-55; Gwinnett − 1837; Habersham − 1834-36; Hancock − 1835; Heard − 1837; Henry − 1829-32, 1855; Jackson − 1834, 1860; Jasper − 1829, 1831-37; Jones − 1829-37; Lee − 1845; Lincoln − 1837; McIntosh − 1859; Madison − 1837; Monroe − 1837; Morgan − 1859, 1860; Muscogee − 1837, 1859, 1860; Polk − 1859; Rabun − 1842, 1860; Schley − 1860; Screven − 1855; Talbot − 1859; Towns − 1859; Upson − 1845, 1860; Ware − 1826, 1832-33; Warren − 1832-35, 1841; Washington − 1832, 1835, 1838, 1866; Wayne − 1833-34, 1841; Wilkes − 1832-35; Wilkinson − 1841, 1860.

The R.J. Taylor, Jr., Foundation has published an index to the records that appear on these two reels, except those after 1850. Other poor school and academy lists of students not on the above microfilm and not in the Foundation's index include some in the County Files, File II, in the Central Research Library; filed under specific counties in the Microfilm Library's county records card files; and in the loose county records available in the Central Research Library through the Historical Research Advisor.

† **State Census Records** under the sub-heading "Executive Department."
Georgia conducted its own censuses in 1786 and roughly every seven years
from 1798 to 1879, with special state censuses held in counties created
from Indian lands during intervening years. Georgia censuses contain only
a fraction of the information found in federal census records, usually only
the name of the head and the number of persons in each household. The
state census records available in the Microfilm Library are for the following
counties: Chatham — 1845, 1852; Dooly — 1845; Forsyth — 1845; Jasper
— 1852; Laurens — 1838; Lumpkin — 1838?; Newton — 1838; Richmond
(Augusta) — 1852; Taliaferro — 1827; Tattnall — 1838; Terrell — 1859;
Warren — 1845.

The R.J. Taylor, Jr., Foundation has published the above censuses for Chatham, Dooly, Forsyth, Lumpkin, Taliaferro, and Warren Counties and has published an index to the above for Laurens, Newton, and Tattnall Counties.
Other state census records are filed under their respective county in the county
records files of the Microfilm Library. State census records have also been
found in the Telamon Cuyler Collection of Special Collections, University of
Georgia libraries, Athens, and other little-known sources, and have been published. State census records are being discovered in the loose county records
currently being brought into the Archives from across the state.

† **Military Records** under the sub-heading "Adjutant General." These include
register of officers in the Georgia state troops, 1900-1936 (reel 185-5); rosters, Mexican Border troubles, 1916 (reel 187-5 & 6); military commission
books, 1798-1860 (some for an earlier period are filed under the sub-heading "Executive Department"); muster roll of the 2nd Brigade, 1st Division,
1815-1818 (reel 60-62); and other military records.

† **Autobiographical Questionnaires** of prominent Georgians under the sub-
heading "Secretary of State — Georgia Department of Archives and History" (reels 154-1 through 15). These questionnaires were first sent out in
the 1920s and are still sent today to get information for **Georgia's Official
and Statistical Register**. Some of the earlier ones were sent to descendants
of deceased persons, some of whom had died in 1890 or earlier. These
papers are rich in genealogical data.

Researchers should note that only the last two reels of this series contain the questionnaires about leading Georgia women. Following the questionnaires are genealogical file folders (reels 154-16 through 25) that, like
the autobiographical questionnaires, were filmed in alphabetical order.

† **State Prison Records** are under the sub-heading "Board of Corrections."
Records of convicts, 1852-1897, that provide the names of each inmate,
county convicted, state of birth, and other information are included here.
The Historical Research Advisor in the Central Research Section has these
records going back to 1817. The Microfilm Library also has the physicians'
reports on the convicts, 1884-1897.

Records of Inmate Burials at Central State Hospital for the Insane, 1880-
1957, are under the sub-heading "Department of Health" (reel 223-24).

Military Records Books on microfilm reels 40-16 through 18. These are handwritten manuscript compilations of Georgia military records. Volume one contains miscellaneous military records from 1779 through 1839 and is also available as a typescript in the Central Research Library. Volume two, 1808-1829; volume three, 1829-1841; volume four, 1841-1862; and volume five, 1861-1877, are primarily military commissions; but volume six, 1872-1902, is miscellaneous records.

† **Governors Proclamations**, 1754-1825, on microfilm reels 40-40 and 40-41, filed under the sub-heading "Executive Department." The proclamations are valuable because they provide the date of death of persons who were murdered but their killers fled justice. The proclamations also provide physical descriptions of the murderers. Governors proclamations for later years are available through the Historical Research Advisor in the Central Research Section. Also see Robert S. Davis, Jr., "Georgia Murders, Murderers, and Murder Victims, 1823-1840," **Georgia Genealogical Society Quarterly** vol. 15 (1979), pp. 103-15.

† **Georgia Treasury Department Records**, 1782-1813, including records of payment for services and supplies provided during the American Revolution. Some of these records are indexed.

FEDERAL RECORDS

Besides the federal census records, the Archives also has a large miscellaneous collection (about 500 catalogue cards) of other federal records, much of which appears to have been donated by patrons over the years. Among the more important of these records are the censuses of the Creeks and Cherokees and other Indian records; and the Revolutionary War pension claims for Georgia soldiers. The latter does not include all of the pension papers, but as with the copies of the pensions you order from the National Archives, these are only a few representative pages from each pension. Revolutionary War pension claims provide a large and varied amount of personal and military information. A list of the pensioners is: National Genealogical Society, **Index of Revolutionary War Pension Applications in the National Archives** (2nd ed., Washington, D.C.: National Genealogical Society, 1976).

PRIVATE COLLECTIONS, NEWSPAPERS, AND OTHER RECORDS

Private collections and other non-government records are filed in the Microfilm Library's card catalogues under a variety of headings. These are often not cross-referenced, and it is necessary to check card by card to be certain of not missing something of specific interest. The cards usually only contain the collection name, microfilm reel number, and a few words of description. Even so, these collections inadequately catalogued as they are, are the most valuable sources of historical and genealogical data on Georgia ever assembled.

The Microfilm Library, however, contains only what has been loaned or donated, plus the little that their limited budget has allowed them to buy. They **do not** have a collection of **all** church, cemetery, county, and newspaper records.

Below is a list of the major headings under which these records are filed:

† **Bible Records** (about 3,000 cards)

† **Books** (about 850 cards). Includes typescripts and bound, handwritten manuscripts as well as published books.

† **Cemeteries** (about 1,000 cards)

† **Church Records** (about 5,000 cards). Includes individual church histories, church minutes, and association minutes. Researchers should look in the drawer labeled "Counties" (see below) for records of a specific church before consulting this drawer.

† **Civil War** (about 600 cards). Includes sub-headings of battles, muster rolls, CSA records, personal narratives, published records, regimental history, and U.S. armies.

† **Cities** (about 1,200 cards). Includes some city and town government records.

† **Counties** (about 3,000 cards). Separate from the drawers holding cards for county records.

† **Genealogical Information** (about 1,800 cards).

† **Name File** (about 700 cards)

† **Newspapers** (about 2,000 cards). The Georgia Newspaper Project of the University of Georgia libraries, Athens, has a much larger collection of newspapers on microfilm, all of which are available on interlibrary loan to Georgia libraries. The Archives' Microfilm Library has a list of these newspapers. The Archives' collection of Augusta newspapers is particularly incomplete. A more complete collection is available at the Reese Library, Augusta College.

On reels 150-1 through 90 and 151-1 through 19, the Microfilm Library has an index to Savannah newspapers, 1836-1845. The Periodical Room in the Central Research Section has this index for 1763-1830, and the Georgia Historical Society and the University of Georgia libraries at Athens have still more of this index. The Central Research Library also has copies of published indexes or abstracts of records of some other Georgia newspapers.

† **Out of State and Foreign Records** (about 600 cards)

† **Private Papers** (about 2,000 cards)

† **Subject File** (about 1,400 cards). Includes several records on Indians, filed by tribe.

The Microfilm Library also has the Leon Hollingsworth Genealogical Collection on microfilm. This collection consists of roughly 45,000 note cards on Georgia families. The R.J. Taylor, Jr., Foundation has published a list of family names in this collection. The Archives also has on reels 160-5, 21-12, 32-64, and 160-8 approximately 300 items from the 50,000 records of the Telamon Cuyler Collection of Special Collections, University of Georgia libraries, Athens. Although these are loose state records, they are filed in the Microfilm Library as a private collection. This sampling from the Cuyler Collection consists of early military records (including the American Revolution) and documents on the travels of Georgia's records during the Revolution.

The Microfilm Library also has on microfilm a few representative pages from each of the claims of Georgia Loyalists seeking redress from the British Government for property losses during the American Revolution that resulted from their loyalty to the British. These claims are rich in information on colonial Georgia, and the evidence in these claims often mentions persons who were not Loyalists and who remained in Georgia. For more complete copies of the Loyalist Claims, microfilm copies may be borrowed from the Public Archives of Canada through inter-library loan.

The Microfilm Library also has the incoming passenger lists for the Port of New York, January 2, 1820-August 12, 1853 — a gift to the Archives by the Reverend Silas Emmett Lucas, Jr. However, these lists are not indexed but are arranged by name of ship. Sometimes, naturalization records can provide the date and name of the ship on which a person arrived, aiding in the location of the person in these records.

4
OTHER SOURCES

SURVEYOR GENERAL DEPARTMENT

This department is in the same building as the Archives but is a separate department, and unlike the Archives, it is **not** open on Saturdays. Among the genealogically important records here are:

† Recorded copies of Georgia's 1,474,699 land grants and plats (surveys). Indexed.

† Loose land records, including certificates for bounties based upon Revolutionary War service. These are filed alphabetically. The loose land plats are arranged by county.

† Records of Georgia land lotteries, including an index to the lots won in the first, 1805, land lottery. This was not published with the list of winners. Indexed. The Surveyor General Department also has records of fraudulent draws in the lotteries.

† 6,000 maps, with special emphasis on those of Georgia. Arranged by time period.

† Dr. John H. Goff Collection of files on Georgia forts, ferries, and roads. Arranged alphabetically by location. See Marion R. Hemperley, **The John H. Goff Collection** (Atlanta: Georgia Surveyor General Department Descriptive Inventory no. 2, 1971).

† Book of Revolutionary War bounty grants issued in Franklin and Washington Counties (this has been published in the **Georgia Genealogist**).

† Receipt book for now-lost colonial and state land grants issued in 1775 and 1778 (to be published in the Georgia **Genealogical Society Quarterly**).

† Receipt book for bounty land grants that was published by Ruth Blair in 1928. Parts of this manuscript are apparently lost as are the succeeding volumes. Like the bounty certificates, this record provides information on Revolutionary War service.

† Miscellaneous records of the creation of and changes in militia districts and Georgia county and state boundary changes and disputes.

The Surveyor General Department sells several valuable publications on their records, including abstracts of all Georgia's surviving colonial land grants (and plats). This latter series is particularly useful when compared with the information found in the published and unpublished volumes of the **Colonial Records of the State of Georgia** series. The unpublished volumes and the cumulative index to those published are in the Central Research Library. The following is a current list of publications for sale (prices are subject to change):

† **Georgia State Boundary Documents: Florida-Georgia Boundary, A Calendar,** by Pat Bryant, 116 pp., $5.00.

† **Pre-Nineteenth Century Maps in the Collection of the Georgia Surveyor General Department,** by Janice G. Blake, 169 pp., $5.00. (The department is currently preparing a new catalogue to their maps for 1800 to 1850, including new editions to their pre-1800 map collection.)

† **Entry of Claims for Georgia Landholders, 1733-1755,** by Pat Bryant, 254 pp., $5.00.

† **Georgia Counties: Their Changing Boundaries,** by Pat Bryant, 164 pp., $5.00.

† **Handbook of Georgia Counties,** by Marion R. Hemperley, 24 pp., $1.00.

† **Georgia Bounty Land Grants,** by Alex M. Hitz, 12 pp., $1.00.

† **Authentic List of All Land Lottery Grants Made to Veterans of the Revolutionary War by the State of Georgia,** by Alex M. Hitz, 78 pp., $2.00.

† **Georgia Militia Districts,** by Alex M. Hitz, 7 pp., $1.00.

† **English Crown Grants in Georgia, 1755-1775,** by Marion R. Hemperley and Pat Bryant, 9 vol. covering Georgia's 12 parishes, $5.00 each or $25.00 for 9 vol. set.

† **Map of Colonial Georgia, 1773-1777,** by Marion R. Hemperley, $2.00.

† **Map of Georgia, Early Roads and Trails, circa 1730-1850,** by Marion R. Hemperley, $2.00.

SOURCES FOR VITAL STATISTICS RECORDS

Some Georgia counties and cities were allowing individuals to voluntarily (officially) record births and deaths long before the state of Georgia began requiring such registrations in 1919. Some of these early records are on microfilm at the Archives, catalogued under their respective counties and cities in the Microfilm Library (see Chapter 7). For example, birth records for the city of Gainesville in Hall County start in 1865 and death records begin in 1909. These are catalogued under "Gainesville" in the "Cities" card catalogue and are available on microfilm reel 245-65. However, other such records must be requested locally. Most birth records are severely restricted. City of Atlanta birth records, beginning in 1887; and death records, starting in 1896, must be requested from the Fulton County Health Department, 99 Butler Street, Atlanta, Georgia 30303. City of Savannah birth records that start in 1890 can be ordered from the Chatham County Health Department, P.O. Box 6148, Savannah, Georgia 31405. Columbus-Muscogee County birth records, starting in 1869; and death records, beginning in 1890, may be ordered from the Muscogee County Health Department, 1958 Eighth Avenue, Columbus, Georgia

31901. Birth records for the city of Macon begin in 1891, and death records start in 1882. However, the early birth records are not available to the public. Death records can be ordered from Macon-Bibb County Department of Health, 770 Hemlock Street, Macon, Georgia 31298.

Federal census records provide information on births, deaths, and marriages for the census years 1850, 1860, 1870, and 1880. These are available in the Microfilm Library.

Georgia began keeping birth and death certificates statewide on January 1, 1919. The Vital Records Unit, Georgia Department of Human Resources, Room 217-H, Health Building, 47 Trinity Avenue, Atlanta, Georgia, controls these records and also provides free brochures on obtaining certified copies, for a fee, of birth and death certificates. However, **by Georgia law, birth certificates will only be issued to the following:**

† The person whose record is registered.

† Either parent whose name is listed on the certificate.

† The legal representative of the person whose birth is registered.

† The superior court, upon its order.

† Any government agency, state or federal, provided such certificate shall be needed for official purposes.

Death certificates are open to anyone if the name of the deceased, year of death (within three years), and county where the death is recorded can be provided. Georgia death certificates often provide the place of birth and the names of the parents of the deceased.

• **Note:** The Historical Records Survey, **Guide to Public Vital Statistics Records in Georgia** (Atlanta: the author, 1941), on pages 5 and 28, describes sixty-four volumes of birth certificates, 1865-1918; and nine volumes of death certificates, 1865-1918, held by Georgia's Department of Health. Presumably, these are delayed birth and death certificates (records filed after January 1, 1919, of earlier births and deaths). These records are currently not available from either the Vital Statistics Unit or the Archives. It is hoped that some time in the near future at least these death records will be turned over to the Archives and made available to the public, since they cannot be used as official substitutes for death certificates.

In the 1940s and 50s, the Department of Health and the Department of Education alternately kept some original school census records from the early 1900s that were often used for obtaining delayed birth certificates. No one today seems to know what has become of these censuses although a rumor has been circulating that they were sent back to their respective counties in the 1950s and may be found today in the records of local boards of education. Hopefully, the Archives will find these records and have them microfilmed and made available for genealogical research.

LIBRARIES

The following are the major research libraries with large Georgia collections. However, almost every regional and local public library in Georgia has locally oriented genealogical collections, and many have private manuscript collections. Manuscript collections in Georgia college libraries tend to deal only with the college's history and biographical information on alumni, although some also have locally oriented historical and genealogical collections.

Researchers should always write or call a library or archives before making a visit, to guarantee that the repository will be open. This is particularly true of college libraries and any branch of state government in Georgia.

• **Note:** Researchers should be aware that some libraries catalogue their Civil War holdings separately from their other collections, with no cross reference. This problem even exists with newspapers.

Athens

University of Georgia libraries, Athens, Georgia 30602. Special Collections has thousands of collections of Georgia manuscripts, photographs and prints, maps, and rare books. These collections are catalogued, although poorly cross referenced. Some of the descriptions in the catalogue are incomplete and misleading. The larger collections are especially poorly catalogued. Their Telamon Cuyler Collection consists of 50,000 loose Georgia state and county records arranged by governor, county, and subject. Of particular interest to genealogists is the LeConte Genealogical Collection with its thousands of cards and files on Georgia families. The Georgia Room has the largest collection of Georgia books available and also has biographical files on thousands of prominent Georgians, past and present. The Georgia Room also has Georgia county files (including WPA compilations of laws dealing with specific Georgia counties) and card indexes to the **Georgia Historical Quarterly** and the **Georgia Alumni Record.** The latter is a publication dealing with the alumni of the University of Georgia. The Microfilm Library has the largest collection of Georgia newspapers available on microfilm, the Lyman C. Draper Collection of records and interviews dealing with the American frontier, and census records for the entire South. The Government Documents Center has some of the volumes of **The American State Papers** and the **Official Register** of federal employees (including postmasters) for 1821, 1822, and 1833. The early volumes of the **Official Register** gave the place of birth of each employee. Also see Emory University Libraries, Atlanta.

Atlanta Area

† Atlanta Historical Society, P.O. Box 12423, Atlanta, Georgia 30355. Located at 3099 Andrews Drive, near West Paces Ferry Drive, their library has extensive manuscript collections that cover the entire state of Georgia, but their holdings are primarily Atlanta-Fulton County oriented. They also have books, Atlanta city directories, and Atlanta newspapers. They have a resident historian for answering requests for information by mail. A guide to their manuscript collections is entitled **Guide to the Manuscript Collections of the Atlanta Historical Society,** by D. Louise Cook (Atlanta: The Society, 1976).

† Atlanta Public Library, One Margaret Mitchell Square, Atlanta, Georgia 30303. Their Special Collections has a card index to published biographical sketches of Georgians, past and present; a card index to articles on promi-

nent black Americans; a large collection of books on black history; the most complete set of the valuable **American-Biographical Index to Genealogical, Biographical and Local History** (Middletown, Conn., 1952- ___) available in Georgia; a large collection of works on Virginia; and much more.

† Trevor Arnett Library, Atlanta University, 173 Chestnut Street, S.W., Atlanta, Georgia 30314. Their Special Collections has the largest collection of books on black history and biography in the Southeast, and their archives has private manuscript collections of prominent black Americans.

† Emory University libraries, Emory University, Emory, Georgia 30338. The Robert W. Woodruff Library has Georgia oriented private manuscript collections and newspapers in their Special Collections. Their Microfilm Library has the Lyman C. Draper Collection (450 volumes of manuscripts relating to frontier America and the South in the American Revolution) and microfilm copies of colonial and Revolutionary War newspapers. Their Government Documents Center has a complete set of **The American State Papers** (the most genealogically significant material in this series, chiefly on the American Revolution, is indexed in **Grassroots of America** by Phillip W. McMullin [Salt Lake City: Gendex Corp., 1972]); a few early published lists of federal employees; and registers of army and navy officers. The Pitts Theological Seminary, Candler School of Theology, has early Methodist newspapers and church records. The Medical Library has copies of publications of early Georgia medical associations.

• **Note:** Although the books in the Woodruff Library are closed to everyone except faculty, students, and visiting scholars; all of the genealogical materials described above are in areas open to the general public. Emory University asks, however, that researchers not consult them for materials available at their local libraries or elsewhere in the Atlanta area.

† Federal Archives and Record Center, 1557 St. Joseph Avenue, East Point, Georgia 30344. The Center has census records (free and slave) for the entire country through 1900; statewide indexes to census records; WW I draft registration records (for persons not actually drafted as well); naturalization records; federal district and circuit court case papers (similar to in genealogical value to the Georgia State Supereme Court case papers described elsewhere); and surviving rosters of Continental troops from the American Revolution. A complete catalogue of their holdings is available.

† Genealogical Center Library, 15 Dunwoody Park Road, Suite 130, Atlanta, Georgia 30308. A private library that charges a fee for its use, the Genealogical Center Library has all the statewide census indexes published by the Accelerated Indexing Systems (the entire country through 1850); genealogical periodicals for the whole United States (3,600 issues of 250 magazines for 1974-77); and a 22,000 card surname index. The Library has special facilities for the blind and handicapped. They are open Wednesdays, Thursdays, and Fridays from 10 a.m. to 3 p.m., and on Thursday nights from 7 p.m. to 9:30 p.m. Genealogy classes are taught on Thursday nights.

† Price Gilbert Memorial Library, Georgia Institute of Technology, Atlanta, Georgia 30332. They have the published indexes to United States patents including names, addresses, and descriptions of inventions for everyone issued patents. Each index covers one year.

† Georgia State Library, 301 Judicial Building, 40 Capitol Square, Atlanta, Georgia 30334. This is the State Library for Georgia and is not to be confused with the library of Georgia State University. Although most of their genealogical books and collections were donated to the Department of Archives and History years ago, they still have many rare books on Georgia, the first annual reports of the Georgia Archives by Dr. Knight, most of the **American State Papers**, and a small historical map collection as well as some old published genealogies.

† Mormon Branch Genealogical Library, 1155 Mt. Vernon Road, Dunwoody, Georgia 30338. This library has a microfilm copy of the card catalogue of the Church of the Latter Day Saints Library in Utah and a microfiche copy of the eighty million name International Genealogical Index. They also have the 1840 federal census for the entire United States. The Mormon Branch Library is open on Tuesdays and Wednesdays from 7 p.m. to 9:30 p.m.

• **Note**: Hours change frequently.

Augusta

Richmond County Historical Society Collection, Reese Library, Augusta College, 2500 Walton Way, Augusta, Georgia 30904. They have Augusta-Richmond County oriented private manuscript and book collections. A guide to these collections is **Library of Richmond County Historical Society** by A. Ray Rowland and Virginia E. de Treville (Augusta: Reese Library, 1978). They also have the most complete collection of Augusta newspapers on microfilm.

Macon

† Georgia Baptist Historical Society, Stetson Library, Mercer University, Macon, Georgia 31201. Largest collection of Georgia Baptist source material and church records.

† Genealogical and Historical Room, Washington Memorial Library, 1180 Washington Avenue, Macon, Georgia 31201. Largest genealogically oriented book collection in Georgia.

Raleigh, North Carolina Area

† Manuscript Department, Perkins Library, Duke University, Durham, North Carolina 27706. Their holdings include the largest Georgia manuscript collections outside of Georgia including more than 3,000 Georgia state papers and records from various Georgia counties. They have a catalogue to most of their collections: **Guide to the Catalogued Collections in the Manuscript Department of the William R. Perkins, Duke University** (Santa Barbara, Calif.: Clio Books, 1980).

† Southern Historical Collection, Wilson Library, University of North Carolina, Chapel Hill, North Carolina 27514. Their holdings include more than 6,200,000 items relating to the history of the South, including the largest number of collections of family papers relating to Georgia in existence. They have published **The Southern Historical Collection: Guide to Manuscripts** (1970) and **The Southern Historical Collection: Supplementary Guide to Manuscripts, 1970-1975** (1975). These guides may be purchased from the Southern Historical Collection. Many of their family papers collections for Georgia and South Carolina are outlined in Wallace R. Draughon and William Perry Johnson, **North Carolina Genealogical Reference: A Research Guide for All Genealogists Both Amateur and Professional** 2nd ed. (Durham: Seeman Printery, 1966).

Savannah

† Georgia Historical Society, 501 Whitaker Street, Savannah, Georgia 31499. The GHS has been collecting Georgia manuscript material longer than any other Georgia library (since 1839). Although their holdings are coastal Georgia oriented, they do have collections from across the state. A comprehensive catalogue to their collections and a comprehensive index to the **Georgia Historical Quarterly** are currently being prepared by the Society for publication. Already available is **Checklist of Eighteenth Century Manuscripts in the Georgia Historical Society** (Savannah: The Society, 1976). The Society has published its most important colonial and Revolutionary War records in their series, **Collections of the Georgia Historical Society**.

† Savannah Public Library, 2002 Bull Street, Savannah, Georgia 31401. Among their holdings are the scrapbooks of Savannah historian Thomas Gamble.

Vidalia

John E. Ladson, Jr. Library, Ohoopee Regional Library, Meadows and Church Streets, Vidalia, Georgia 30474. Includes 25,000 volumes of genealogist Jack Ladson's collections and microfilm of War of 1812 pension records plus microfilm copies of original Georgia County Records, as well as similar microfilm copies for North Carolina and Virginia.

SPECIAL SOURCES

Adoptees (genealogy for and search for parents). Adoptees' Liberty Movement Association, P.O. Box 154, Washington Bridge Station, New York, New York 10033.

Baptist Records. The Georgia Baptist Historical Society Collection, Stetson Memorial Library, Mercer University, Macon, Georgia 31201, has the largest collection of Georgia Baptist newspapers, church minutes, and related records available. They also have an index to the marriages, deaths, and other information in the **Christian Index (1828-____)**, the official publication of the Georgia Baptist Convention.

Corporation Records. Georgia began requiring registration of corporations in the 1880s. These yearly registrations only contain brief data on these businesses. Copies of registrations are open to anyone but must be requested by mail from Corporation Commissioner, Suite 600, Peachtree Center South, Atlanta, Georgia 30303.

Credit Records (with personal data). The R.G. Dun Collection (Dun & Bradstreet Records), Baker Library, Harvard University, Boston, Massachusetts 02163 has records of information used to compile credit ratings in the 1840s through the 1880s that are rich in gossip and personal data. Copies will be made from these records for a fee provided that the researcher can give the name, county and state of residence of the person whose records are being sought. These records cover the entire United States.

Documents (having them preserved, donated, or loaned for copying). The Georgia Department of Archives and History, 330 Capitol Avenue, S.E., Atlanta, Georgia 30334, accepts donations and loans of Georgia-related private manuscripts, newspapers, or church minutes. Materials **loaned** are microfilmed and returned to their owners free of charge, but the microfilm copy remains at the Archives for use by researchers. **Donations** of books are gladly accepted.

The Document Conservation Center, 3099 Andrews Drive, N.E., P.O. Box 11991, Atlanta, Georgia 30355, Telephone 404/261-6754, located in the same building as the Atlanta Historical Society, does document restoration and preservation work for libraries and private individuals for a fee.

Newspapers. The Georgia Newspaper Project microfilms old Georgia newspapers and makes them available to Georgia libraries on interlibrary loan. Microfilm copies are also available at the University of Georgia Library for use by the general public. A computer printout of the newspapers copied so far is available for a fee from Georgia Newspaper Project, University of Georgia Library, Athens, Georgia 30602. They also accept donations and loans of newspapers for microfilming.

Quaker Records. From the late 1760s to the early 1800s, Georgia had a Quaker community at Wrightsboro, in present-day McDuffie County. The records of this settlement are in the Quaker Collection, Guilford College Library, Greensboro, North Carolina 27410. The library answers requests by mail for information from these records.

Genealogical information on the Wrightsboro Quakers has been abstracted in volume 1, pp. 1047-1051, of William Wade Hinshaw, **Encyclopedia of American Quaker Genealogy**, 6 vols. (1936; rep. ed. Baltimore: Genealogical Publishing Company, 1969). The Wrightsboro Foundation, c/o Dorothy Jones, 633 Hemlock Dr., Thomson, Ga. 30824, publishes booklets, brochures, and other publications on the Quakers and other settlers of Wrightsboro.

Social Security Information. Under certain restrictions, data is available on individuals from the Social Security Administration, P.O. Box 57, Baltimore, Maryland 21235. These records were started in 1936.

Vital Statistics Records for U.S. citizens who were born in or died outside the United States and for persons of foreign birth adopted by U.S. citizens. Copies of reports of birth for U.S. citizens born outside the country can be obtained, under certain restrictions, from the Authentication Officer, U.S. Department of State, Washington, D.C. 20520. Birth certificates of alien children legally adopted by U.S. citizens can be obtained from Immigration and Naturalization Services (INS), U.S. Department of Justice, Washington, D.C. 20536, if the information is on file. Death certificates for U.S. citizens who died in foreign countries are available from the Office of Special Consular Services, U.S. Department of State, Washington, D.C. 20520, unless the deceased was a member of the military. Reports of deaths in foreign countries of members of the U.S. Coast Guard must be obtained from   Commandant, P.S., U.S. Coast Guard, Washington, D.C. 20226. Such records for all other branches of the service should be requested from the Secretary of Defense, Washington, D.C. 20301.

Indians. The Office of Indian Affairs, Georgia Department of Archives and History, 330 Capitol Avenue, S.E. Atlanta, Georgia 30334, provides free pamphlets on Georgia's Indian heritage, will give brief answers to simple questions about **Georgia** Indian research, and is currently preparing a list of Indian source material available at the Archives. The Federal Records Center, 1557 St. Joseph Avenue, East Point, Georgia 30344, currently provides a handout on sources for Indian research.

Professional Researchers. The Georgia Department of Archives and History (330 Capitol Avenue, S.E., Atlanta, Georgia 30334), the Atlanta Public Library (One Margaret Mitchell Square, Atlanta, Georgia 30303), the **Georgia Genealogical Magazine** (P.O. Box 738, Easley, South Carolina 29640), and many public libraries and county offices in Georgia provide free lists of persons willing to do genealogical research for a fee. **None of these institutions takes responsibility for insuring the quality of the work performed by the persons on their list.** All negotiations are between the individual and the researchers. The Board for Certification of Genealogists, 1307 New Hampshire Avenue, Washington, D.C. 20036, provides lists of certified genealogists for Georgia and other areas. The Georgia Secretary of State, 214 State Capitol, Atlanta, Georgia 30334, publishes "Georgia Directory of State and County Officers," which provides the names and addresses of current county officials in Georgia. Most libraries have directories to public libraries in Georgia and across the country.

Others. Useful materials for Georgia research can be found in na'.onal repositories such as the National Archives, the Library of Congress, and the Church of the Latter Day Saints (the Mormons) Library. Guides to these libraries are available. Also, The Georgia Secretary of State, 214 State Capitol, Atlanta, Georgia 30334, publishes "Georgia Directory of State and County Officers," which provides names and addresses of county officials responsible for county records. The Historic Preservation Section, Georgia Department of Natural Resources, 270 Washington Street, Atlanta, Georgia 30334, publishes a list of Georgia historical societies, statewide and local. These materials may be ordered by mail.

REFERENCE BOOKS

The following is a list of some of the better known nationwide reference books used by genealogists. Researchers may contact their local or regional library about other bibliographies and catalogues.

June A. Babbel, **Lest We Forget: A Guide to Genealogical Research in the Nation's Capital** (Annandale, Va.: Annandale Stake of the Church of Jesus Christ of the Latter Day Saints, 1976).

Meredith B. Colket, Jr., and Frank Bridges, **Guide to Genealogical Records in the National Archives** (Washington, D.C.: National Archives, 1964).

P. William Filby, **American and British Genealogy and Heraldry: A Selected List of Books** (Chicago: American Library Association, 1975).

Val D. Greenwood, **The Researcher's Guide to American Genealogy** (Baltimore, Md.: Genealogical Publishing Co., 1975).

F. Wilbur Helmbold, **Tracing Your Ancestry** (Birmingham, Ala.: Oxmoor House, 1976).

Marion J. Kaminkow, **Genealogies in the Library of Congress: A Bibliography** 3 vols. (Baltimore, Md.: Magna Carta Book Co., 1972). [The Magna Carta Book Co. is currently preparing a bibliography of genealogies not in the Library of Congress. Individuals who have information about libraries that have such books should send the names of the books and the addresses of the libraries to Magna Carta Publishing Company, 5502 Magnolia Avenue, Baltimore, Maryland 21215.]

Marion J. Kaminkow, **United States Local Histories in the Library of Congress** 2 vols. (Baltimore, Md.: Magna Carta Book Co., 1972).

Bill R. Linder, **How to Trace Your Family History** (New York: Everest House, 1978).

Donna McDonald, **Directory of Historical Societies and Agencies in the United States and Canada** (Nashville, Tenn.: American Association for State and Local History, 1978).

Mary K. Meyer, **Directory of Genealogical Societies in the U.S.A. and Canada with an Appended List of Independent Genealogical Periodicals** (Pasadena, Md.: The Author, 1978).

Anita C. Milner, **Newspaper Genealogy Columns Directory** (Escondido, Cal.: The Author, 1979).

National Union Catalogue of Manuscripts (Ann Arbor, Mich.: J.W. Edwards, 1959- ____). [Multi-volumed catalogue to manuscript collections across the country. New volumes are added each year.]

Hugh Peskett, **Discovering Your Ancestors: A Quest for Your Roots** (New York: Arco Publishing Co., 1978).

Kip Sperry, **A Survey of American Genealogical Periodicals and Periodical Indexes** (Detroit, Mich.: Gale Research Co., 1978).

Jeane E. Westin, **Finding Your Roots** (New York: Ballantine Books, 1978).

Ethel W. Williams, **Know Your Ancestors: A Guide to Genealogical Research** (Rutland, Vt.: Charles E. Tuttle Co., 1974).

Netti S. Yantis, **Genealogical Books in Print: A Catalogue of In-Print Titles, Useful and Interesting to Those Doing Genealogical Research** (Springfield, Vt.: The Author, 1975).

• **Note:** Because local history and genealogy is a live and growing hobby, any bibliography or guide in this field must by necessity be out of date to some degree, even before publication.

5
PUBLISHERS AND PERIODICALS

[An asterisk (*) indicates publishers who consider unsolicited manuscripts]

PUBLISHERS
(Researchers should write to publishers for catalogues.)

Major Genealogical

Georgia Pioneers, P.O. Box 1028, Albany, Georgia 31702

Genealogical Publishing Company,* 111 Water Street, Baltimore, Md. 21202

Mary Warren, Heritage Papers, Danielsville, Ga. 30633

National Genealogical Society, 1921 Sunderland Pl., NW, Washington, D.C. 20036

The Reprint Company,* P.O. Box 5401, Spartanburg, S.C. 29601 (Georgia and county histories)

Taylor Publishing Company,* P.O. Box 6217, Marietta, Ga. 30065 (county histories)

The R.J. Taylor, Jr., Foundation, P.O. Box 38176, Capitol Hill Station, Atlanta, Ga. 30334

Southern Historical Press,* P.O. Box 738, Easley, S.C. 29640 (formerly Georgia Genealogical Reprints)

Others (Genealogical and Historical)

Accelerated Indexing Systems, P.O. Box 2127, Salt Lake City, Utah 84110 (statewide indexes to federal census records)

Ancestors Unlimited, P.O. Box 490336, College Park, Ga. 30349

Ashantilly Press, Darien, Ga. 31305 (emphasis on Georgia history)

Beehive Press,* 321 Barnard Street, Savannah, Ga. 31401 (emphasis on Georgia history)

Ted O. Brooke, 79 Wagonwheel Court, Marietta, Ga. 30062 (statewide indexes to Georgia wills)

Cherokee Publishing Company,* P.O. Box 1081, Covington, Ga. 30209

Lynda S. Eller, P.O. Box 249, Lanett, Ala. 36863 (books on Heard County)

Sybil McRay, P.O. Box 491, Gainesville, Ga. 30501 (books on Hall County)

Mercer University Press,* Macon, Ga. 31207 (emphasis on Georgia history)

John Moseley, P.O. Box 888305, Atlanta, Ga. 30338 (1880 federal census records for counties created from original Washington County)

Rhea Cumming Otto, 8816 Ferguson Avenue, Savannah, Ga. 31406 (publishing the 1850 federal census of Georgia, county by county)

Diane Dieterle, Roots Publishing Co., Box 476, Mableton, Ga. 30059

Carroll Scruggs, Drawer 278, Helen, Ga. 30545 (publishes book of Georgia historical markers)

University of Georgia Press,* Athens, Ga. 30602 (emphasis on Georgia history)

University of North Carolina Press,* P.O. Box 2288, Chapel Hill, N.C. 27514 (emphasis on history)

W.H. Wolfe Associates,* 1141 Warren Hall Lane, N.E., Atlanta, Ga. 30319 (publishes county histories)

Frances Wynd, 2009 Gail Avenue, Albany, Ga. 31707

PERIODICALS

Genealogical

(All periodicals offer subscriptions. Write for prices. Those marked with a + accept memberships.)

Newsletter (started 1976), Carole Merritt, ed. African-American Family History Association,+ 2077 Bent Creek Way, S.W., Atlanta, Ga. 30311

Ancestoring (quarterly, started 1980 [Richmond County area]), Mrs. Raymond J. Adamson, ed. Augusta Genealogical Society,+ P.O. Box 3743, Augusta, Ga. 30904

Ancestors Unlimited (quarterly started 1979 [emphasis on the Henry, Fayette, and Clayton County area]), Ancestors Unlimited,+ P.O. Box 490336, College Park, Ga. 30349

Armchair Researcher (quarterly, started 1980 [on counties south and west of Atlanta]), Joel Dixon Wells, ed. Rt. 2, Box 895, Hampton, Ga. 30228

Carroll County Genealogical Quarterly (started 1980), Mrs. Kermit B. Cox, pres. Carroll County Genealogical Society,+ Rt. 2, Box 274, Carrollton, Ga. 30117

Central Georgia Genealogical Society Quarterly (started 1979). Central Georgia Genealogical Society,+ P.O. Box 2024, Warner Robins, Ga. 31093

Coweta Chatter (quarterly, started 1974). Norma Gunby, ed., Rt. 1, Hwy. 54, Sharpsburg, Ga. 30277

Douglas County Genealogy (quarterly, started 1978), Joe Braggett, ed., 8823 Rose Ave., Douglasville, Ga. 30134

Family Puzzlers (weekly, started 1964) Mary Warren, ed., Heritage Papers, Danielsville, Ga. 30633

Family Tree (quarterly newsletter, started 1979), Northwest Cobb Genealogical Society,+ P.O. Box 1413, Marietta, Ga. 30061

Georgia Genealogical Magazine (quarterly, started 1961). Silas E. Lucas, Jr., ed., Southern Historical Press, P.O. Box 738, Easley, S.C. 29640

Georgia Genealogical Society Quarterly (started 1964). Georgia Genealogical Society,+ P.O. Box 38066, Atlanta, Ga. 30334

Georgia Genealogist (quarterly, started 1970). Mary Warren, ed., Heritage Papers, Danielsville, Ga. 30633

Georgia Pioneers (quarterly, started 1964). Mary Carter, ed., P.O. Box 1028, Albany, Ga. 31702

Gwinnett Historical Society Newsletter (started 1975). Gwinnett Historical Society,+ P.O. Box 261, Lawrenceville, Ga. 30246

Heard Heritage (quarterly, started 1976 [on Heard **County** area]). Lynda S. Eller, ed., P.O. Box 249, Lanett, Ala. 36863

Huxford Genealogical Society Quarterly (started 1974 [emphasis on south Georgia-Wiregrass area]). Lois A. McAlpin, ed., Huxford Genealogical Society,+ P.O. Box 246, Homerville, Ga. 31634

Genealogical Society of Original Muscogee County Newsletter (started 1980). Published by Edge R. Reid, ed., Genealogical Society of Original Muscogee County,+ 1112 Sixteenth Ave., Columbus, Ga. 31906

North West Georgia Historical and Genealogical Society Quarterly (started 1968). Jewel J. Dyer, ed., North West Georgia Historical and Genealogical Society,+ P.O. Box 2484, Rome, Ga. 30161

They Were Here (quarterly, started 1965). Frances A. Wynd, ed., 2009 Gail Ave., Albany, Ga. 31707

Whitfield-Murray County Historical Quarterly (started 1977 [formerly the Murray-Whitfield County Historical Quarterly]). Whitfield-Murray Historical and Genealogical Society,+ Crown Garden and Archives, 715 Chattanooga Ave., Dalton, Ga. 30720

Historical Periodicals

Georgia Historical Quarterly (covers all of Georgia). Georgia Historical Society,+ 501 Whitaker Street, Savannah, Ga. 31499

Richmond County History (quarterly). Richmond County Historical Society,+ c/o Reese Library, Augusta College, 2500 Walton Way, Augusta, Ga. 30904

Foxfire (on history and culture in north Georgia). Foxfire Fund, Inc., Rabun Gap, Ga. 30568

Georgia Baptist Viewpoints (bi-annually). Georgia Baptist Historical Society,+ Box 776, Washington, Ga. 30673

Atlanta Historical Journal, Atlanta Historical Society,+ P.O. Box 12432, Atlanta, Ga. 30355 (covers all of Georgia, but special emphasis on Atlanta)

Newsletter of the Georgia Association of Historians. Georgia Association of Historians,+ c/o Dr. Edwin Bridges, Georgia Department of Archives and History, 330 Capitol Ave., S.E., Atlanta, Ga. 30334

Papers of the Athens Historical Society. Athens Historical Society,+ P.O. Box 1752, Athens, Ga. 30603

• **Note:** The Historic Preservation Section, Georgia Department of Natural Resources, 270 Washington St., Atlanta, Ga. 30334, publishes a list of local Georgia historical societies

Publications on the Georgia Archives and Records

Newsletter (free). Georgia Department of Archives and History, 330 Capitol Ave., S.E., Atlanta, Ga. 30334

Georgia Archive. Society of Georgia Archivists,+ Box 261, Georgia State University, Atlanta, Ga. 30303

6
MAPS SHOWING THE CREATION OF GEORGIA COUNTIES

All maps, except where noted, are provided through the courtesy of
the Georgia Surveyor General Department

Transition from Districts and Towns into
Parishes in 1758 and 1765 to Counties in 1777

1732-1758 Districts & Towns	1758-1765 Parishes	1765-1777 Parishes	1777 Counties
District of Augusta	St. Paul	St. Paul	Richmond
District of Halifax	St. George	St. George	Burke
District of Abercorn	St. Matthew	St. Matthew	Effingham
District of Goshen	St. Matthew	St. Matthew	Effingham
District of Ebenezer	St. Matthew	St. Matthew	Effingham
District of Ogechee (above Canoochee River)	St. Philip	St. Philip	Effingham
District of Ogechee (below Canoochee River)	St. Philip	St. Philip	Chatham
Town of Hardwick	St. Philip	St. Philip	Chatham
Town of Savannah	Christ Church	Christ Church	Chatham
District of Savannah	Christ Church	Christ Church	Chatham
Sea Islands north of Great Ogechee River	Christ Church	Christ Church	Chatham
Town of Sunbury	St. John	St. John	Liberty
District of Midway	St. John	St. John	Liberty
District of Newport	St. John	St. John	Liberty
St. Catherines Island	St. John	St. John	Liberty
Bermuda Island	St. John	St. John	Liberty
Town of Darien	St. Andrew	St. Andrew	Liberty
District of Darien	St. Andrew	St. Andrew	Liberty
Sapelo Island	St. Andrew	St. Andrew	Liberty
Eastwood Island	St. Andrew	St. Andrew	Liberty
Sea Islands between Great Ogechee & Altamaha Rivers	St. Andrew	St. Andrew	Liberty

COLONIAL GEORGIA
1773 - 1777
BY
MARION R. HEMPERLEY
1979

Town of Frederica	St. James	St. James	Liberty
District of Frederica	St. James	St. James	Liberty
Great St. Simons Island	St. James	St. James	Liberty
Little St. Simons Island	St. James	St. James	Liberty
Sea Islands south of Altamaha River	St. James	St. James	Liberty

Between Altamaha & Turtle River	St. David	Glynn
Between Turtle & Little Satilla Rivers	St. Patrick	Glynn
Between Little Satilla & Great Satilla Rivers	St. Thomas	Camden
Between Great Satilla & St. Marys River	St. Mary	Camden

[Horatio Marbury & William H. Crawford. **Digest of the Laws of Georgia** (Savannah 1802), pp. 150-153]

[State of Georgia. **1777 Constitution**, Section 242]

LOCAL AREA MAPS

The Georgia Department of Transportation, Two Capitol Square, Atlanta, Georgia 30334, sells statewide road maps and maps of individual counties. The latter maps show locations of present-day churches and cemeteries.

The Georgia Surveyor General Department, 330 Capitol Avenue, S.E., Atlanta, Georgia 30334, has a large collection of Georgia maps including early county and town lot maps.

The Branch of Distribution, Eastern Region, U.S. Geological Survey, 1200 South Eads Street, Arlington, Virginia 22202, sells topographical maps and other maps of Georgia.

• **Note:** Union Army maps prepared during the Civil War campaigns in Georgia are so detailed that they often include names of families living in specific areas. Some of the best of these were compiled in **The Official Military Atlas of the Civil War** by George B. Davis, et al. (1891; rep. ed. New York: Arno Press, 1978).

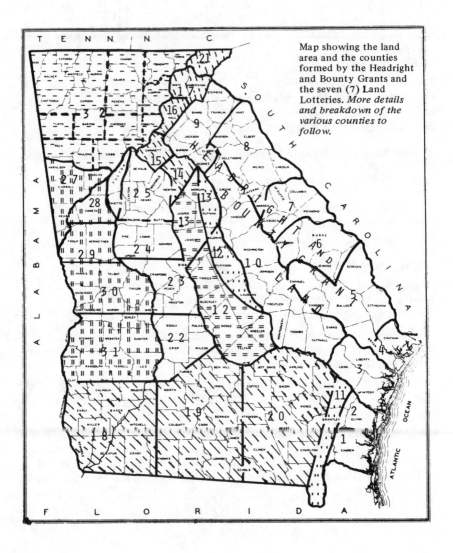

Map showing the land area and the counties formed by the Headright and Bounty Grants and the seven (7) Land Lotteries. *More details and breakdown of the various counties to follow.*

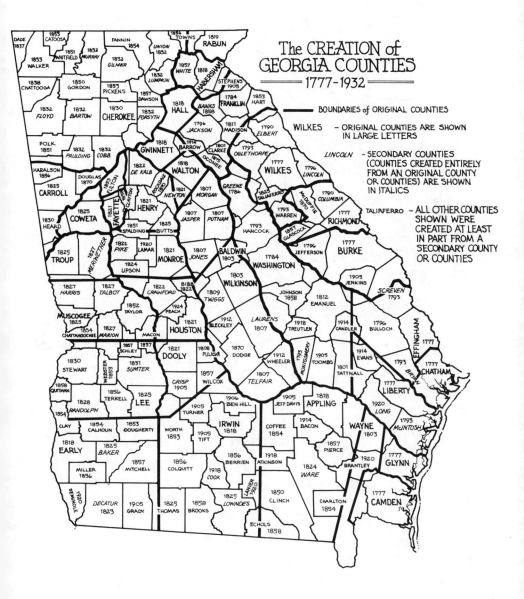

The CREATION of
GEORGIA COUNTIES
1777-1932

COUNTIES OF STATE OF GEORGIA

Reference map of regions used in the following maps of Georgia communities, counties, and militia districts.

UNITED STATES
DEPARTMENT OF THE INTERIOR
GEOLOGICAL SURVEY

STATE OF GEORGIA

Scale 1:1,000,000
1 inch equals approximately 16 miles

Datum is mean sea level

Compiled, edited, and published by the Geological Survey.   1927 North American datum
Lambert conformal conic projection based on standard parallels 33° and 45°

LEGEND

⊕ State capital
◉ County seat
○ City, town, or village
✈ Scheduled service airport
☐ Built-up area shown for towns over 10,000 population

SOURCE DATA

U. S. Dept. of the Interior—Geological Survey topographic maps
U. S. Dept. of the Army—Corps of Engineers topographic maps

BASE MAP

POPULATION KEY

ATLANTA .... more than 100,000
MACON .... 50,000 to 100,000
Rome .... 10,000 to 50,000
Statesboro .... 2,500 to 10,000
Andersonville .... less than 2,500

Population indicated by size of letters

FOR SALE BY U. S. GEOLOGICAL SURVEY, WASHINGTON, D. C. 20242
COMPILED IN 1963
EDITION OF 1966

North West Georgia

The "Cherokee Strip," "Cherokee Country," "Original Cherokee County,"
or "Pioneer Georgia."

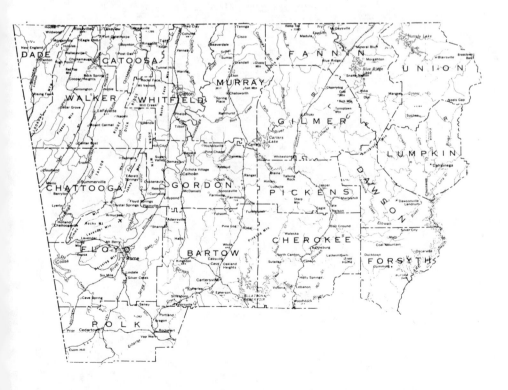

North East Georgia

The "Ceded Lands" and "Original Franklin County"
are included on this map.

East Central Georgia

"Old Colonial Georgia" and "Original Washington County"
are included below.

West Central Georgia
"West" Georgia

South West Georgia

South East Georgia
"Wiregrass" Georgia

GEORGIA

MINOR CIVIL DIVISIONS-MILITIA DISTRICTS

SCALE

10   0   10   20   30   40 MILES

CIRCLES INDICATE INCORPORATED AND UNINCORPORATED PLACES
HAVING UNDER 2500 INHABITANTS
UNINCORPORATED PLACE NAMES ARE IN ITALICS

NOTE: In most instances of a new county being created, any existing militia districts within the new county were abolished and new militia districts were created for the newly created county.

North West Georgia

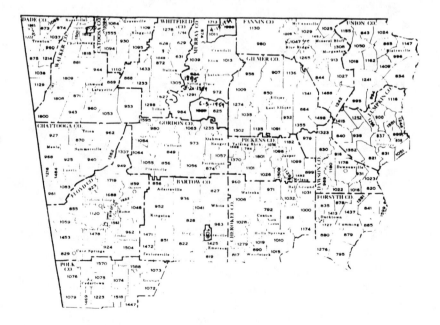

North East Georgia

East Central Georgia

West Central Georgia

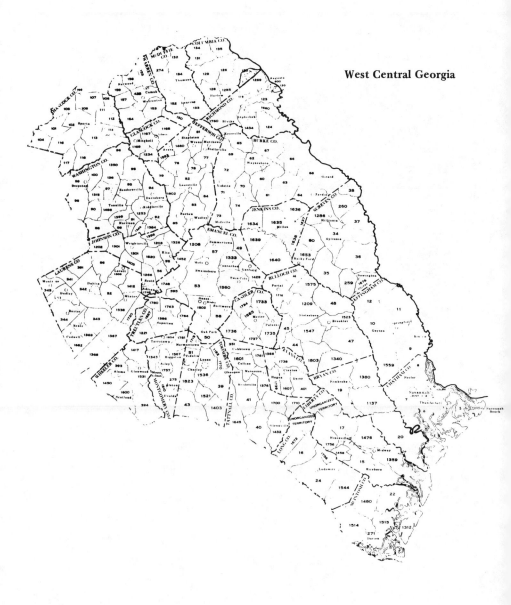

South West Georgia

South East Georgia

7

BASIC DATA ON GEORGIA COUNTIES AND
COUNTY RECORDS ON MICROFILM
AT THE GEORGIA ARCHIVES

SUMMARY

The following is a basic summary of the county records on microfilm in the Microfilm Library of the Georgia Department of Archives and History. It is **not an item by item list** as space limitations prevent such an exact listing here. However, the Southern Historical Press hopes to some day publish such a list. Abbreviations are used to save space and are explained on the following pages. Many more types of estate records exist than are included here, but researchers can almost always assume that if annual returns, inventories and appraisements, and wills exist for a county for a certain period; then so do the records not included in this list — such as guardianships, letters, testamentary, and dismissals.

In using this section, researchers are cautioned of the following:

† The Microfilm Library's card catalogue is not consistent in use of terms, and many records may appear under a variety of names **not** listed here. For this reason and because of other shortcomings of the Microfilm Library's card catalogue, researchers should never presume a particular record has not been microfilmed until they have checked every card in the catalogue for the county they are researching (see the description of the county records card catalogue of the Microfilm Library in Chapter 3).

† Many of the county records that the Archives has microfilmed are no longer kept by their respective counties. Many have been turned over to the Archives for safekeeping and others have been destroyed, either by accident or by county officials needing space. Researchers should contact the Archives Government Records Office, the Microfilm Library, or county officials before making a visit to a courthouse to see original records.

† Many records were lost before they could be microfilmed or were accidentally overlooked by the persons doing the filming. The following list of county records on microfilm includes the years that courthouses were destroyed or damaged to such a degree that records may have been destroyed. Information on some years that records were lost was unavailable, and some records were destroyed while being loaned by county officials. While a gap is then created, not all of the records were destroyed. Many personal copies of deeds and wills were re-recorded after courthouse fires.

† The following publications available from the Surveyor General Department, 330 Capitol Ave., S.E., Atlanta, Georgia 30334, provide information on changes in county boundaries in Georgia from 1777 to 1932:

Pat Bryant, **Georgia Counties: Their Changing Boundaries** (Atlanta: State Printing Office, 1977).

Marion R. Hemperley, **Handbook of Georgia Counties** (Atlanta: State Printing Office, 1980). [The more important information found in the Bryant book but cheaper, smaller, easier to use, and corrected.]

ABBREVIATIONS

Except where noted, all abbreviations refer to bound books of records.

*	The Microfilm Library's card catalogue indicates that the records are indexed or appear in alphabetical order. The term "index" in county records generally means that the names appear only in rough alphabetical order by the first letter of each person's last name.
**	Records are not indexed for some years.
Amnst	Amnesty Records — information on individuals who signed amnesty oaths after the Civil War to participate in the special election of 1867 to choose a constitutional convention for bringing Georgia back into the Union. The amount of information found in these records varies considerably.
Aptc	Apprenticeships (see glossary of terms)
AnRns	Annual Returns (see glossary)
Bast	Bastardy Records — bonds posted by fathers of illegitimate children. Usually gives the names of the father, mother, and child.
Birth	Birth Records — usually gives name and date of birth plus names of parents. Early county birth records are often incomplete.
Cen	County Copies of Federal, State, or Local Census Records. County copies of federal records often do not contain all the information found in federal copies.
Conf	Confederate Service or Pension Records. Despite some of the dates shown, almost none of these records were compiled in 1861-1865; nearly all were created in the early 1900s.
Death	Death Records — usually provides the name and date of death. Early county death records are often incomplete.
Deed	Deeds and Mortgages (see glossary). Deed records, particularly early ones, sometimes provide the names of heirs to an estate or previous state and county of residence. Deed indexes described in this section are alphabetical indexes; not the indexes by land lot that some counties also have.
Est	Estate Records — wills, administrations, annual returns, guardians bonds, inventories, etc. — any or all records dealing with the property of a person who has died or requires a guardian.

FPC Free Persons of Color Records — names of free Negroes or Mulattos and their guardians.

Home Homestead Records — requests by individuals or families for exemptions from taxes or obligations to creditors because of poverty. These records often provide personal data and information on children, such as names of parents and ages.

Inf Inferior Court Minutes — a county-level court presided over by local justices and juries. The court appointed administrators, dismissed executors and administrators, appointed guardians, and regulated estates in other ways. The court also functioned as a county government and a civil court, including regulating taverns, repairing roads, and maintaining county buildings. The Inferior Court was created in December of 1789 and was abolished in 1868. Its functions regarding estate records are now performed by the Judge of Probate (formerly known as the Court of Ordinary). See Warren Grice, "The Old Inferior Court," **Journal of the Georgia Bar Association** vol. 5 (1942), pp. 5-14.

InvA Inventories and Appraisements (see glossary)

Jury Jury Lists or Registers — lists adults, usually male residents. These are useful in proving that a person lived in a certain place at a certain time and can provide clues to when a person became an adult.

LdCt Land Court Minutes (see glossary)

LLoty Land Lottery — county copies of lists of all local participants in Georgia's land lotteries. With the exception of the first, 1805, lottery, all of the published statewide lists only identify the winners. These records are sometimes useful for proving when a person moved to a certain county, married, had children, or if they served in the American Revolution.

Liq Liquor or Tavern Licenses — issued by the Inferior Court to individuals to allow the retailing of certain alcoholic beverages and to collect the local tax on such sales.

Lun Lunacy Records — usually provides the name of the person declared insane plus his residence. Sometimes also gives information on their care or confinement.

Mar Marriage Records — usually shows names of groom and bride (maiden name also), date, and presiding official. Georgia began requiring marriage licenses in 1804, but some counties were allowing voluntary registration as early as the 1780s. Loose marriage records often include licenses that were never recorded in books of record. Marriage licenses, by tradition and by law, are recorded in the bride's county.

Nat Naturalizations — records of foreign born persons receiving U.S. citizenship, usually showing the country of birth.

OInd Index to Ordinary (state) Records.

OMin Minutes of the Court of Ordinary — records of the official body that regulated all matters dealing with estates after 1868. The Court of

Ordinary replaced the Inferior Court in these functions and is today itself the Probate Court.

Paup   Paupers Records — those dealing with poor people, usually in attempting to obtain public relief at the county level.

PhR   Register of Physicians, Druggists, Embalmers, Dentists, etc. — In some counties, separate registers are kept for each profession.

Pony   Pony Homestead Records — similar to regular homestead, but dealt with certain personal, movable property and not with houses, land, livestock, etc.

Sch   School Records — providing at least the names of students and sometimes their ages and names of parents or guardians. These include county copies of poor school and academy lists.

SlavR   Register of persons bringing slaves into Georgia. Provides information on migrations to Ga.

SMisc   Miscellaneous Superior Court Records — usually loose papers that include civil and criminal court case papers and loose deeds. Court case papers often include genealogically valuable plaintiffs petitions and testimony not found in the superior court minutes.

SMin   Superior Court Minutes — highest civil and criminal court on the county level and, until 1846, on the state level. Superior Court minutes are also useful because of the jury lists they contain and because of relationships implied in the abstracts of court cases recorded in the minutes. Usually, the minutes do not contain the same detailed information found in the loose court case papers. In the Archives' Microfilm Library, the dockets to Superior Court minutes are sometimes mistakenly identified as being the minutes.

TMSup   Twelve Months Support or Year's Support (see Year's Support in the glossary). In the Microfilm Library's card catalogue, both terms are used — sometimes even within the same county.

Vote   Voter Lists or Registers — has the same value as jury lists.

WWI   World War I Service or Discharge Records. Some counties also have these for later wars.

Wills   (See glossary.) Many wills are recorded in other books of record as well, including miscellaneous estate books, inferior court records, mixed estate records, etc. See Ted O. Brooke, **In the Name of God, Amen: Georgia Wills: An Index** (Marietta: the author, 1976). Mr. Brooke is currently preparing a revised edition of this work and a second volume to cover wills up to 1900.

COUNTY DATA

• There will be **no list of records** for counties created **after 1900**. The Georgia Department of Archives and History has not yet made their microfilm copies of these counties' records available to researchers.

Appling:
Created December 15, 1818, from Indian lands ceded in 1814 and 1818, #42 in order of creation; county seat, Baxley 31513; courthouse fire, 1851.

Ordinary		Superior Court	
AnRns,	1873-1935**	Deed,	1828-1907*,
Conf,	1861-1865		1907-1915
Est,	1856-1956	Deed,	1833-1914
(Index)		(Index)	
FPC,	1843-1856	Jury,	1904-1907
Home,	1859-1957	PhR,	1856-1934*
Inf,	1857-1882	SMin,	1868-1895,
InvA,	1897-1945*		1895-1922*
Lun,	1911-1920*		
Mar,	1869-1952*		
OMin,	1879-1951**		
PhR,	1897-1919		
Sch,	1859-1887		
TMSup,	1893-1894,		
	1897-1953*		
Wills,	1877-1937*		

Atkinson:
Created November 5, 1918, from Coffee and Clinch Counties; #151 in order of creation; county seat, Pearson 31642.

Bacon:
Created November 3, 1914, from Appling, Pierce, and Ware Counties; #149 in order of creation; county seat, Alma 31510.

Baker:
Created December 12, 1825, from Early County; #66 in order of creation; county seat, Newton 31770; courthouse fire, 1872?; flood, 1925 & 1929.

Ordinary		Superior Court	
AnRns,	1872-1920*	Deed,	1866-1873,
Home,	1883-1944*		1870-1908*
InvA,	1875-1918*	Deed,	1850-1902
Mar,	1874-1953*	(Index)	
OMin,	1874-1924*	SMin,	1879-1900*,
TMSup,	1882-1924*		1899-1914
Wills,	1868-1962*	WWI,	1922-
Wills,	1868-1918*		
(original)			

Baldwin:
Created May 11, 1803, from Indian lands ceded in 1802 and 1805; #29 in order of creation; county seat, Milledgeville 31061; courthouse fire, 1861.

Ordinary		Superior Court	
Aptc,	1866-1872	Deed,	1861-1902**

AnRns,	1813-1901**	Deed,	1861-1900
Est,	1807-1939	(Index)	
(Index)		PhR,	1875-1963
FPC,	1832-1864	SMin,	1861-1903*,
Home,	1868-1905*		1912*
Inf,	1806-1868**	WWI,	no date shown
InvA,	1807-1900*		
LdCt,	1854-1869*		
LLoty,	1820-1821		
Liq,	1831-1890		
Mar,	1806-1925*		
Mar,	1806-1874		
(Index)			
OMin,	1807-1900*		
PhR,	1908-1926		
Sch,	1852-1867		
TMSup,	1830-1900*		
Wills,	1806-1936*		

Banks:
Created December 11, 1858, from Habersham and Franklin Counties; #127 in order of creation; county seat, Homer 30547.

Ordinary		Superior Court	
AnRns,	1859-1910*	Conf,	1892-1903
	1917-1937*	Deed,	1859-1936*
Conf,	1890-1924	Deed,	1859-1912
Home,	1867-1962	(Index)	
InvA,	1859-1910*	Jury,	1896-1904*
LdCt,	1873-1927*	SMin,	1859-1902
Mar,	1859-1907*	Vote,	1898
OMin,	1859-1911*	WWI,	no date shown
TMSup,	1886-1930*		
Wills,	1859?-1911?		

Barrow:
Created November 3, 1914, from Gwinnett, Walton, and Jackson Counties; #147 in order of creation; county seat, Winder 30680.

Bartow:
Created December 3, 1832, from Cherokee County; #86 in order of creation; county seat, Cartersville 30120; courthouse fire, 1864.
• Bartow was Cass County until the name was officially changed on December 6, 1861.

Ordinary		Superior Court	
AnRns,	1853-1901*	Deed,	1837-1902
Conf,	1861-1865	Deed,	1837-1962
Home,	1874-1905*,	(Index)	
	1868-1951	SMin,	1865-1903
Inf,	1865-1868	WWI,	1917-1919

InvA,	1853-1908*
Mar,	1836-1907**
OMin,	1853-1904
Wills,	1836-1922

Ben Hill:
Created November 6, 1906, from Irwin and Wilcox Counties; #144 in order of creation; county seat, Fitzgerald 31750.

Berrien:
Created February 25, 1856, from Lowndes, Irwin, and Coffee Counties; #115 in order of creation; county seat, Nashville 31639.

Ordinary		**Superior Court**	
AnRns,	1858-1911*	Deed,	1850-1901*
Conf,	1891-1922	Deed,	1850-1928
Home,	1873-1899*	(Index)	
InvA,	1862-1910*	PhR,	1872-1953
Mar,	1856-1967**	SMin,	1856-1905
OMin,	1856-1906	WWI,	1922-
Pony,	1899-1930*		
Sch,	1858-1863*		
TMSup,	1897-1925*		
Wills,	1855-1956*		

Bibb:
Created December 9, 1822, from Jones, Monroe, and Twiggs Counties; #55 in order of creation; county seat, Macon 31202.

Ordinary		**Superior Court**	
Aptc,	1866-1899	Deed,	1822-1908**
AnRns,	1823-1900*,	Deed,	1823-1919
	1906-1907	(Index)	
Conf,	1890-1926*	SMin,	1825-1909
Est,	1823-1964	(Index)	
(Index)		SMin,	1823-1900**
Home,	1868-1902*	WWI,	1922*-
Inf,	1824-1864*		
InvA,	1881-1914*		
Mar,	1828-1929*,		
	1936, 1963, 1964		
Mar,	1823-1963		
(Index)			
OMin,	1827-1900*		
Sch,	1860		
Wills,	1823-1929*,		
	1933*		

Bleckley:
Created October 2, 1912, from Pulaski County; #145 in order of creation; county seat, Cochran 31014.

Brantley:
Created November 2, 1920, from Charlton, Pierce, and Wayne Counties; #156 in order of creation; county seat, Nahunta 31553.

Brooks:
Created December 11, 1858, from Lowndes and Thomas Counties; #129 in order of creation; county seat, Quitman 31643.

Ordinary		Superior Court	
AnRns,	1859-1905*	Deed,	1859-1916
Conf,	1890-1908	Deed,	1857-1925
Home,	1877-1940*	(Index)	
InvA,	1859-1922*	PhR,	1856-1953
Mar,	1859-1966**	SMin,	1859-1908*
Mar,	1859-1966	Vote,	1910
(Index)		WWI,	no date shown*
OMin,	1859-1909*		
TMSup,	1860-1926*		
Vote,	1898-1900		
Wills,	1860-1964*		

Bryan:
Created December 19, 1793, from Chatham County; #19 in order of creation; county seat, Pembroke 31321; courthouse fire, 1866.
• Bryan County was significantly enlarged with land from Effingham County in 1794.

Ordinary		Superior Court	
AnRns,	1882-1943	Deed,	1799-1920
Est,	18??-1939	Deed,	1793-1937
(Index)		(Index)	
Home,	1873-1919	Jury,	1924-1943
Inf,	1794-1811,	PhR,	1880-1946
	1833-1853	SMin,	1794-1923
InvA,	1865-1952	Vote,	1914
Liq,	1850-1867,		
	1871-1917		
Lun,	1910-1924		
Mar,	1865-1948**		
OMin,	1865-1896		
Pony,	1897-1951		
TMSup,	1876-1903		
WWI,	1917-1952		
Wills,	1870-1933		

Bulloch:
Created February 8, 1796, from Bryan and Screven Counties; #21 in order of creation; county seat, Statesboro 30458; courthouse fire, 1864.

Ordinary		Superior Court	
AnRns,	1817-1968**	Deed,	1796-1969

Conf,	no date shown	Deed,	1796-1967
Est,	1795-1900	(Index)	
(Index)		Home,	1868-1899
Home,	1873-1916,	Inf,	1812-1836
	1919-1966*	PhR,	1881-1958
Inf,	1812-1834	SMin,	1806-1969
InvA,	1874-1946*	WWI,	1917-1919
Liq,	1854		
Lun,	1899-1966**		
Mar,	1795-1969**		
Mar	1795-1900		
(Index)			
OInd,	1800s		
OMin,	1815-1967		
OMin	1795-1900		
(Index)			
Pony,	1899-1919		
Sch,	1846-1864,		
	1878-1890		
TMSup,	1893-1953*		
Vote,	1865-1898		
WWI,	1917-1919		
Wills,	1795-1969*		

Burke:

Created February 5, 1777, from colonial Georgia. Boundaries originally were those of St. George Parish; #3 in order of creation; county seat, Waynesboro 30830; courthouse fire, 1825, 1843, 1856, and 1870.

Ordinary		Superior Court	
Aptc,	1867-1919	Deed,	1843-1900
AnRns,	1856-1900	Deed,	1844-1900
Conf,	1880-1916	(Index)	
Inf,	1830-1863	SMin,	1835-1902
(Docket)		WWI,	1917-1919
InvA,	1856-1926*		
Mar,	1855-1900*		
Mar	1855-1940		
(Index)			
OMin,	1849-1907*		
TMSup,	1868-1903*		
Vote,	1890, 1902, 1904		
Wills,	1853-1930*		

Butts:

Created December 24, 1825, from Henry and Monroe Counties; #70 in order of creation; county seat, Jackson 30233.

Ordinary		Superior Court	
AnRns,	1826-1887**	Conf,	no date shown

Home,	1867-1954		Deed,	1826-1916,
Inf,	1826-1881**			1971-1972
InvA,	1826-1918**		Deed,	1825-1912
Lun,	1898-1908		(Index)	
Mar,	1826-1948**		Home,	1867-1874*
Mar,	1876-1896		Liq,	1873-1881
(Index)			PhR,	1873-1881
OMin.	1844-1903*		SMin,	1834-1881
PhR,	1881-1942			
TMSup,	1881-1927*			
Wills,	1826-1948*			

Calhoun:
Created February 20, 1854, from Baker and Early Counties; #111 in order of creation; county seat, Morgan 31766; courthouse fire, 1888 and 1920.

Ordinary			Superior Court	
AnRns,	1869-1924		Deed,	1854-1902
Conf,	no date shown		Deed,	1854-1920
Home,	1867-1895		(Index)	
Inf,	1854-1875		Home,	1868-1927
Liq,	1873-1888		PhR,	1881-1908
Mar,	1880-1908		SMin,	1852,
OMin,	1854-1896			1859-1906
Wills,	1855-1890			

Camden:
Created February 5, 1777, from colonial Georgia. Original boundaries included St. Thomas and St. Mary Parishes; #8 in order of creation; county seat, Woodbine 31569.

Ordinary			Superior Court	
AnRns,	1809-1918		Deed,	1786-1958
Cen,	1860, 1870		Deed,	1786-1955
FPC,	1819-1843		(Index)	
Home,	1869-1880		LdCt,	1787-1849
Inf,	1794-1914		Liq,	1841-1860,
InvA,	1794-1908			1916
Liq,	1887-1916		Nat,	1793-1860
Mar,	1819-1955*,		PhR,	1856-1954
	1955-1966		SlavR,	1818-1847
Mar,	1954-1965		SMisc,	1790-1924
(Index)			SMin,	1797-1901,
Militia Records,				1901-1957*
	1817			
Nat,	1903-1920			
OMin,	1802-1948			
Receipts for Military Service,				
	1817			
SlavR,	1818-1847			

WWI,   1917-1918,
           1931-1935
Wills,   1795-1829*,
           1868-1945*

Campbell:
Created December 20, 1828, from Coweta, Carroll, DeKalb, and Fayette Counties. Campbell County was abolished on January 1, 1932, and became south Fulton County. The story of Campbell County records is strange. In 1931, the loose records and tax digests were transferred to the Ga. Dept. of Archives & History. However, in 1938 and 1939, they were taken by Fulton County officials. During the last few years, the records have again been moved, many given to the Atlanta Historical Society by Fulton County. Researchers may check with the Fulton County courthouse and the Atlanta Historical Society about specific records.

Ordinary		Superior Court	
Aptc,	1868-1890	Deed,	1828-1931
AnRns,	1829-1931**	(Index)	
Conf,	1890-1928	Deed,	1829-1931
Est,	1828-1931	Home,	1868-1892*
(Index)		PhR,	1881-1920
Home,	1873-1898*	SMin,	1856-1931**
Inf,	1829-1873**		
InvA,	1829-1931**		
Mar,	1829-1931		
Mar	1827-1931		
(Index)			
OMin,	1868-1931*		
PhR,	1881-1925*		
Pony,	1897-1931*		
TMSup,	1852, 1931		
Wills,	1833-1931*		
Wills	1833-1948		
(Index)			

Candler:
Created November 3, 1914, from Bulloch, Emanuel, and Tattnall Counties; #148 in order of creation; county seat, Metter 30439.

Carroll:
Created June 9, 1825, from Indian land ceded in 1826 and 1827; #65 in order of creation; county seat, Carrollton 30117; courthouse fire, 1927.
• Almost all of Carroll County's earliest estate records (including wills) are in "Inferior Court Record Book A" microfilm reel 171-45. This book is identified in the general estate index as "Record of Court of Ordinary Book A." These records cover 1829-1845. [Information provided by Ted O. Brooke.]

Ordinary		Superior Court	
Aptc,	1890-1935*	Deed,	1827-1901**

AnRns,	1829-1901**		Deed,	1828-1934
AnRns,	1831-1885		(Index)	
(Index)			PhR,	1881-1962
Birth,	1875		SMin,	1857-1903**
Conf,	1890-1912		WWI,	1917
Death,	1875			
Est,	1826-1939			
(Index)				
Home,	1869-1894*			
Inf,	1827-1862			
InvA,	1829-1902			
Mar,	1827-1904*			
OMin,	1852-1910			
PhR,	1881-1944			
Pony,	1883-1913*			
TMSup,	1881-1902*			
Wills,	1829-1922			

Catoosa:
Created December 5, 1853, from Walker and Whitfield Counties; #99 in order of creation; county seat, Ringgold 30736.

Ordinary		**Superior Court**	
AnRns,	1860-1902	Board of Education	
Est,	1874-1975	Records Identifying	
(Index)		Teachers,	1875-1896
Inf,	1854-1861	Deed,	1854-1867,
InvA,	1874-1928		1867-1902*
Mar,	1858-1910*	Deed,	1854-1867;
OMin,	1854-1920		1893-1901
Wills,	1874-1961*	(Index)	
		Jury,	1874-1920
		PhR,	1881-1933
		SMin,	1854-1870;
			1870-1903*

Charlton:
Created February 18, 1854, from Camden County, #110 in order of creation; county seat, Folkston 31537; courthouse fire, 1877; February 19, 1928.

Ordinary		**Superior Court**	
AnRns,	1854-1912	Deed,	1878-1906
Est,	1882-1954*	Deed,	1852-1915
(loose)		(Index)	
Home,	1873-1908*;	PhR,	1894-1958
	1913	SMin,	1879-1888;
Inv.A,	1854-1912		1887-1920*
Mar,	1854-1961**	WWI,	1920-
OMin,	1854-1911**		
Wills,	1868-1966*		

Chatham:
Created February 5, 1777, from colonial Georgia. Original boundaries included all of Christ Church and part of St. Philip Parishes; #5 in order of creation; county seat, Savannah 31402.
• The William R. Perkins Library, Duke University, has loose Chatham County records scattered among their Georgia Papers collection. Also, colonial books of record contain a great deal of information on early Chatham families.

Ordinary		Superior Court	
AnRns,	1780s?-19??	Aliens Exempt from	
Birth,	1803-1847	Military Duty,	
Cen,	1845		1862-1864
Conf,	1890-1925	Deed,	1785-1900
Death,	1803-1847	Deed,	1785-1903
Death,	1733-	(Index)	
(Index)		Home,	1868-1902
Est,	1777-1852*	LLoty,	1819-1821
(Loose)		Nat,	1823-1910,
FPC,	1780-1865	Nat,	1789-1908
Home,	1876-1922	(Index)	
Inf,	1790-1845	PhR,	1881-1919
InvA,	1783-1925	Prison Records,	
LLoty,	1832		1891-1899
Lun,	1854-1949	SMin,	1782-1900,
Mar,	1805-1866,		1902-1905*
	1877-1902*		
Mar,	1733-1837,		
(Index)	1806-1877		
Mar	1808-1924*		
(Loose)			
Nat,	1824-1906		
(titles vary)			
OMin,	1800-1901		
Pony,	1876-1922		
TMSup,	1890-1920		
Wills,	1775-1936		

Chattahoochee:
Created February 13, 1854, from Muscogee and Marion Counties; #108 in order of creation; county seat, Cusseta 31805.

Ordinary		Superior Court	
AnRns,	1854-1910*	Deed,	1854-1918**
Cen,	1880	Deed,	1854-1904
Conf,	1890-1920	(Index)	
Home,	1863-1940*	Jury,	1879-1902
Inf,	1854-1868*	SMin,	1854-1902*
InvA,	1854-1940*	Vote,	1896-1900,
Mar,	1854-1860,		1907-1909
	1854-1947*	WWI,	1917-

OMin,	1854-1920*
Sch,	1857-1884*
Wills,	1854-1935*

Chattooga:

Created December 28, 1838, from Floyd and Walker Counties; #92 in order of creation; county seat, Summerville 30747.

Ordinary		Superior Court	
Aptc,	1866-1907	Conf,	1861-1865
(free black children)		Deed,	1839-1902
AnRns,	1851-1910*	Deed,	1839-1937
Bast,	1897-1912*	(Index)	
Birth,	1874-1876*	PhR,	1882-1927*
Death,	1875-1876*	SMin,	1867-1903
Est,	1839-1939	WWI,	1922-
(Index)			
Home,	1871-1922*		
Inf,	1839-1864		
InvA,	1851-1904*		
Mar,	1839-1939*		
OMin,	1862-1912*		
TMSup,	1899-1929*		
WWI,	1917-1919		
Wills,	1856-1924*		

Cherokee:

Created December 21, 1830, from Indian land ceded in 1835; #78 in order of creation; county seat, Canton 30114; courthouse fire, 1865 and March 1927.

Ordinary		Superior Court	
Aptc,	1866-1904	Deed,	1833-1913,
AnRns,	1848-1911**		1915-1917
Cen,	1870	Deed,	1832-1920
Conf,	1859-1871,	(Index)	
	1914-1919	SMin,	1832-1903
Home,	1868-1875,	WWI,	1917-
	1875-1915*		
Inf,	1832-1888		
InvA,	1848-1924*		
Mar,	1841-1910		
OMin,	1848-1901		
Paup,	1859-1871		
Wills,	1866-1921		

Clarke:

Created December 5, 1801, from Jackson County; #26 in order of creation; county seat, Athens 30601.

• Clarke County estate records are not organized in the same manner as other Ga. counties; they are more complete than this list indicates. Also, Mary Warren has published some War of 1812 rosters for Clarke County in **Georgia Genealogist**, issue #28 providing name, age, and physical description of each recruit. Original rosters are in the Telamon Cuyler Collection, Special Collections, University of Georgia libraries.

Ordinary		Superior Court	
Aptc,	1802-1822;	Deed,	1802-1960
	1837-1911	Deed,	1801-1960
AnRns,	1800s?-1959	(Index)	
Birth,	1808-1852;	Jury,	1879-1911
	1875-1876	LdCt,	1834-1875
Cen,	1850; 1860;	SMin,	1801-1880;
	1880		1880-1903*
Chain Gang			1903-1958
Records,	1883-1886	WWI,	1918
Conf,	1861-1869;		
	1884-1934		
Death,	1875-1876		
Deed,	1807-1814		
Est,	no date shown		
(Index)			
FPC,	1847-1862		
Home,	1846-1943		
Inf,	1802-1856;		
	1866		
InvA,	1811-1828;		
	1850-1871		
Lun,	1895-1909		
Mar,	1805-1956*		
OInd,	1889-1946		
OMin,	1851-1960		
OMin,	1889-1946		
(Index)			
Paup,	1883-1886		
PhR,	1895-1910		
Pony,	1884-1926		
Powers of Attorney,			
	1807-1814;		
	1835-1868		
Sch,	1852-1876;		
	1876-1879		
TMSup,	1881-1952		
Vote,	1890-1894*;		
	1896-1898;		
	1908		
Wills,	1802-1955		

Clay:

Created February 16, 1854, from Early and Randolph Counties; #109 in order of creation; county seat, Ft. Gaines 31751.

	Ordinary
Aptc,	1866-1867*
(free persons of color)	
Conf,	1889-1958
Home,	1876-1918*
InvA,	1854-1947*
Mar,	1854-1933*
OMin,	1854-1875; 1875-1897*
Wills,	1852-1963*; 1966*

	Superior Court
Deed,	1854-1922*
PhR,	1881-1955*
SMin,	1854-1905*
WWI,	1917-1922*

Clayton:
Created November 30, 1858, from Fayette and Henry Counties; #125 in order of creation; county seat, Jonesboro 30236; courthouse fire, 1864.

	Ordinary
AnRns,	1860-1863, 1874-1919
Birth,	1875
Conf,	1890-1927
Est,	1859-1938
(Index)	
Home,	1859-1940
Inf,	1859-1878
InvA,	1859-1957
Liq,	1859-1873
Mar,	1859-1918*
Mar,	1859-1961
(Index)	
Sch,	1860-1875
TMSup,	1882-1928
Wills,	1859-1921

	Superior Court
Deed,	1859-1914
Deed,	1859-1952
(Index)	
Jury,	1882-1918
PhR,	1882-1917
SMin,	1859-1914
Vote,	1898, 1900-1902, 1904-1920
WWI,	1917-1922

Clinch:
Created February 14, 1850, from Ware and Lowndes Counties; #94 in order of creation; county seat, Homerville 31634; courthouse fire, 1856; 1867.

	Ordinary
AnRns,	1867-1889 1889-1945*
Conf,	1896-1930
Home,	1872-1957*
Inf,	1868-1901
InvA,	1869-1960*
Mar,	1867-1965*
OMin,	1867-1921*
TMSup,	1892-1923*

	Superior Court
Aptc,	1866-1896*
Conf,	1862
Deed,	1868-1927*
(some missing)	
Deed,	1850-1867
(Index)	
	1858-1966
Home,	1866-1896*
PhR,	1893-1963

Vote,	1896-1898;	SMin,	1867-1884,
	1900; 1904		1885-1906*
	1914-1915	Vote,	1889-1894,
Wills,	1868-1966*		1898, 1916-1941
		WWI,	1919

Cobb:

Created December 3, 1832, from Cherokee County; #83 in order of creation; county seat, Marietta 30060; courthouse fire, 1864.

• Cobb records are reportedly on microfilm at the Ga. Dept. of Archives & History. **However,** Cobb County currently refuses to allow this microfilm to be made available to researchers.

Ordinary	Superior Court
Miscellaneous,	
1868-1907	
(some records are pre-Civil War)	

Coffee:

Created February 9, 1854, from Clinch, Ware, Telfair, and Irwin Counties; #107 in order of creation; county seat, Douglas, 31533; courthouse fire, 1898, 1938.

• Some pre-1900 Coffee County records survived the fire and are at the court-house, but the Georgia Archives has not microfilmed these records.

Colquitt:

Created February 25, 1856, from Thomas and Lowndes Counties; #114 in order of creation; county seat, Moultrie 31768; courthouse fire, 1881.

• Where are the Colquitt County estate records for 1881-1902? Does the fact that the new courthouse dates from 1903 have anything to do with these missing records?

Ordinary		Superior Court	
AnRns,	1905-1922*	Deed,	1881-1910*
Birth,	1875*	Deed,	1881-1911
Death,	1875*	(Index)	
Home,	1883-1933*	PhR,	1886-1966*
InvA,	1903-1930*	SMin,	1881-1907*
Mar,	1891-1956*	WWI,	1923-
	1956-1967		
Mar,	1953-1967		
(Index)			
OMin,	1902-1922*		
Pony,	1903-1913*		
TMSup,	1903-1918*		
Wills,	1900-1967*		

Columbia:

Created December 10, 1790, from Richmond County; #12 in order of creation; county seat, Appling 30802.

Ordinary		Superior Court	
AnRns,	1809-1919*	Deed,	1791-1818*,
Cen,	1879, 1880		1881-1824,
Conf,	1890-1913,		1822-1904*
	1920-1926,	Deed,	1791-1911
	1931-1933	(Index)	
Est,	1833-1856	Jury,	1794-1802,
(Index)			1879-1910*
FPC,	1819-1836	PhR,	1881-1901*
Home,	1876-1948*	SMin,	1790-1908
Inf,	1791-1868	WWI,	1917-1919*
Inf,	1796-1805		
(Index)			
InvA,	1790-1804, 1804-1959*		
Jury,	1840-1846		
LLoty,	1805, 1807, 1821		
Liq,	1852-1871		
Mar,	1807-1967*		
Mar,	1787-1935*		
(loose)			
OMin,	1799-1824*, 1824-1828, 1834-1913*		
Sch,	1828-1849		
SlavR,	1818-1835		
TMSup,	1858-1898*, 1899-1940*		
Vote,	1895-1897, 1909-1912		
Wills,	1790-1963*		
Wills	1789-1930		
(Loose)			

Cook:
Created November 5, 1918, from Berrien County; #153 in order of creation; county seat, Adel 31620.

Coweta;
Created June 9, 1825, from Indian lands ceded in 1826 and 1827; #64 in order of creation; county seat, Newnan 30263.

Ordinary		Superior Court	
Aptc,	1866-1911*	Deed,	1827-1904*
AnRns,	1829-1911*	Deed,	1827-1832
Conf,	1890-1941	(Index)	
Death,	1927-1966	Home,	1874-1914*
(Index)		PhR,	1881-1961
Est,	1827-1966	SMin,	1828-1866,
(Index)			1866-1908*
Home,	1874-1915*	WWI,	1922-
Inf,	1829-1838,		
	1838-1857*,		
	1855-1873		
InvA,	1828-1910*		

Mar,	1827-1966*
Mar,	1827-1966
(Index)	
OMin,	1857-1916*
PhR,	1880-1935
Sch,	1853-1858
TMSup,	1857-1922*
Vote,	1905, 1908
Wills,	1828-1966*

Crawford:
Created December 9, 1822, from Houston County; #57 in order of creation; county seat, Knoxville 31050; courthouse fire, 1829.

Ordinary		Superior Court	
AnRns,	1836-1928**	Deed,	1830-1902**
Cen,	1850	Deed,	1830-1940
Conf,	1914-1962*	(Index)	
Est,	1868-1905	SMin,	1830-1900
(Index)		WWI,	1919-
Home,	1866-1946*		
Inf,	1830-1863		
InvA,	1833-1837, 1836-1913*		
Mar,	1823-1845, 1873-1943*		
	1888 (Index)		
OMin,	1880-1918*		
TMSup,	1871-1893*		
Wills,	1835-1948*		

Crisp:
Created August 17, 1905, from Dooly County; #136 in order of creation; county seat, Cordele 31015.

Dade:
Created December 25, 1837, from Walker County; #91 in order of creation; county seat, Trenton 30752; courthouse fire, 1865 and 1895.

Ordinary		Superior Court	
AnRns,	1853-1914**	Deed,	1849-1902**
Conf,	1908-1952	Deed,	1887-1928
InvA,	1853-1914**	(Index)	
Mar,	1866-1962*	SMin,	1854-1906*
OMin,	1853-1919*	WWI,	1922-
Paup,	1885-1902		
Vote,	1909-1916, 1920-1928		
Wills,	1884-1948*		

Dawson:
Created December 3, 1857, from Lumpkin and Gilmer Counties; #118 in order of creation; county seat, Dawsonville 30534.

	Ordinary		Superior Court
AnRns,	1858-1962	Deed,	1858-1903
Conf,	1890-1920	Deed,	1858-1934
Home,	1868-1898	(Index)	
InvA,	1858-1962	Divorce Rec.,	
Mar,	1858-1961*		1857-1880
OMin,	1858-1922	PhR,	1881-1907
Pony,	1898-1950	SMin,	1858-1905
TMSup,	1896-1962		
Wills,	1857-1959*		

Decatur:
Created December 8, 1823, from Early County; #58 in order of creation; county seat, Bainbridge 31717.

	Ordinary		Superior Court
AnRns,	1835-1901	Conf (Donations to	
Cen,	1850-1860	Confederate Soldiers),	
Conf,	1890-1926		1860s
Home,	1871-1878	Deed,	1823-1919
Inf,	1829-1864	Deed,	1823-1960
LLoty,	1832	(Index)	
Mar,	1824-1905*	Home,	1868-1927
Mar,	1824-1942	Jury,	1869-1877
(Index)		PhR,	1881-1911
OMin,	1824-1900	SMin,	1825-1901
Vote,	1886, 1888,	Vote,	1902
	1892, 1894		
Wills,	1824-1913		

DeKalb:
Created December 9, 1822, from Fayette, Gwinnet, and Henry Counties; #54 in order of creation; county seat, Decatur 30030; courthouse fire, 1842, 1898, 1916.

	Ordinary		Superior Court
AnRns,	1842-1902	Deed,	1842-1905*
Conf,	1890-1938	Deed,	1840-1910
Est,	1840-1929	(Index)	
(Index)		Nat,	1918
Inf,	1824-1870*	PhR,	1895-1933
Inf,	1823-1859	SMin,	1836-1905*
(Index)		WWI,	1917-1919,
InvA,	1842-1904*		1922-
Mar,	1840-1908		
Mar,	1840-1928		
(Index)			
OMin,	1870-1901*		
OMin,	1840-1929		
(Index)			

PhR,	1881-1930
TMSup,	1874-1908*
Wills,	1841-1919*

Dodge:

Created October 26, 1870, from Pulaski, Telfair, and Montgomery Counties; #134 in order of creation; county seat, Eastman 31023.

Ordinary		**Superior Court**	
Aptc,	1880-1926*	Deed,	1871-1909*
AnRns,	1871-1905*	Deed,	1871-1934
Conf,	1920-1939*	(Index)	
Est,	1871-1966	Home,	1872-1941*
(Index)		Nat,	1904-1911
Home,	1873-1921*	PhR,	1881-1962
InvA,	1871-1955*	SMin,	1871-1889,
Mar,	1871-1966*		1889-1911*
Mar,	1871-1966	WWI,	1922-
(Index)			
OMin,	1871-1900*		
Paup,	1892-1904		
TMSup,	1873-1965		
Vote,	1888-1900*, 1892*, 1894-1896*, 1898-1902*, 1904*, 1906*, 1908-1914*, 1919-1920*, 1926*		
Wills,	1875-1966*		

Dooly:

Created May 25, 1821, from Indian lands ceded in 1821; #48 in order of creation; county seat, Vienna 31092; courthouse fire, 1847.

Ordinary		**Superior Court**	
Aptc,	1873-1919*	Deed,	1847-1888*,
AnRns,	1847-1909*		1888-1900
Conf,	1880-1925	Deed,	1888-1902
Home,	1868-1916*	(Index)	
Inf,	1847-1896**	PhR,	1880-1964*
InvA,	1837-1912*	SMin,	1847-1885,
Mar,	1856-1908*		1886-1901*
OMin,	1847-1902*		
TMSup,	1886-1910*		
Wills,	1847-1901*		

Dougherty:

Created December 15, 1853, from Baker County; #102 in order of creation; county seat, Albany 31701.

Ordinary		**Superior Court**	
AnRns,	1849-1917	Deed,	1854-1902
Home,	1881-1912	Deed,	1859-1902
Inf,	1854-1869	(Index)	

InvA,	1854-1919	PhR,	1868-1951
Liq,	1880-1892	SMin,	1856-1899
Mar,	1854-1905*	WWI,	1922-
OMin,	1854-1901		
TMSup,	1884-1958		
Wills,	1854-1925		

Douglas:
Created October 17, 1870, from Campbell and Carroll Counties; #131 in order of creation; county seat, Douglasville 30134; courthouse fire, 1896 and 1957.

Ordinary		**Superior Court**	
AnRns,	1871-1912*	Deed,	1871-1904*
Conf,	1920-1934	Deed,	1871-1917
Home,	1889-1919	(Index)	
InvA,	1871-1933*	PhR,	1881-1963*
Mar,	1871-1941*	SMin,	1871-1904*
OMin,	1871-1873,	WWI,	1921-
	1882-1912*		
TMSup,	1883-1959*		
Wills,	1870-1932*		

Early:
Created December 15, 1818, from Indian land ceded in 1814; #40 in order of creation; county seat, Blakely 31723; courthouse fire, 1896.

Ordinary		**Superior Court**	
AnRns,	1850-1906	Deed,	1821-1900
Birth,	1875-1877*	SMin,	1820-1854,
Conf,	1861-1865		1857-1902*
Death,	1875		
Home,	1860-1900		
Inf,	1820-1882		
InvA,	1822-1914		
Mar,	1820-1915*		
OMin,	1866-1902		
Vote,	1896, 1898, 1900		
Wills,	1822-1839, 1839-1941*		

Echols:
Created December 13, 1858, from Lowndes and Clinch Counties; #130 in order of creation; county seat, Statenville 31648; courthouse fire, 1897.

Ordinary		**Superior Court**	
AnRns,	1898-1967*	Deed,	1867-1910*
InvA,	1898-1960*	Deed,	1897-1909
Mar,	1898-1967*	(Index)	
OMin,	1880-1917*	PhR,	1907-1940
TMSup,	1899-1964*	SMin,	1898-1914*

Vote,	1895-1896, 1910-1912	Vote,	1896, 1898, 1900, 1902
Wills,	1875-1952*		

Effingham:

Created February 5, 1777, from colonial Georgia. Original boundaries included St. Matthew and part of St. Philip Parishes; #4 in order of creation; some records stolen during Civil War.

Ordinary		Superior Court	
AnRns,	1817-1919	Deed,	1786-1918
Coroner's Records,	1916-1950	Deed, (Index)	1786-1918
Est, (Index)	1791-1934	Home,	1860-1934
Inf,	1832-1872	Jury,	1910-1932
InvA,	1827-1949	LdCt,	1829-1907
Lun,	no date shown	PhR,	1881-1953
Mar,	1791-1819, 1819-1943*	SMin,	1821-1901
Mar, (Index)	1790-1935		
Militia Records,	1900-1904		
Misc. Records,	1791-1834*		
(includes lunacy)			
OMin,	1827-1922*		
Pony,	1873-1901*		
TMSup,	1866-1940		
Vote,	1911-1932		
WWI,	1922-		
Wills,	1829-1950		

Elbert:

Created December 10, 1790, from Wilkes County; #13 in order of creation; county seat, Elberton 30635.

• Mary Warren has published a War of 1812 roster for Elbert County in Georgia Genealogist, #28, p. 12, that provides the name, place of birth, age, and physical description of each soldier. The original roster is in the Telamon Cuyler Collection, Special Collections, University of Georgia libraries.

Ordinary		Superior Court	
Amnst,	1865	Conf,	1861
Aptc,	1809-1816*, 1830-1881, 1867-1903	Deed,	1791-1912
		Deed, (Index)	1793-1912
AnRns,	1791-1907*	Home,	1867-1933
Birth,	1875-1878	Jury,	1867-1872,

Conf,	1890-1905,		1882-1898
	1909-1932	LdCt,	1834-1859
Death,	1875-1878	LdCt,	1822-1833
Est,	1828-1835*	(Docket)	
(Index)		SlavR,	1822-1847
FPC,	1819-1858	SMin,	1790-1904
Home,	1868-1897	WWI,	1918-
Inf,	1791-1902		
InvA,	1791-1829*, 1897, 1915*		
LdCt	1822-1833		
(docket)			
LLoty,	1807, 1821, 1827, 1832		
Liq,	1839-1858		
Lun,	1897-1909		
Mar,	1804-1913*		
Mar	1821-1835*		
(Index)			
Militia Officers,			
	1809-1818		
OMin,	1791-1910		
Pony,	1897-1933		
TMSup,	1856-1924*		
Wills,	1791-1919*		

Emanuel:
Created December 10, 1812, from Bulloch and Montgomery Counties: #39 in order of creation; county seat, Swainsboro 30401; courthouse fire, 1841, 1855, 1857, 1919, 1938.

Ordinary		Superior Court	
AnRns,	1836-1850,	Deed,	1830-1961
	1866-1907	Deed,	1840-1961
	1907-1960	(Index)	
Birth,	1822-1863	Home,	1869-1916
FPC,	1855	Jury,	1896-1902
Home,	1877-1913	LdCt,	1858-1867
Inf,	1841-1859	PhR,	1888-1959
InvA,	1812-1956*	SMin,	1810-1961
Liq,	1856-1875		
Mar,	1817-1916*		
OMin,	1841-1961		
PhR,	1893-1899		
Sch,	1823-1880		
TMSup,	1857-1961*		
Wills,	1815-1961*		

Evans:
Created November 3, 1914, from Bulloch and Tattnall Counties; #150 in order of creation; county seat, Claxton 30417.

Fannin:
Created January 21, 1854, from Gilmer and Union Counties; #106 in order of creation; county seat, Blue Ridge 30513; courthouse fire, 1936 or 1937.

Ordinary		Superior Court	
AnRns,	1866-1916*	Deed,	1854-1891,
Conf,	1914-1928		1891-1902*
InvA,	1865-1903*	Deed,	1854-1936
Mar,	1854-1864*,	(Index)	
	1866-1901*	Home,	1869-1917*
OMin,	1865-1867,	SMin,	1854-1881,
	1867-1908*		1887-1904*
TMSup,	1866-1900*	WWI,	1923-
WWI,	1917-1919*		
Wills,	1854-1865*, 1868-1929*		

Fayette:
Created May 15, 1821, from Indian lands ceded in 1821; #51 in order of creation; county seat, Fayetteville 30214.

Ordinary		Superior Court	
AnRns,	1824-1911	Cen,	1880
Cen,	1870, 1880	Deed,	1823-1903
Conf,	1861-1949	Deed,	1821-1900
Home,	1869-1922	(Index)	
Inf,	1823-1862	PhR,	1892-1952
InvA,	1824-1911	SMin,	1827-1914
Liq,	1883-1885	WWI,	1918-1922
Mar,	1823-1913*		
OMin,	1823-1903		
Pony,	1883-1919		
Sch,	1928, 1933, 1938		
TMSup,	1879-1941		
Wills,	1823-1953		

Floyd:
Created December 3, 1832, from Cherokee County; #87 in order of creation; county seat, Rome 30161.

Ordinary		Superior Court	
AnRns,	1842-1902	Deed,	1833-1903
Conf,	1861-1865,	Deed,	1833-1934
	1890-1940,	(Index)	
	1906-1933	Home,	1868-1933
Inf,	1837-1875	Sch,	1858-1859
InvA,	1842-1901	SMin,	1840-1901
Liq,	1898-1928	WWI,	1917*-
Lun,	1898-1909		
Mar,	1834-1904*		
Mar	1850-1888		
(Loose)			

OMin,	1837-1846, 1852-1859, 1866-1904
Paup,	1850-1869
Sch,	1830-1880
TMSup	1883-1912
Vote,	1896
Wills,	1852-1918

Forsyth:
Created December 3, 1832, from Cherokee County; #80 in order of creation; county seat, Cumming 30130; courthouse fire, 1973.

Ordinary		Superior Court	
Aptc,	1865-1874	Deed,	1832-1835,
AnRns,	1858-1866*,		1835-1904*
	1869-1901*	Deed,	1887-1901
Home,	1868-1903*	(Index)	
Inf,	1843-1865	PhR,	1881-1959*
InvA,	1848-1905*	SMin,	1832-1903
Mar,	1833-1848*,	WWI,	1917-1919*,
	1852-1900*		1922-
Mar,	1834-1910*		
(Loose)			
OMin,	1852-1901*		
Sch,	1848-1875*		
TMSup,	1883-1916*		
Wills,	1833-1848*, 1856-1939*		

Franklin:
Created February 25, 1784, from Indian lands ceded in 1783; #9 in order of creation; county seat, Carnesville 30521.
• Pre-1850 records are at the Georgia Archives and have been compiled into indexed typescripts. The loose records are at the William R. Perkins Library, Duke University, although they are on microfilm at the Archives. The Perkins Library, however, also has loose Franklin County records scattered among its Georgia Papers Collection. Special Collections, University of Georgia libraries, Athens, Ga., also has a collection of loose Franklin County records.

Ordinary		Superior Court	
AnRns,	1801-1903	Deed,	1785-1904
Conf,	1862-1865,	Deed,	1785-1902
	1921	(Index)	
Home,	1868-1904*	Nat,	1914
Inf,	1790-1812	PhR,	1881-1961
	1826-1875*	SlavR,	1818-1831
InvA,	1786-1823,	SMin,	1814-1883**,
	1823-1903*		1883-1901
Loose Original		WWI,	1917-1919,
Papers,	1790-1881		1929
Mar,	1805-1938**		

Mar,	1805-1850
(Index)	
OMin,	1786-1813*, 1801-1823, 1823-1905*
Pony,	1898-1938*
Sch,	1823-1827 (receipts), 1844-1850
TMSup,	1800-1898, 1899-1929*
Wills,	1786-1911*

Fulton:
Created December 20, 1853, from DeKalb County. On January 1, 1932, Campbell and Milton Counties became part of Fulton County; #104 in order of creation; county seat, Atlanta 30303.
• Some Fulton County records are now kept by the Atlanta Historical Society.

Ordinary		Superior Court	
Aptc,	1899-1913*	Deed,	1854-1906*
AnRns,	1854-1901*	Deed,	1854-1910
Est,	1854-1921	(Index)	
(Index)		Home,	1873-1960*
Inf,	1854-1862	Home,	1874-1960
InvA,	1854-1906*	(Index)	
Mar,	1854-1921*	Nat,	1878-1906*
Mar,	1854-1921	PhR,	1897-1957*
(Index)		PhR,	1853-1962
OMin,	1854-1902*	(Index)	
Wills,	1854-1924*	SMin,	1854-1901*
Wills,	1833-1948	WWI,	1917-1919
(Index)			

Gilmer:
Created December 3, 1832, from Cherokee County; #84 in order of creation; county seat, Ellijay, 30540.

Ordinary		Superior Court	
AnRns,	1849-1904	Deed,	1833-1960
Conf,	1885-1911	Deed,	1866-1955
Home,	1833-1959	(Index)	
Inf,	1835-1868	SMin,	1833-1905
InvA,	1836, 1853-1909	WWI,	1918-1960
Jury,	1857-1860, 1880-1896		
Mar,	1835-1960*		
OMin,	1856-1908		
Paup,	1842-1873		
PhR,	1881-1956		
Pony,	1877-1923		
Sch,	1835-1840, 1852-1863		
TMSup,	1868-1959*		
Vote,	1895-1896, 1898		
Wills,	1836-1960*		

Glascock:
Created December 19, 1857, from Warren County; #120 in order of creation; county seat, Gibson 30810.

Ordinary		Superior Court	
Aptc,	1857-1888*	Deed,	1858-1916*
AnRns,	1857-1925*	Deed,	1887-1924
Cen,	1880	(Index)	
Conf,	1890-1933	Home,	1868-1869*
Home,	1874-1910*	PhR,	1898-1933
Inf,	1858-1888	SMin,	1858-1874,
InvA,	1858-1924*		1874-1921*
Mar,	1858-1920,		
	1906-1966*		
OMin,	1858-1917		
TMSup,	1858-1916		
Vote,	1909		
Wills,	1859-1966*		

Glynn:
Created February 5, 1777, from colonial Georgia. Original boundaries included all of St. David and St. Patrick Parishes; #7 in order of creation; county seat, Brunswick 31520; courthouse fire, c. 1830; storm, 1896.

Ordinary		Superior Court	
AnRns,	1866-1921*	Deed,	1765-1908
Conf,	1914-1924	Deed,	1859-1926
Home,	1870-1881,	(Index)	
	1905-1920	Home,	1884-1927
Inf,	1813-1870	Jury,	1901-1915
InvA,	1792-1921	PhR,	1881-1959
Mar,	1818-1933*	SMin,	1787-1792,
OMin,	1870-1923*		1877-1916
Prescription Records/		WWI,	1917-
Alcoholic Medicines,			
	1908-1911		
TMSup,	1907-1947		
Wills,	1810-1916		

Gordon:
Created February 13, 1850, from Floyd and Cass (now Bartow) Counties; #93 in order of creation; county seat, Calhoun 30701; courthouse fire, 1864; storm, 1888.

Ordinary		Superior Court	
AnRns,	1866-1902*	Conf,	1861-1865*
Conf,	1890-1906*,	Deed,	1850-1922*
	1911-1936*	Deed,	1887-1917
Home,	1870-1921*	(Index)	
Inf,	1850-1872	SMin,	1850-1872,

InvA,	1856-1888,			1872-1906*
	1888-1908*	WWI,		1917-1919,
Mar,	1864-1966*			1922-
OMin,	1855-1904*			
PhR,	1881-1924*			
TMSup,	1865-1917*			
Wills,	1856-1964*			

Grady:
Created August 17, 1905, from Decatur and Thomas Counties; #137 in order of creation; county seat, Cairo 31728.

Greene:
Created February 3, 1786, from Washington County; #11 in order of creation; county seat, Greensboro 30642; courthouse destroyed by Indians in 1787.
• Most of the early Greene County records are at the William R. Perkins Library, Duke University, although microfilm copies are available at the Georgia Archives.

Ordinary		Superior Court	
AnRns,	1792-1813,	Deed,	1785-1885
	1806-1850*	Deed,	1785-1889
Conf,	no date shown	(Index)	
Death,	c. 1811-1833	SMisc,	1798-1900
Home,	1868-1935	(Loose)	
Inf,	1787-1860*	SMin,	1792-1905
InvA,	1786-1890*		
LdCt,	1794-1798		
LLoty,	1806, 1825, 1832		
Liq,	1820-1935		
Mar,	1786-1908*		
OMin,	1852-1893		
TMSup,	1856-1896		
Wills,	1786-1921*		

Gwinnett:
Created December 15, 1818, from Indian lands ceded in 1817 and 1818; #44 in order of creation; county seat, Lawrenceville 30245; courthouse fire, 1871.

Ordinary		Superior Court	
AnRns,	1856-1902	Deed,	1871-1901
Conf,	1890-1935,	(Includes recorded pre-1871	
	1861-1865*	deeds, some going back to 1835)	
Est,	1856-1920	Deed,	1871-1917
(Index)		(Index)	
Home,	1858-1914	PhR,	1881-1962
Inf,	1819-1874	SMin,	1871-1902
InvA,	1856-1912	WWI,	1919-
Mar,	1843-1908*		

```
Mar,        1818-1965
(Index)
Mar (Loose), 1835-1838
OMin,       1858-1880, 1874-1906*
Sch,        1884
Vote,       1898
Wills,      1847-1917*
```

Habersham:
Created December 15, 1818, from Indian lands ceded in 1817 and 1818, #46 in order of creation; county seat, Clarkesville 30523; courthouse fire, 1856, 1898, 1923.
• Marriage Books A, B, and D have survived for Habersham County but were too tightly bound to be microfilmed.

Ordinary		Superior Court	
AnRns,	1854-1901	Deed,	1819-1900*
AnRns,	1819-1957	Deed,	1818-1848
(Index)		(Index)	
Conf,	1897-1911,	Home,	1869-1934*
	1924-1937	PhR,	1881-1914*
Home,	1885-1899*	SMin,	1819-1901
	1890-1915	WWI,	1918-1921*
Inf,	1824-1905		
Inf (Index), 1819-1964			
InvA,	1863-1880, 1885-1928		
InvA (Index), 1819-1961			
Mar,	1868-1945*		
Mar (Index), 1824-1964			
OMin,	1824-1905		
OMin (Index), 1819-1964			
TMSup,	1877-1918		
WWI,	no date shown*		
Wills,	1838-1894		

Hall:
Created December 15, 1818, from Indian lands ceded in 1817 and 1818, #45 in order of creation; county seat, Gainesville 30501; courthouse fire, 1851, 1882; tornado, 1936.
• City of Gainesville birth records, starting in 1865; and death records, starting in 1900, are on microfilm reel 245-65, Georgia Archives.

Ordinary		Superior Court	
AnRns,	1890-1903	Deed,	1819-1902
Conf,	1914-1938	Deed,	1819-1934
Est,	1819-1937	(Index)	
(Index)		PhR,	1881-1966*
Home,	1867-1903**	SMin,	1834-1881,
Inf,	1822-1873		1881-1901*
InvA,	1819-1903*	WWI,	1919*-

```
Lun,        1900-1914*
Mar,        1819-1964*
Mar (Index), 1819-1966
OMin,       1830-1903
Pony,       1901-1913*
Sch,        1838-1847
TMSup,      1850-1929*
Wills,      1819-1966**
```

Hancock:

Created December 17, 1793, from Washington and Greene Counties; #15 in order of creation; county seat, Sparta 31087.

Ordinary		Superior Court	
AnRns,	1797-1903	Deed,	1793-1934
AnRns, (Index)	1797-1853	Deed, (Index)	1794-1909
Conf,	1890-1939	SMin,	1794-1900
Est, (Index)	1793-1900	SMin, (Index)	1829-1849
FPC,	1855-1862		
Home,	1877-1894		
Inf,	1800-1871		
InvA,	1794-1880		
Jury,	1833-1918		
LLoty,	1805, 1820, 1825, 1832		
Lun,	1845-1885, 1896-1925*		
Mar,	1808-1880, 1880-1962*		
OMin,	1794-1903		
Pony,	1873-1893		
TMSup,	1885-1959		
Vote,	1895-1900		
WWI,	1917-		
Wills,	1794-1909		

Haralson:

Created January 26, 1856, from Polk and Carroll Counties; #112 in order of creation; county seat, Buchanan 30113; courthouse fire, January 13, 1889.

Ordinary		Superior Court	
AnRns,	1884-1902	Deed,	1830-1900
Conf,	no date shown	Deed, (Index)	1888-1902
Home,	1869-1934	SMin,	1855-1903
Inf,	1856-1868		
InvA,	1865-1937		
Liq,	1856-1896		
Mar,	1865-1909*		
Mar (Loose)	1856-1882*		
OMin,	1856-1905		

Pony,	1893-1905
TMSup,	1894-1911
Vote,	1896-1897
WWI,	1917-1919
Wills,	1865-1919

Harris:

Created December 14, 1827, from Troup and Muscogee Counties; #72 in order of creation; county seat, Hamilton 31811; courthouse fire, 1865 (set on fire by Union troops; fire quickly extinguished).

Ordinary		Superior Court	
Aptc,	1866-1867	Conf,	1861-1865
AnRns,	1829-1908	Deed,	1828-1947
Conf,	1890-1925	Deed,	1928-1910
Est,	1828-1940	(Index)	
(Index)		PhR,	1881-1952
Home,	1848-1942*	SMin,	1828-1909
Inf,	1828-1868	WWI,	1917-
InvA,	1829-1908		
Mar,	1828-1923*		
OMin,	1828-1908		
TMSup,	1857-1937		
Wills,	1833-1849, 1850-1932*		

Hart:

Created December 7, 1853, from Franklin and Elbert Counties; #101 in order of creation; county seat, Hartwell 30643; courthouse fire, 1900, 1967 (no loss; records in adjoining building).

• The Hart County Superior Court denied the Georgia Department of Archives and History permission to microfilm the Superior Court records.

Ordinary	
AnRns,	1857-1903*
Conf,	1861-1865, 1921-1926, 1933
Est,	1854-1945
(Index)	
Home,	1879-1921*
InvA,	1857-1916*
Mar,	1854-1923*
OMin,	1854-1908*; index, 1854-1945
TMSup,	1862-1920*
Wills,	1854-1934*

Heard:

Created December 22, 1830, from Troup, Coweta, and Carroll Counties; #76 in order of creation; county seat, Franklin 30217; courthouse fire, 1893.

Ordinary		Superior Court	
AnRns,	1894-1920*	Deed,	1894-1914
Conf,	1920-1937*	Deed,	1894-1914
Home,	1894-1929*	(Index)	

InvA,	1894-1920*		SMin,	1894-1914*
Mar,	1886-1965*		WWI,	1917-1919*,
OMin,	1894-1914*			1922-
TMSup,	1894-1925*			
Wills,	1894-1965*			

Henry:

Created May 15, 1821, from Indian lands ceded in 1821; #52 in order of creation; county seat, McDonough 30253; courthouse fire, 1824; some records destroyed by Federal troops during the Civil War.

Ordinary		Superior Court	
AnRns,	1836-1949	Deed,	1822-1917
Conf,	1861-1929	Deed,	1822-1917
Est,	1821-1939	(Index)	
(Index)		Jury,	1888-1914
Home,	1866-1894	PhR,	1881-1957
Inf,	1822-1891	SMin,	1822-1906
InvA,	1821-1954		
Lun,	1897-1909		
Mar,	1822-1945*		
Mar,	1821-1939		
(Index)			
OMin,	1825-1891, 1930-1944		
Pony,	1884-1949		
Sch,	1903, 1908, 1913, 1918		
TMSup,	1857-1893		
WWI,	1917-1952		
Wills,	1822-1952		

Houston:

Created May 15, 1821, from Indian lands ceded in 1821; #49 in order of creation; county seat, Perry 31069.

Ordinary		Superior Court	
Aptc,	1866-1930	Deed,	1822-1901
AnRns,	1824-1901*	Deed,	1822-1943
Home,	1873-1915	(Index)	
Inf,	1822-1836,	Home,	1868-1925
	1850-1961*	PhR,	1885-1937
InvA,	1834-1919	SMin,	1822-1902
Liq,	1834-1862	SMin,	1871-1888
(free persons of color)		(Index)	
Mar,	1833-1919*	WWI,	1922-
OMin,	1852-1903*		
Sch,	1841-1871		
Wills,	1827-1926*		

Irwin:

Created December 15, 1818, from Indian lands ceded in 1814 and 1818; #41 in order of creation; county seat, Ocilla 31774.

Ordinary		Superior Court	
AnRns,	1822-1899,	Deed,	1821-1903**
	1899-1923*	Deed,	1821-1900
Conf,	1890-1924	(Index)	
Inf,	1820-1878	Home,	1869-1924*
InvA,	1822-1923	PhR,	1882-1945*
Mar,	1820-1927*	SMin,	1820-1893,
OInd,	1821-1956		1898-1902*
OMin,	1820-1883,	WWI,	1921*-
	1891-1902*		
Transcripts of old records,			
	1820-1904*		
TMSup,	1863-1896*		
Wills,	1821-1951*		

Jackson:
Created February 11, 1796, from Franklin County, #22 in order of creation; county seat, Jefferson 30549.
• The original loose papers of Jackson County are in the Special Collections, University of Georgia libraries, Athens.

Ordinary		Superior Court	
Aptc,	1872-1906	Deed,	1796-1902
AnRns,	1800-1903	Deed,	1796-1906
Birth,	1875	(Index)	
Conf,	1894-1939	Jury,	1873, 1874,
Death,	1875		1876, 1878-1880
Home,	1868-1922**	Liq,	1880-1884
Inf,	1796-1865	PhR,	1881-1928
InvA,	1796-1903*	SMin,	1796-1904
Ld. Ct.	1796-1075,	WWI,	1917
	1871-1877		
LLoty,	1806, 1825, 1832		
Liq,	1851-1884		
Mar,	1805-1911**		
OMin,	1868-1904		
Paup,	1879-1901		
Pony,	1896-1913		
Sch,	1852-1863		
SlavR,	1818-1830		
TMSup,	1875-1908		
Wills,	1796-1919		

Jasper:
Created December 10, 1807, from Baldwin County; #31 in order of creation; county seat, Monticello 31064.
• Jasper County was Randolph County until the name was changed on December 10, 1812. The present-day Randolph was created on December 20, 1828.

Ordinary		Superior Court	
AnRns,	1823-1905	Deed,	1807-1901
Conf,	Misc. Dates	Deed,	1808-1835,
Est,	1809-1941		1837-1938
(Index)		(Index)	
Home,	1866-1924	PhR,	1881-1911
Inf,	1820-1868	SMin,	1807-1832,
InvA,	1852-1902*		1832-1906*
LLoty,	1825		
Mar,	1808-1900*		
OMin,	1812-1832, 1845-1902*		
Pony,	1873-1905		
TMSup,	1875-1912		
Wills,	no date shown; seem to start 1797		

Jeff Davis:
Created August 18, 1905, from Appling and Coffee Counties; #140 in order of creation; county seat, Hazelhurst 31539.

Jefferson:
Created February 20, 1796, from Burke and Warren Counties; #23 in order of creation; county seat, Louisville 30434; courthouse fire, 1861.
• Jefferson County Inventory and Appraisement Book B, 1813?-1815? was missing from the courthouse on the day the records were microfilmed.

Ordinary		Superior Court	
AnRns,	1815-1922	Deed,	1797-1799,
Cen,	1880		1803-1808,
Conf,	1890-1952		1865-1925
Death,	1875	Deed,	1865-1912
FPC,	1818, 1820-1822	(Index)	
	1840-1859	Home,	1868-1939
Inf,	1796-1868	Jury,	1799-1848
InvA,	1801-1812,	SMisc,	1796-1800,
	1816-1923*		1803-1812,
LLoty,	1825, 1831		1815-1891
Liq,	1839-1864,	SMin,	1796-1824,
	1916-1917		1872-1920*
Map,	1879	Vote,	1897, 1902
Mar,	1803-1957*		
OMin,	1801-1861,		
	1865-1921		
Pony,	1868-1939		
Sch,	1870-1880		
TMSup,	1897-1931		
Wills,	1777-1945*		

Jenkins:
Created August 17, 1905, from Bulloch, Burke, Emanuel, and Screven Counties; #138 in order of creation; county seat, Millen 30442; courthouse fire, 1919.

Johnson:

Created December 11, 1858, from Washington, Emanuel, and Laurens Counties; #128 in order of creation; county seat, Wrightsville 31096.

Ordinary		Superior Court	
AnRns,	1858-1916*	Deed,	1859-1909*
Bast,	1884-1915	Deed,	1859-1902
Conf,	1861-1865,	(Index)	
	1890-1929	Home,	1868-1909*
Home,	1868-1903*	PhR,	1881-1946
Inf,	1859-1941*	SMin,	1859-1903
InvA,	1859-1941*	Vote,	1898-1908*
LdCt,	1862-1909	WWI,	1922*-
Mar,	1859-1966*		
Mar,	1873-1876		
(Loose)			
OMin,	1859-1904*		
Pony,	1897-1960*		
TMSup,	1886-1925*		
Wills,	1859-1961*		

Jones:

Created December 10, 1807, from Baldwin County, #32 in order of creation; county seat, Gray 31032.

• Five boxes of loose Jones County records are in the Telamon Cuyler Collection, University of Georgia libraries, Athens. A small group that once were part of the Cuyler Collection are in the Manuscripts Section of the Georgia Archives.

Ordinary		Superior Court	
AnRns,	1809-1944	Deed,	1808-1906*
Cen,	1820, 1850,	Deed,	1807-1966
	1870, 1880	(Index)	
Conf,	1890-1944	Home,	1866-1959*
	1861-1862*	PhR,	1881-1904,
FPC,	1818-1830		1912-1962
Inf,	1809-1822,	Slave Deeds Index,	
	1824-1861		1791-1864
	1864-1874	SMin,	1808-1903*
InvA,	1809-1903*	WWI,	1917-1920
LLoty,	1820-1832		
(Index)			
Mar,	1809-1942*		
Mar,	1864-1919		
(Index) (Female)			
OMin,	1808-1818*, 1814-1873, 1866-1902*		
Sch,	1829-1861		
TMSup,	1865-1924*		
Wills,	1809-1951*		

Lamar:
Created November 2, 1920, from Monroe and Pike Counties; #158 in order of creation; county seat, Barnesville 30204.

Lanier:
Created November 2, 1920, from Berrien, Lowndes, and Clinch Counties; #155 in order of creation; county seat, Lakeland 31635.

Laurens:
Created December 10, 1807, from Wilkinson County; #34 in order of creation; county seat, Dublin 31021.

Ordinary		Superior Court	
Aptc,	1866-1900	Deed,	1808-1900
AnRns,	1811-1901*	Deed,	1808-1900
Conf,	1890-1938	(Index)	
Home,	1868-1928*	Mar,	1851-1868*
Inf,	1808-1870	PhR,	1891-1917*
InvA,	1808-1908**	SMin,	1816-1903
LLoty,	1820	WWI,	no date shown*
Mar,	1809-1823, 1826-1935*		
OMin,	1853-1872, 1872-1903*		
PhR,	1889-1903		
TMSup,	1871-1900**		
Wills,	1809-1926*		

Lee:
Created June 9, 1825, from Indian lands ceded in 1825 and 1826; #61 in order of creation; county seat, Leesburg 31763; courthouse fire, 1856 and 1872.

Ordinary		Superior Court	
AnRns,	1852-1916*	Deed,	1826-1832, 1858-1902*
Conf,	1890-1922	Deed,	1858-1915
Home,	1868-1911*	(Index)	
Inf,	1858-1878*	PhR,	1912-1939*
InvA,	1852-1916*	SMin,	1858-1904*
Mar,	1867-1905*		
OMin,	1858-1910*		
Wills,	1854-1955*		

Liberty:
Created February 5, 1777, from colonial Georgia. Originally included St. John, St. Andrew, and St. James Parishes; #6 in order of creation; county seat, Hinesville 31313.
• The Liberty County Historical Society and Georgia Southern College have microfilmed some Liberty County records not copied by the Georgia Archives.

Ordinary		Superior Court	
Aptc,	1866-1873,	Deed,	1777-1920
	1866-1884	Deed,	1777-1958
AnRns,	1812-1817*,	(Index)	
	1863-1864,	SMin,	1784-1897,
	1874-1923*		1897-1935*
Conf,	no date shown		
FPC,	1852-1864		
Home,	1872-1952		
Inf,	1799-1871		
InvA,	1789-1955*		
LdCt.	1804-1837		
Mar,	1819-1956*		
Mar,	1784-1895		
(Loose)			
OMin,	1826-1881, 1890-1940		
PhR,	1882-1924		
Sch,	1852-1875, 1885-1907		
TMSup,	1874-1927*		
Vote,	1896-1899		
Wills,	1789-1942*		
Wills,	1780-1880*		
(Loose)			

Lincoln:
Created February 20, 1796, from Wilkes County; #24 in order of creation; county seat, Lincolnton 30817.

Ordinary		Superior Court	
Aptc,	1804-1831,	Deed,	1796-1968
	1866-1915	Deed,	1796-1905,
Amnst,	1865	(Index)	1906-1946
AnRns,	1806-1968	Jury,	1879-1959
Conf,	1890-1920	PhR,	1881-1915
Est,	1796-1899	SMin,	1796-1966
(Index)			
FPC,	1819-1863		
Home,	1867-1930		
Inf,	1797-1868, 1802-1867(?)*		
InvA,	1807-1953		
LdCt,	1796-1917		
Liq,	1882-1885		
Lun,	1898-1953**, 1955-1968*		
Mar,	1806-2955		
Mar,	1925-1968		
(Index)			
OInd,	1800-1939		
OMin,	1799-1908, 1948-1968*		
Sch,	1852-1870		

TMSup,	1852-1968*
Vote,	1896
WWI,	1917-1918
Wills,	1796-1968

Long:
Created November 2, 1920, from Liberty County; #157 in order of creation; county seat, Ludowici 31316.

Lowndes:
Created December 23, 1825, from Irwin County, #68 in order of creation; county seat, Valdosta 31601.
• The Lowndes County Superior Court denied the Georgia Archives permission to microfilm the Superior Court records.

Ordinary

Affidavits giving ages or birthdays of children in cotton mills,	
	1891-1895
AnRns,	1862-1903**
Conf,	1910-1912*, 1914-1928*
InvA,	1862-1876, 1870-1914*
Mar,	1870-1934
OMin,	1870-1908*
Pony,	1882-1910*
TMSup,	1862-1876, 1873-1952*
Wills,	1871-1965*

Lumpkin:
Created December 3, 1832, from Cherokee County; #81 in order of creation; county seat, Dahlonega 30533.

Ordinary

		Superior Court	
AnRns,	1844-1906	Deed,	1833-1901
Birth,	1875	Deed,	1833-1856
Cen,	1860	(Index)	
Death,	1875	SMin,	1833-1901
FPC,	1848-1864	WWI,	1917-1919
Home,	1866-1912		
Inf,	1833-1859		
InvA,	1844-1906		
Liq,	1833-1887		
Mar,	1833-1847, 1850-1908*		
Mar,	1828*, 1830-1908*		
(Loose)			
OMin,	1835-1921		
Pony,	1845-1962		
Sch,	1847-1884		
TMSup,	1886-1936		
Wills,	1833-1923*		

Macon:
Created December 14, 1837, from Houston and Marion Counties; #90 in order of creation; county seat, Oglethorpe 31068; courthouse fire, 1857.

Ordinary		Superior Court	
AnRns,	1857-1901	Deed,	1857-1902
Conf,	1861-1920	Deed,	1887-1909
Death,	1956-1963	(Index)	
(Index)		PhR,	1895-1954
Home,	1866-1932	SMin,	1856-1901
InvA,	1872-1913	WWI,	1917-
Mar,	1858-1901*		
OMin,	1857-1908		
TMSup,	1861-1935		
Wills,	1856-1937		

Madison:
Created December 5, 1811, from Oglethorpe, Clarke, Jackson, Franklin, and Elbert Counties; #38 in order of creation; county seat, Danielsville 30633.

Ordinary		Superior Court	
Amnst,	1865	Deed,	1812-1907*
Aptc,	1868-1940*	Deed,	1812-1905
AnRns,	1816-1875**,	(Index)	
	1879-1939	Home,	1867-1917*
Cen,	1820	PhR,	1881-1929
Conf,	1890-1931	SMin,	1812-1874,
Dower Records,			1874-1900*
	1829-1939	WWI,	1922*-
Home,	1827-1897		
Inf,	1812-1887*		
InvA,	1813-1878*, 1877-1920		
Liq,	1881		
Mar,	1812-1909*		
OMin,	1860-1885, 1885-1906*		
Pony,	1897-1919*		
Sch,	1828-1871		
TMSup,	1866-1897, 1897-1926*		
Wills,	1812-1922*		

Marion:
Created December 14, 1827, from Lee and Muscogee Counties; #74 in order of creation; county seat, Buena Vista 31803; courthouse fire, 1845.

Ordinary		Superior Court	
AnRns,	1839-1865,	Deed,	1846-1965*
	1853-1941*	Deed,	1845-1965
Cen,	1860	(Index)	
Conf,	1890-1948	Home,	1866-1924
Home,	1866-1950*	SMin,	1846-1911*

Inf,	1842-1875*	Vote,	1898, 1900, 1903,
InvA,	1839-1853,	(colored)	1906
	1852-1904*	WWI,	no date shown
Mar,	1844-1953*		
OMin,	1854-1958*		
TMSup,	1864-1904*		
Wills,	1846-1940*		

McDuffie:
Created October 18, 1870, from Warren and Columbia Counties; #132 in order of creation; county seat, Thomson 30824.

Ordinary		Superior Court	
Aptc,	1874-1909	Deed,	1871-1900
AnRns,	1871-1915	Deed,	1871-1960
Conf,	1890-1931	(Index)	
Home,	1871-1909	Jury,	1871-1896
InvA,	1871-1927	PhR,	1881-1960
Mar,	1870-1911	SMin,	1871-1913
Mar,	1870-1960	WWI,	1917-
(Index)			
OMin,	1871-1905		
TMSup,	1871-1913		
Vote,	1886-1894		
(colored)			
Wills,	1872-1927		

McIntosh:
Created December 19, 1793, from Liberty County, #18 in order of creation; county seat, Darien 31305; courthouse fire, 1864, 1872, 1931.

Ordinary		Superior Court	
Conf,	1896-1923	Deed,	1873-1920
Death,	1875	Deed,	1873-1942
InvA,	1887-1911	(Index)	
Mar,	1869-1957*	Home,	1870-1920
OMin,	1873-1957	Jail Records,	
PhR,	1860-1901		1886-1927
Wills,	1873-1915	Jury,	1906-1942
		Liq,	1882-1889
		SMin,	1873-1922
		Vote,	1877-1922
		WWI,	1919-

Meriwether:
Created December 14, 1827, from Troup County; #71 in order of creation; county seat, Greenville 30222; cyclone March 3, 1893; courthouse fire, 1976 (no records lost).
• The Manuscripts Section of the William R. Perkins Library, Duke University, has two volumes of names of persons who registered for the 1832 land lottery from Meriwether County. These are not on microfilm at the Georgia Archives.

Ordinary		Superior Court	
Aptc,	1865-1888*	Deed,	1828-1918
AnRns,	1828-1902*	Deed,	1827-1963
Conf,	1861-1863,	(Index)	
	1896-1956	PhR,	1881-1961
Est,	1828-1963	SMin,	1828-1905
(Index)		WWI,	1917-1919*
Home,	1866-1910		
Inf,	1829-1890		
InvA,	1828-1886*		
Mar,	1828-1902*		
OMin,	1877-1890		
PhR,	1881-1926		
Powers of Attorney,			
	1865-1888*		
Sch,	1898, 1903, 1913		
TMSup,	1866-1905		
WWI,	1918		
Wills,	1831-1903		

Miller:
Created February 26, 1856, from Baker and Early Counties; #116 in order of creation; county seat, Colquitt 31737; courthouse fire, 1873; Oct. 10, 1904; Dec. 2, 1974.

Ordinary		Superior Court	
AnRns,	1871-1913*	Deed,	1873-1912*
Birth,	1875-1876*	Deed,	1874-1916
Death,	1875-1876*	(Index)	
InvA,	1880-1913*	PhR,	1881-1952*
Mar,	1892-1966*	SMin,	1904-1912*
Vote,	1906-1908	WWI,	1922-*
Wills,	1871-1965*		

Milton:
Created December 18, 1857, from Cherokee, Cobb, and Forsyth Counties. The county was abolished. Records are now kept by Fulton County.
• Milton County was abolished on January 1, 1932. The area is today the northern part of Fulton County. The loose records and tax digests were kept by the Ga. Archives from 1931 to 1938 before being transferred to Fulton County. Within the last few years, some Milton County records have been given to the Atlanta Historical Society. Researchers may contact the Fulton courthouse and the Society about specific records.

Ordinary		Superior Court	
AnRns,	1866-1931*	Deed,	1867-1931
Conf,	1911-1929	Deed,	1867-1931
Est,	1867-1931	(Index)	
(Index)		Home,	1883-1912*

Home,	1868-1905*	SMin,	1861-1931,
Inf,	1858-1884,	SMin,	1861-1929
	1884-1904*	(Index)	
InvA,	1858-1931*		
Mar,	1865-1874, 1875-1932*		
Mar,	1867-1931		
(Index)			
OMin,	1872-1880, 1881-1931*		
Pony,	1901-1931*		
TMSup,	1882-1931*		
Wills,	1865-1932*, 1936		
Wills,	1833?-1948*		
(Index)			

Mitchell:

Created December 21, 1857, from Baker County; #121 in order of creation; county seat, Camilla 31730; fire, 1869.

Ordinary		Superior Court	
Aptc,	1882-	Deed,	1858-1907
AnRns,	1867-1879*,	Deed,	1856-1878,
	1883-1912*		1888-1906
Conf,	1889-1897,	(Index)	
	1914-1925	Home,	1868-1913
Home,	1870-1881*	SMin,	1858-1902*
InvA,	1896-1948*	WWI,	1924-*
Mar,	1867-1960*		
OMin,	1858-1907*		
TMSup,	1881-1913*		
Wills,	1868-1965*		

Monroe:

Created May 15, 1821, from Indian lands ceded in 1821; #50 in order of creation; county seat, Forsyth 31029.

Ordinary		Superior Court	
Aptc,	1869-1890	Deed,	1822-1901
AnRns,	1823-1905	Deed,	1822-1921
Conf,	no date shown	(Index)	
Home,	1868-1956	Jury,	1892-1912
Inf,	1826-1849	PhR,	1881-1915
InvA,	1851-1954	SMin,	1826-1902
Mar,	1824-1958*		
Mar,	1824-1958		
(Index)			
Mar,	1850-1899*		
(Loose)			
OMin,	1824-1903		
Pony,	1921-1932		
TMSup,	1882-1952		
Wills,	1824-1958*		

Montgomery:
Created December 19, 1793, from Washington County; #20 in order of creation; county seat, Mt. Vernon 30445.
• The Georgia Archives has records of some Montgomery County schools for 1884-1889 in their Private Papers, Microfilm Library, reel 199-45.

Ordinary		Superior Court	
AnRns,	1850-1910	Deed,	1794-1903
Conf,	1890-1924	Deed,	1790-1916
Home,	1874-1919	(Index)	
Inf,	1809-1818,	Home,	1861-1931
	1820-1870	Jury,	1882-1912
InvA,	1801-1906	PhR,	1881-1923
Lun,	1896-1909	SMin,	1807-1904
Mar,	1810-1946**	WWI,	1917-1919
Mar,	1811-1960		
(Index)			
OMin,	1809-1903		
PhR,	1886-1917		
TMSup,	1886-1919		
Vote,	1902, 1909-1912		
Wills,	1806-1903		

Morgan:
Created December 10, 1807, from Baldwin County; #30 in order of creation; county seat, Madison 30650.

Ordinary		Superior Court	
Aptc,	1866-1877	Deed,	1808-1903
AnRns,	1808-1903	Deed,	1808-1903
Cen,	1870, 1880	(Index)	
Conf,	1890-1930	Jury,	1886-1904
Home,	1866-1921,	SMin,	1808-1903
	1868-1921*,		
	1877-1956		
Inf,	1808-1860		
InvA,	1808-1903		
Jail Rec.,	1877-1937		
LLoty,	1827 (incomplete)		
Liq,	1840-1846		
Mar,	1806-1818, 1821-1904*		
Mar,	1818-1868*		
(Loose)			
OMin,	1808-1901		
PhR,	1886		
SlavR,	1818-1824		
Vote,	1898, 1905		
Wills,	1806-1899		
Wills	1807-1865*		
(Loose)			

Murray:
Created December 3, 1832, from Cherokee County; #85 in order of creation; county seat, Chatsworth 30705.

Ordinary		Superior Court	
AnRns,	1835-1914*	Deed,	1833-1901*
Conf,	1861-1865,	Deed,	1833-1964
	1820-1938	(Index)	
Home,	1874-1932*	Jury,	1837, 1839
Inf,	1834-1862	Parole Records,	
InvA,	1835-1914*		1919-1923
Mar,	1834-1907*	PhR,	1877-1955
OMin,	1853-1869,	SMin,	1833-1907**
	1869-1905*	WWI,	1917*-
TMSup,	1882-1918*		
Wills,	1840-1922*		

Muscogee:
Created June 9, 1825, from Indian land ceded in 1826; #62 in order of creation; county seat, Columbus 31902; courthouse fire, Oct. 15, 1838 (total loss).

Ordinary		Superior Court	
AnRns,	1839-1903	Conf,	no date shown
Conf,	1919-1965	Deed,	1837-1901
Home,	1868-1906*	Deed,	1838-1905*
InvA,	1839-1909*	(Index)	
Mar,	1838-1929*	Nat,	1919
OInd,	1889-1925	PhR,	1881-1926*
OMin,	1838-1902*	SMin,	1838-1907**
TMSup,	1879-1887*		
Wills,	1838-1964*		

Newton:
Created December 24, 1821, from Jasper, Walton, and Henry Counties; #53 in order of creation; county seat, Covington 30209; courthouse fire, 1883.

Ordinary		Superior Court	
AnRns,	1822-1902	Deed,	1822-1902
Cen,	1880	Deed,	1821-1904
Conf,	1860-1865,	(Index)	
	1890-1929	PhR,	1881-1959
Home,	1850-1865,	SMin,	1822-1904
	1874-1889,		
	1864-1954		
Inf,	1823-1876		
InvA,	1822-1915		
Mar,	1822-1904*		
OMin,	1859-1903		
PhR,	1882-1961		
Pony,	1889-1918		

TMSup	1856-1961
Vote,	1895-1897
Wills,	1823-1936*

Oconee:

Created February 25, 1875, from Clarke County; #135 in order of creation; county seat, Watkinsville 30677; courthouse fire, January 1887.

Ordinary		Superior Court	
AnRns,	1875-1915*	Deed,	1875-1911*
Conf,	1862,	Deed,	1875-1939
	1890-1920*	(Index)	
Home,	1875-1912*	SMin,	1875-1892,
InvA,	1885-1954*		1892-1913*
Lun,	1878-1897	WWI,	1922*-
Mar,	1875-1966*		
OMin,	1875-1905*, 1892-1912		
TMSup,	1875-1930*		
Wills,	1875-1960*		

Oglethorpe:

Created December 19, 1793, from Wilkes County; #17 in order of creation; county seat, Lexington 30648; courthouse fire, 1941.

• Mary Warren has published some War of 1812 rosters for this county in **Georgia Genealogist**, #28, that provide the name and physical description of each recruit. The originals are in the Telamon Cuyler Collection, Special Collections, Univeristy of Georgia libraries.

Ordinary		Superior Court	
Aptc,	1866-1903	Attorney's Roll,	
AnRns,	1798-1903		1795-1886
Birth,	1875-1878	Deed,	1794-1901
Conf,	1881-1895	Deed,	1794-1901
Home,	1868-1905	(Index)	
Inf,	1794-1839,	PhR,	1881-1944
	1842-1858,	SMisc,	1820-1902
	1863-1869	SMin,	1794-1904
InvA,	1793-1911**		
Jury,	1870-1893		
LLoty,	1805, 1806, 1820, 1832		
Lun,	1851-1888		
Mar,	1794-1908**		
Mar,	1793-1830		
(Index)			
OMin,	1794-1904		
Paup,	1851-1888		
Pony,	1867-1910		
Sch,	1829-1861		
TMSup,	1856-1903		

Vote,	1886-1893
WWI,	1917-1919
Wills,	1793-1873*

Paulding:
Created December 3, 1832, from Cherokee County; #88 in order of creation; county seat, Dallas 30132.

Ordinary		Superior Court	
AnRns,	1885-1908*	Deed,	1848-1902*
Bast,	1880-1911*	Deed,	1881-1882
Conf,	1890-1940*	(Index)	
Home,	1866-1915*	PhR,	1881-1961
InVa,	1896-1945*	SMin,	1859-1905
Lun,	1895-1920*	WWI,	1917-
Mar,	1833-1964*		
OMin,	1866-1932		
PhR,	1876-1911*		
Pony,	1876-1911*		
TMSup,	1895-1919*		
Vote,	1896*, 1898*, 1900*, 1921		
Wills,	1850-1965*		

Peach:
Created November 4, 1924, from Houston and Macon Counties; #159 in order of creation; county seat, Fort Valley 31030.

Pickens:
Created December 5, 1853, from Cherokee and Gilmer Counties; #100 in order of creation; county seat, Jasper 30143; courthouse fire, 1947 — almost no record loss.

Ordinary		Superior Court	
AnRns,	1854-1911*	Deed,	1854-1901
Conf,	1890-1912*	Deed,	1854-1919
Home,	1868-1881*	(Index)	
Inf,	1865-1894	Jury,	1879-1902*
InvA,	1854-1923*	PhR,	1861-1950*
Mar,	1854-1878	SMin,	1854-1890,
Mar,	1871-1931?		1890-1907*
(Loose)		WWI,	1917-1919
OMin,	1854-1894,		
	1868-1911*		
Pony,	1895-1928*		
TMSup,	1880-1923*		
Wills,	1854-1935*		

Pierce:
Created December 18, 1857, from Ware and Appling Counties; #119 in order of creation; county seat, Blackshear 31516; courthouse fire, 1875.

Ordinary			Superior Court	
Conf,	1890-1924		Deed,	1871-1913
Est,	1871-1940		Deed,	1871-1914
Home,	1892-1940		(Index)	
InvA,	1875-1911		PhR,	1883-1944
Jury,	1880-1902		SMin,	1872-1909
Mar,	1875-1917*		WWI,	1922-
OMin,	1870-1907			
Pony,	1892-1950			
Sch,	1892-1902			
Vote,	1896-1916			
WWI,	1917-1919			
Wills,	1872-1941			

Pike:

Created December 9, 1822, from Monroe County; #56 in order of creation; county seat, Zebulon 30295.

Ordinary			Superior Court	
AnRns,	1824-1900		Deed,	1823-1903
Conf,	1890-1959		Deed,	1823-1906
Home,	1868-1908		(Index)	
Inf,	1825-1873		Home,	1868-1908*
InvA,	1824-1854,		Jury,	1837-1839
	1854-1872*		PhR,	1898-1941
Mar,	1823-1912*		SMin,	1823-1903
OInd,	no date shown			
OMin,	1856-1901			
Sch,	1841-1866			
TMSup,	1882-1924			
Wills,	1823-1914*			

Polk:

Created December 20, 1851, from Paulding and Floyd Counties; #95 in order of creation; county seat, Cedartown 30125.

Ordinary			Superior Court	
Aptc,	1866-1891*		Deed,	1852-1907*
AnRns,	1851-1908*		Home,	1867-1916*
Conf,	1890-1929		PhR,	1881-1963
Home,	1853-1904*		Smin,	1852-1856,
Inf,	1854-1860			1857-1901*
InvA,	1866-1950*		WWI,	1922*-
Lun,	1895-1912*			
Mar,	1854-1965*			
OMin,	1865-1910*			
Pony,	1895-1912			
TMSup,	1886-1917*			
Vote,	1945			
Wills,	1848-1963*			

Pulaski:
Created December 13, 1808, from Laurens County; #36 in order of creation; county seat, Hawkinsville 31036.

Ordinary			Superior Court	
AnRns,	1817-1956		Deed,	1807-1919
Birth,	1875*		Deed,	1807-1939
Bast,	1841-1875		(Index)	
Conf,	no date shown		Jury,	1809-1827,
FPC,	1840-1865			1876-1880,
Home,	1868-1915			1882-1892
Inf,	1809-1867		PhR,	1881-1954
InvA,	1817-1910		SMin,	1809-1935
LLoty,	1832		Vote,	1886
Liq,	1882-1906		WWI,	no date shown
Lun,	1899-1918			
Mar,	1810-1956*			
OMin,	1813-1816, 1818-1925			
Pony,	1915-1928			
Sch,	1841-1850, 1857-1868, 1895-1897			
SlavR,	1818-1865			
TMSup,	1863-1913			
Wills,	1810-1935			

Putnam:
Created December 10, 1807, from Baldwin County; #33 in order of creation; county seat, Eatonton 31024.

Ordinary			Superior Court	
Aptc,	1869-1880		Conf,	no date shown
AnRns,	1808-1916*		Deed,	1808-1810,
Conf,	1890-1929*,			1810-1864*
	1879-1937		Deed,	1806-1911
Est,	1808-1964		(Index)	
(Index)			Inf,	1810-1822
Home,	1869-1879,		PhR,	1881-1953
	1881-1915*		SMin,	1808-1846,
Inf,	1819-1846			1846-1901*
InvA,	1808-1911*		WWI,	no date shown
Mar,	1808-1964*			
Mar,	1808-1940			
(Index)				
OMin,	1808-1902			
Sch,	1825-1859			
TMSup,	1864-1963*			
Wills,	1808-1964*			

Quitman:
Created December 10, 1858, from Randolph and Stewart Counties; #126 in order of creation; county seat, Georgetown 31754; courthouse fire, 1920.

Ordinary		Superior Court
Mar,	1875-1891	
Mar,	1875-1891	
(Index)		
OMin,	1864-1902	

Rabun:
Created December 21, 1819, from Indian land ceded in 1819; #47 in order of creation; county seat, Clayton 30525.

Ordinary		Superior Court	
AnRns,	1855-1877,	Deed,	1821-1904
	1877-1910*	Deed,	1821-1940
Cen,	1860	(Index)	
Conf,	1891-1910,	Inf,	1856-1878
	1916-1919	(Docket)	
Home,	1871-1914	SMin,	1829-1905
Inf,	1826-1882	WWI,	1919-
InvA,	1855-1877,		
	1869-1896*		
Liq,	1861-1875		
Mar,	1820-1920*		
OMin,	1831-1889		
Sch,	1857-1858		
Wills,	1857-1867, 1863-1930*		

Randolph:
Created December 20, 1828, from Lee County; #75 in order of creation; county seat, Cuthbert 31740.
• Jasper County was named Randolph until the name was changed on December 10, 1812.

Ordinary		Superior Court	
AnRns,	1861-1912	Cen,	1870
Birth,	1875-1877	Deed,	1837-1901
Cen,	1870	Deed,	1889-1903
Conf,	no date shown	(Index)	
Inf,	1845-1879*	Home,	1866-1913
Liq,	1839-1882	Jury,	1841-1859
Mar,	1837-1838,	SMin,	1841-1856,
	1836-1902*		1859-1890
OMin,	1852-1871*		
TMSup,	1857-1858		
Wills,	1835-1916		

Richmond:
Created February 5, 1777, from colonial Georgia. Originally included all of St. Paul Parish; #2 in order of creation; county seat, Augusta 30903.
• Manuscripts Section, William R. Perkins Library, Duke University, has Richmond County loose records scattered through their Georgia Papers Collection.

Ordinary		Superior Court	
AnRns,	1797-1798, 1857-1881	Deed,	1788-1901
Birth,	1823-1896	Deed, (Index)	1787-1901
Cen, (Augusta)	1852	Home,	1868-1921
		Jury,	1851-1900
Home,	1867-1868, 1879-1909	LdCt,	1784-1787, 1853-1870
Inf,	1786, 1790-1872	SlavR,	1818-1837
		SMin,	1782-1904
InvA,	1799-1901		
Jury,	1826-1830		
LLoty,	1832		
Mar,	1806-1900*		
Mar, (Loose)	1785-1849*		
OMin,	1791-1898		
TMSup,	1799-1901*		
Wills,	1777-1905; Index, 1777-1957		

Rockdale:
Created October 18, 1870, from Newton and Henry Counties; #133 in order of creation; county seat, Conyers 30207.

Ordinary		Superior Court	
AnRns,	1876-1906*	Deed,	1870-1907*
Conf,	1890-1952	Deed, (Index)	1870-1908
Home,	1871-1904*		
InvA,	1897-1938*	SMin,	1871-1905*
Mar,	1871-1878, 1876-1902* 1876-1909	WWI,	no date shown
OMin,	1871-1908*		
TMSup,	1881-1898, 1898-1922*		
Wills,	1870-1916*		

Schley:
Created December 22, 1857, from Marion and Sumter Counties; #122 in order of creation; county seat, Ellaville 31806.

Ordinary		Superior Court	
AnRns,	1858-1907*	Conf,	no date shown
Home,	1870-1897*	Deed,	1858-1899*, 1896-1906
Inf,	1858-1891*		
InvA,	1858-1869*, 1859-1882, 1882-1914*	Deed, (Index)	1858-1900
		PhR,	1881-1950*
Mar,	1858-1913*	SMin,	1858-1911*
OMin,	1858-1901*	WWI,	1917*-
Wills,	1858-1905*		

Screven:
Created December 14, 1793, from Burke and Effingham Counties; #14 in order of creation; county seat, Sylvania 30467; courthouse fire, 1860s, 1896.

Ordinary		Superior Court	
AnRns,	1821-1854,	Deed,	1794-1910
	1882-1915	Deed,	1794-1906
Home,	1871-1936	(Index)	
Inf,	1811-1868	Jury,	1879-1912
InvA,	1878-1918	PhR,	1881-1958
Jury,	1856, 1858,	SMin,	1816-1901
	1860	WWI,	1919-
Mar,	1821-1902*		
OMin,	1811-1904		
TMSup,	1896-1933		
Vote,	1897		
Wills,	1810-1929		

Seminole:
Created November 2, 1920, from Decatur and Early Counties; #154 in order of creation; county seat, Donaldsonville 31745.

Spalding:
Created December 20, 1851, from Pike, Fayette, and Henry Counties; #96 in order of creation; county seat, Griffin 30223.

Ordinary		Superior Court	
AnRns,	1851-1905	Deed,	1852-1899*,
Conf,	1914-1928		1890-1901
Home,	1867-1920*	Deed,	1852-1881
Inf,	1852-1864*	(Index)	
InvA,	1852-1946*	Home,	1868-1930*
Lun,	1897-1909*	SMin,	1852-1911*
Mar,	1852-1966*	Vote,	1895-1896
OMin,	1852-1905*	WWI,	1921*-
PhR,	1900-1949		
Pony,	1897-1915*		
Sch,	1852-1864		
TMSup,	1858-1925*		
Wills,	1852-1966*		

Stephens:
Created August 18, 1905, from Franklin and Habersham Counties; #141 in order of creation; county seat, Toccoa 30577.

Stewart:
Created December 23, 1830, from Randolph County; #77 in order of creation; county seat, Lumpkin 31815; courthouse fire, 1922 — no loss.

Ordinary		Superior Court	
AnRns,	1827-1920	Deed,	1828-1907*
Death,	no date shown	Deed,	1828-1905

Home,	1858-1941*	(Index)	
Inf,	1827-1873**	Jury,	1869*,
InvA,	1827-1903**		1870, 1872
Mar,	1825-1961**	PhR,	1881-1958
Mar,	1828-1895	SMin,	1824-1847,
(Index)			1827-1837*,
OMin,	1856-1903		1843-1902*,
Sch,	1852-1858		1919*
WWI,	1936-1943	WWI,	1925*-
Wills,	1831-1944*		

Sumter:
Created December 26, 1831, from Lee County; #79 in order of creation; county seat, Americus 31709.

Ordinary		Superior Court	
Aptc,	1867-1871	Deed,	1831-1915
AnRns,	1850-1882	Deed,	1831-1917
Birth,	1875-1876*	(Index)	
Conf,	1903-1952	Jury,	1871-1873,
Home,	1866-1901		1879-1880,
Inf,	1832-1857		1882-1892
InvA,	1842-1904		1894-1916
Jury,	1836-1843	Nat,	1906-1918
Liq,	1882-1891	SMin,	1842-1900
Mar,	1831-1897*		
Mar,	1831-1937		
(Index)			
OMin,	1829-1902		
PhR,	1838-1919		
TMSup,	1857-1901		
Vote,	1909, 1911-1913		
Wills,	1838-1926*		

Talbot:
Created December 14, 1827, from Muscogee County; #73 in order of creation; county seat, Talbotton 31827; courthouse fire, 1890 — no loss.

Ordinary		Superior Court	
AnRns,	1828-1926	Deed,	1828-1900
Conf,	1895-1899	Deed,	1888-1902
Death,	1875*	(Index)	
Home,	1868-1920	Jury,	1879-1902
Inf,	1828-1882	PhR,	1899-1953
InvA,	1831-1924	SMin,	1828-1900
Liq,	1828-1833	WWI,	1918-
Mar,	1828-1903*		
OMin,	1828-1909		
Wills,	1828-1928		

Taliaferro:
Created December 24, 1825, from Wilkes, Warren, Hancock, Greene, and Oglethorpe Counties; #69 in order of creation; county seat, Crawfordville 30631.

Ordinary		Superior Court	
Aptc,	1866-1844	Deed,	1826-1900
AnRns,	1827-1913	Deed,	1826-1900
Birth,	1875-1876*	(Index)	
Cen,	1827, 1850,	LdCt,	1826-1858
	1860, 1880	PhR,	1881-1911
Conf,	1890-1920	SMin,	1826-1901
Death,	1875-1876*	WWI,	1917-1960
FPC,	1796-1864		
Home,	1826-1905		
Inf,	1826-1832, 1853-1867		
InvA,	1826-1937		
Jury,	1880-1910		
LLoty,	1832		
Mar,	1826-1973*		
OMin,	1854-1903		
PhR,	1881-1899		
Sch,	1828-1867		
Vote,	1892-1903		
Wills,	1826-1949		

Tattnall:
Created December 5, 1801, from Montgomery County; #25 in order of creation; county seat, Reidsville 30453.

Ordinary		Superior Court	
AnRns,	1857-1913	Deed,	1802-1913*
Conf,	1914-1924	Deed,	1802-1938
Home,	1868-1878	(Index)	
Inf,	1805-1868	Home,	1868-1909
InvA,	1836-1862,	PhR,	1881-1933
	1873-1917	SMin,	1805-1916
Lun,	1893-1909	WWI,	1919-
Mar,	1806-1932		
OMin,	1853-1913		
Pony,	1883-1911		
Sch,	1852-1865, 1928, 1933, 1938		
TMSup,	1858-1923		
Wills,	1854-1939*		

Taylor:
Created January 15, 1852, from Talbot, Macon, and Marion Counties; #98 in order of creation; county seat, Butler 31006.

Ordinary		Superior Court	
AnRns,	1858-1911	Deed,	1852-1902

Conf,	1890-1928	Deed,	1852-1918
Est,	no date shown	(Index)	
Home,	1887-1931	PhR,	1894-1913
Inf,	1852-1869	SMin,	1852-1903
InvA,	1852-1952	WWI,	1922-1962
Mar,	1852-1937		
OMin,	1866-1913		
TMSup,	1852-1952		
Wills,	1853-1917		

Telfair:
Created December 10, 1807, from Wilkinson County; #35 in order of creation; county seat, McRae 31055; courthouse fire, early 1900s.

Ordinary		Superior Court	
AnRns,	1879-1937*	Conf,	1890-1928
Cen,	1880	Deed,	1806-1903
Conf,	1861-1864,	Deed,	1809-1904
	1867	(Index)	
Home,	1894-1923*	Home,	1869-1936*
Inf,	1845-1854*	PhR,	1887-1955*
InvA,	1854-1865,	SMin,	1810-1837,
	1858-1938*		1849-1861,
Liq,	1869-1880		1884-1900
Mar,	1810-1902**	WWI,	1917*-
OMin,	1857-1871*,		
	1871-1892, 1892-1917*		
TMSup,	1898-1961		
Wills,	1869-1921*		

Terrell:
Created February 16, 1856, from Lee and Randolph Counties; #113 in order of creation; county seat, Dawson 31742.

Ordinary		Superior Court	
Aptc,	1866-1920	Deed,	1856-1909
AnRns,	1855-1910	Deed,	1856-1899
Home,	1883-1910	(Index)	
Inf,	1859-1872	Home,	1868-1904
InvA,	1855-1907	SMin,	1856-1900
Mar,	1855-1919		
OMin,	1856-1908		
Paup,	1886		
Sch,	1856, 1884		
TMSup,	1855-1921		
Vote,	1895-1909		
Wills,	1857-1913		

Thomas:
Created December 23, 1825, from Decatur and Irwin Counties; #67 in order

of creation; county seat, Thomasville 31792; courthouse damaged by storm in 1849 — no loss.

Ordinary		Superior Court	
AnRns,	1845-1849,	Deed,	1826-1911
	1853-1901	Deed,	1826-1910
Conf,	no date shown	(Index)	
Est,	1826-1957	PhR,	1884-1957
(Index)		SMin,	1826-1901
FPC,	1858-1894	WWI,	1916-1919
Home,	1868-1912		
Inf,	1849-1860		
InvA,	1847-1931		
Liq,	1869-1907		
Mar,	1826-1921*		
Mar,	1826-1957		
(Index)			
OMin,	1826-1902		
TMSup,	1897-1928		
Vote,	1898		
Wills,	1826-1957		

Tift:
Created August 17, 1905, from Berrien, Irwin, and Worth Counties; #139 in order of creation; county seat, Tifton 31794.

Toombs:
Created August 18, 1905, from Emanuel, Montgomery, and Tattnall Counties; #142 in order of creation; courthouse fire, 1919.

Towns:
Created March 6, 1856, from Union and Rabun Counties; #117 in order of creation; county seat, Hiawassee 30546.

Ordinary		Superior Court	
Amnst,	1865	Deed,	1856-1861*,
AnRns,	1873-1931*		1861-1880,
Conf,	1924-1941		1881-1901*
Est,	1857-1876?	Deed,	1856-1926
(Index)		(Index)	
Home,	1868-1945*	Inf,	1865-1868
InvA,	1899-1941*	(Docket)	
Jury,	1880-1898,	SMin,	1856-1899*,
	1900-1928		1899-1905
Mar,	1856-1893,	WWI,	1917-1919,
	1885-1908*		1922-
OMin,	1856-1906*		
TMSup,	1894-1938*		
Vote,	1898-1900		

Treutlen:
Created November 5, 1918, from Emanuel and Montgomery Counties; #152 in order of creation; county seat, Soperton 30457.

Troup:
Created June 9, 1825, from Indian land ceded in 1826; #63 in order of creation; county seat, LaGrange 30240; courthouse fire, November 4, 1936.

Ordinary		Superior Court	
AnRns,	1828-1902	Deed,	1827-1904
Est,	1828-1953	Deed,	1827-1917
(Index)		(Index)	
Inf,	1828-1840,	SMin,	1832-1905
	1837-1845*	WWI,	1917-1919*
InvA,	1828-1902		
Mar,	1828-1908*		
OMin,	1846-1903		
Wills,	1832-1929*		

Turner:
Created August 18, 1905, from Dooly, Irwin, Wilcox, and Worth Counties; #143 in order of creation; county seat, Ashburn 31714.

Twiggs:
Created December 14, 1809, from Wilkinson County; #37 in order of creation; county seat, Jeffersonville 31044; courthouse fire, Feb. 6, 1901 — total loss.
• The Georgia Archives has a collection of miscellaneous Twiggs County records on microfilm for 1809-1900.

Union:
Created December 3, 1832, from Cherokee County; #82 in order of creation; county seat, Blairsville 30512; courthouse fire, 1859, and some county records and newspapers burned by county commissioner in September 1979.

Ordinary		Superior Court	
Amnst,	1865	Deed,	1860-1906*
AnRns,	1877-1920*	Deed,	1860-1906
Conf,	1863-1865,	(Index)	
	1914-1925,	PhR,	1881-1946*
	1927, 1941	SMin,	1856-1904
Home,	1877-1937*	WWI,	1922-
Inf,	1855-1972		
InvA,	1877-1928*		
Mar,	1833-1933		
OMin,	1838-1903		
Sch,	1859-1864*		
TMSup,	1877-1933*		
Vote,	1895-1904		
Wills,	1877-1942*		

• Pre-1860 Union County deeds exist but were missed when the Archives microfilmed the Union County records. Reportedly, the pre-1860 deeds are now in the possession of the heirs of a local historian who borrowed these records recently and then died before he could return them.

Upson:
Created December 15, 1824, from Crawford and Pike Counties; #59 in order of creation; county seat, Thomaston 30286.

Ordinary		Superior Court	
AnRns,	1825-1948	Deed,	1825-1909
Conf,	1890-1933	Deed,	1825-1901
Home,	1872-1904	(Index)	
Inf,	1825-1854	Home,	1868-1930
InvA,	1825-1929	PhR,	1881-1962
Lun,	1892-1920	SMin,	1825-1944
Mar,	1825-1886,	WWI,	1917-1919
	1866-1908*		
OMin,	1825-1904		
TMSup,	1886-1925		
Wills,	1825-1915		

Walker:
Created December 18, 1833, from Murray County; #89 in order of creation; county seat, LaFayette 30728; courthouse fire, 1883.

Ordinary		Superior Court	
AnRns,	1883-1901*	Deed,	1882-1901
Conf,	1890-1957*	Deed,	1883-1908
Home,	1883-1909*	(Index)	
InvA,	1883-1916*	PhR,	1883-1935
Mar,	1882-1920*	SMin,	1883-1904
OMin,	1883-1906*	SMin,	1883-1904
TMSup,	1883-1906*	(Index)	
Vote,	1899-1900	WWI,	1917-1919*,
Wills,	1883-1956*		1922-

Walton:
Created December 15, 1818, from Indian land ceded in 1818; #43 in order of creation; county seat, Monroe 30655.
• Estate records are more complete than this listing indicates.

Ordinary		Superior Court	
AnRns,	1895-1910	Deed,	1819-1909
Conf,	1861-1865,	Deed,	1819-1909
	1911-1930	(Index)	
Est,	1819-1965	Jury,	1823-1920
(Index)		PhR,	1947-1960
Home,	1824-1914	SMin,	1819-1906
Inf,	1819-1910	SMin,	1820-1943
Liq,	1868-1889	(Index)	

Lun,	1901-1918	WWI,	1917-1919,
Mar,	1820-1934		1922-
Paup,	1905-1907		
Sch,	1829-1939, 1928-1938		
Vote,	1891-1902, 1909-1910		
Wills,	1819?-1923		

Ware:

Created December 15, 1824, from Appling County; #60 in order of creation; county seat, Waycross 31501; courthouse fire, 1874.

Ordinary		**Superior Court**	
AnRns,	1874-1910	Deed,	1874-1905
Conf,	1890-1923	Deed,	1874-1916
Home,	1875-1909	(Index)	
InvA,	1879-1946	Home,	1874-1932
Jury,	1890-1925	PhR,	1894-1941
Lun,	1895-1918	SMin,	1875-1912
Mar,	1874-1953*	WWI,	1919-
OMin,	1874-1911		
TMSup,	1895-1920		
Vote,	1900		
Wills,	1879-1949		

Warren:

Created December 19, 1793, from Wilkes, Columbia, Burke, and Richmond Counties; #16 in order of creation; county seat, Warrenton 30828; courthouse fire, 1909 — no loss, and at least one other fire prior to 1936.

Ordinary		**Superior Court**	
AnRns,	1798-1910	Deed,	1795-1902
Conf,	1890-1932	Deed,	1796-1900
FPC,	1844-1863	(Index)	
Home,	1857-1913	SMin,	1794-1901
Inf,	1815-1868		
InvA,	1794-1857		
Jury,	1870-1892		
Mar,	1794-1902*		
OMin,	1817-1945		
Sch(?),	1856-1872		
TMSup,	1856-1919		
Vote,	1893-1899		
WWI,	1917		
Wills,	1798-1937		

Washington:

Created February 25, 1784, from Indian land ceded in 1783; #10 in order of creation; county seat, Sandersville 31082; courthouse fire, 1855 and 1864.

Ordinary		**Superior Court**	
Aptc,	1829-1876*	Conf,	1896-1920

AnRns,	1843-1912*	Deed,	1865-1904
Cen,	1880, 1890,	Deed,	1866-1915
	1900	(Index)	
Conf,	1861-1865	LdCt,	1784-1787
Home,	1859-1925*	SMin,	1865-1902
Inf,	1843-1869	WWI,	1917-1957*
InvA,	1846-1901*		
Mar,	1828-1903*		
OMin,	1858-1906*		
PhR,	1881-1917		
Sch,	1859-1870		
TMSup,	1861-1906*		
Wills,	1852-1903		

Wayne:
Created May 11, 1803, from Indian land ceded in 1802; #27 in order of creation; county seat, Jesup 31545.
• Estate record books have misleading designations in the Microfilm Library card catalogue.

Ordinary		Superior Court	
AnRns,	1819-1878,	Deed,	1809-1920
	1903-1915	Deed,	1810-1918
Conf,	1890-1919	(Index)	
Home,	1835-1857,	PhR,	1883-1956
	1875-1909	SMin,	1823-1920
Inf,	1823-1868		
Jury,	1880-1906		
Liq,	1868-1885, 1856-1870		
Mar,	1809-1926**		
OMin,	1815-1916		
Paup,	1904-1937		
Pony,	1905-1937		
TMSup,	1886-1919		
Vote,	1896, 1898-1914		
WWI,	1922-		
Wills,	1819-1927		

Webster:
Created December 16, 1853, from Stewart County; #103 in order of creation; county seat, Preston 31824; courthouse fire, 1914.
• Webster County was Kinchafoonee until the name was officially changed on February 21, 1856. Marriage books are lost prior to 1914.

Ordinary		Superior Court	
Aptc,	1866-1869*	Conf,	no date shown
AnRns,	1863-1881,	Deed,	1860-1927*
	1881-1914	Deed,	1860-1932
Conf,	1910,	(Index)	
	1931-1932	SMin,	1903-1913*

Home,	1856	SMin,	1903-1913*
InvA,	1863-1914	WWI,	1917-1919
Mar,	1914-1953		
Mar, (Loose)	1878-1883*, 1909*		
OMin,	1854-1914**		
Pony,	1893-1914*		
Wills,	1854-1910, 1914-1965*		
Wills, (Loose)	1854-1910		

Wheeler:
Created November 5, 1912, from Montgomery County; #146 in order of creation; county seat, Alamo 30411; courthouse fire, 1916.

White:
Created December 22, 1857, from Habersham County; #123 in order of creation; county seat, Cleveland 30528; some ordinary records are believed stolen.

Ordinary		Superior Court	
AnRns,	1859-1902*	Deed,	1858-1903*
Conf,	1861-1865	Deed, (Index)	1890-1915
Home,	1869-1904*		
Inf,	1857-1868	Home,	1888-1919*
InvA,	1859-1929*	Nat,	1909-1914
Mar,	1858-1965*	SMin,	1873-1886,
OMin,	1858-1911*		1886-1902*
Pony,	1894-1949*	WWI,	1917-1919
TMSup,	1887-1919*		
Wills,	1863-1961*		

Whitfield:
Created December 30, 1851, from Murray County; #97 in order of creation; county seat, Dalton 30720; courthouse fire, 1864.

Ordinary		Superior Court	
Aptc,	1881-1918*	Deed,	1852-1903*
AnRns,	1852-1909*	Deed, (Index)	1852-1954
Conf,	1913-1937		
Est, (Index)	1852-1861	PhR,	1881-1949
Home,	1880-1922*	SMin,	1852-1871,
Inf,	1852-1880		1871-1903*
InvA,	1852-1903*	WWI,	1917-1919,
Mar,	1852-1906*		1923-
OMin,	1852-1903*		
Pony,	1868-1881*		
TMSup,	1866-1935*		
Wills,	1852-1960*		

Wilcox:
Created December 22, 1857, from Irwin, Dooly, and Pulaski Counties; #124 in order of creation; county seat, Abbeville 31001.

Ordinary		Superior Court	
Amnst,	1865	Conf,	1861
Conf,	1866-1867,	Deed,	1866-1900
	1881-1882,	Deed,	1863,
	1891-1893		1873-1906
Home,	1873-1882,	(Index)	
	1898-1919	Home,	1869-1884,
Inf,	1866-1877		1886-1904
InvA,	1857-1927	Jury,	1878-1892
Jury,	1868	SMin,	1878-1902
Liq,	no date shown	WWI,	1917-1919
Mar,	1858-1921*		
OMin,	1858-1915		
Paup,	1866		
Sch,	1858-1871		
TMSup,	1891-1931		
Vote,	1894, 1897-1898, 1903, 1908		
Wills,	1858-1957		

Wilkes:
Created February 5, 1777, from colonial Georgia. Original boundaries included all of ceded lands of St. Paul Parish; #1 in order of creation; county seat, Washington 30673; courthouse fire, 1780 — Tories and 1958 — no major loss.
• For information on the loose Wilkes County records see Robert S. Davis, Jr., **The Wilkes County Papers, 1773-1833** (1979). Another collection of loose records has been found in the State Historical Society of Oklahoma and are being published in **Georgia Genealogist**.

Wilkes County estate records are even more complete than the Microfilm Library card catalogue implies.

Mary Warren has published a War of 1812 roster for Wilkes County in **Georgia Genealogist**, #28, pp. 12-3, that provides name, place of birth, age, and physical description of each soldier. The original roster is in the Telamon Cuyler Collection, Special Collections, University of Georgia libraries.

Ordinary		Superior Court	
Aptc,	1868-1938*	Deed,	1785-1901
AnRns,	1805-1903	Deed,	1785-1918
Conf,	1861-1865	(Index)	
Est,	1777-1925	Jury,	1826,
(Index)			1869-1878
FPC,	1819-1826	PhR,	1881-1951
Home,	1868-1876	SMin,	1778-1904
Inf,	1790-1882		
InvA,	1794-1925		
LdCt,	1784-1854		

LLoty,	1805, 1807, 1820, 1821, 1827, 1832 (Gold)
Liq,	1839-1872
Lun,	1888-1908
Mar,	1792-1905*
Mar, (Loose)	1792-1832**
OMin,	1799-1903
Paup,	1800-1867
Pony,	1877-1956
Sch,	1829, 1841-1845
SlavR,	1818-1822
TMSup,	1881-1913
Vote,	no date shown
WWI,	1917-
Wills,	1786-1921

Wilkinson:
Created May 11, 1803, from Indian land ceded in 1802 and 1805; #28 in order of creation; county seat, Irwinton 31042; courthouse fire, 1829, 1854, 1864, 1924.
• Pre-1900 Wilkinson County books of records have survived but have not been microfilmed by the Georgia Archives, but they do have on microfilm a collection of loose Wilkinson County records.

Worth:
Created December 20, 1853, from Dooly and Irwin Counties; #105 in order of creation; county seat, Sylvester 31791; courthouse fire, 1879, 1893.

Ordinary		Superior Court	
AnRns,	1879-1912*	Deed,	1892-1911*
Conf,	1890-1927, 1930	Deed, (Index)	1892-1912
InvA,	1879-1913*	Home,	1896-1916
Mar-wh.,	1854-1907*	Jury,	1879-1904
Mar-bl.,	1908-1967*	PhR,	1893-1962
OMin,	1879-1911*	SMin,	1879-1910*
Pony,	1899-1940*	WWI,	1917-
TMSup,	1897		
Wills,	1865-1957*		

8

CENSUS RECORDS
PUBLISHED, UNPUBLISHED, OR INDEXED

The following is a list of Georgia census records at the Department of Archives and History other than those available on microfilm, compiled by the author although compared against a similar Archives list. Very few published or compiled census records reproduce all the information found in the originals. When the words "Index Only" appear, only the names of the persons in the census are shown, and usually the page number in the census where the family or person can be found. Often, the names are not in alphabetical order. When "Index Only" does **not** appear, more information is usually given. Substitutes for census records are usually only lists of persons living in the area when the census was taken.

The Georgia Archives has on microfilm all the surviving Georgia census records to 1900, inclusive; as well as those for many other states. Although the 1790, 1800, 1810, and the 1890 federal census records for Georgia have been lost, as well as the 1820 census for Twiggs, Rabun, Franklin, and part of Columbia Counties; the Archives has on microfilm county copies of the 1800 Oglethorpe and 1890 Washington County federal census plus the surviving fragments of the 1890 census for Muscogee County. They also have the soundex indexes to the 1880 and 1900 federal censuses.

The censuses listed in this bibliography as being compiled by Rhea Cumming Otto may be ordered from her at 8816 Ferguson Avenue, Savannah, Georgia 31406. The reference numbers shown with each book in this section are those used by the Georgia Archives.

Georgia – General

† First Settlers (substitute). E. Merton Coulter and Albert B. Sayne, **A List of Early Settlers of Georgia** (Athens, 1949). G 975.8 Co.

† First Settlers (substitute). Pat Bryant, **Entry of Claims for Georgia Land-holders, 1733-1755** (Atlanta, 1975) G 333.3 G35e

† Colonial Georgia (substitute). Pat Bryant and Marion R. Hemperley, **English Crown Grants in Georgia, 1755-1775,** 9 vols. (Atlanta, 1972-1974). Abstracts of colonial grants and surviving plats. G 333.3 G35e

† Colonial Georgia (substitute-index). Florence Shirley Hodges, "Master Index to English Crown Grants in Georgia, 1755-1775," (typescript, n.d.). Does not include index to vol. 9, St. Paul Parish. G 333.3 G35e v. 10

† Colonial Georgia − 1783-1815 (Substitute). **Index to the Headright and Bounty Grants of Georgia, 1756-1909** (Vidalia, 1970). Available from the Southern Historical Press, Easley, S.C. G 333.1 Land 1756-1909

† Colonial Georgia (substitute). Allen D. Candler, Lucian Lamar Knight, and William Northen, **The Colonial Records of the State of Georgia**, 39 vols. (Atlanta, 1904-1916). Only vols. 1-19 and 21-26 have been published; those remaining are only in typescript. SEE BELOW. G 973.2 Co.

† Colonial Georgia (substitute-index). "Index to Candler's **The Colonial Records of Georgia**," (typescript, n.d.). Index only to the published vols., 1-19 and 21-26. The typescript unpublished vols. are indexed separately. G 973.2 Co.

† 1790 Federal Census (substitute). Delwyn Associates, **Substitutes for Georgia's Lost 1790 Census** (Albany, 1975). DESK

† 1800 Federal Census (substitute). Virginia S. and Ralph V. Wood, **1805 Georgia Land Lottery** (Cambridge, 1964). Every adult head of a family in Georgia for 12 months prior to March, 1803, was qualified to participate in this lottery. All persons who applied for draws are listed. Available through Southern Historical Press, Easley, S.C. G 333.1 Land 1805

† 1820 Federal Census (Index to Heads of Families). Georgia Historical Society, **Index to United States Census of Georgia for 1820** (Savannah, 1963). The 1820 federal census has not survived for Franklin, Twiggs, Rabun, and part of Columbia Counties. Accelerated Indexing Systems, 3346 S. Orchard Dr., Bountiful, Utah, has also published an index to the surviving 1820 federal census of Ga., but theirs also includes the page numbers where the names can be found, not just the county. Ga. Archives does not have a copy of this index. Each of these has names not found in the other.

† 1830 Federal Census (Index to Heads of Families). Alvaretta Kenan Register **Index to the 1830 Census of Georgia** (Baltimore, 1974). DESK

† 1840 Federal Census (Index to Heads of Families). Barbara Woods and Eileen Sheffield, **1840 Index to Georgia Census** (1969). DESK

† 1840 Federal Census (Index to Heads of Families). Ronald Vern Jackson and Gary Ronald Teeples, **Georgia 1840 Census Index** (Utah, 1977). DESK

† 1840 Federal Census (Index to Northwest Georgia counties). Homer H. Bradley, II, "The Georgia Cherokee Strip 1840 U.S. Census," **Georgia Genealogical Society Quarterly** 5 (1969): 1-82. Index to the 1840 federal census of Bartow (Cass), Chattooga, Cherokee, Cobb, Dade, Floyd, Forsyth, Gilmer, Lumpkin, Murray, Paulding, Union, and Walker Counties. PERIODICAL ROOM AND DESK

† 1840 and 1850 Federal Census (corrections). "Additions and Corrections A.I.S. Georgia 1840, 1850 Census Index" (typescript, n.d.). DESK

† 1850 Federal Census (Index to Heads of Families). Ronald Vern Jackson, Cary Ronald Teeples, and David Schaefermeyer, **Georgia 1850 Census Index** (Utah, 1976). DESK

† 1850 Federal Census (corrections). Kenneth H. Thomas, Jr., "Corrections to A.I.S. Georgia Census Index," **Georgia Genealogical Society Quarterly** 16 (1980) pp. 181-2. PERIODICAL ROOM

† 1850 Federal Census (mortality schedules). Aurora C. Shaw, **1850 Georgia Mortality Schedules** (1971). Persons who died during the year. Available from the Southern Historical Press, Easley, S.C. G 975.8 S53e

† 1850 Federal Census (Index to Heads of Families, 25 counties). Rhea Cumming Otto, **1850 Census of Georgia** (Savannah, 1975). Index to heads of families in Burke, Dooly, Camden, Early, Effingham, Elbert, Emanuel, Fayette, Floyd, Glynn, Gordon, Greene, Jefferson, Laurens, Lee, Liberty, Lincoln, Lumpkin, Macon, McIntosh, Marion, Talbot, Tattnall, Telfair, and Warren. DESK

† 1880 and 1900 Federal Census (Index). Microfilm Library, Ga. Archives has soundex indexes to the 1880 and 1900 federal censuses; 1880 only includes families with small children, but 1900 includes everyone. Also on microfilm are all the surviving Ga. census records to 1900, inclusive.

Appling County

† 1820 Federal Census. Aurora C. Shaw, **1820 U.S. Census: Appling County** (Jacksonville, n.d.). Not available at the Georgia Archives.

† 1820 Federal Census (corrections). Folks Huxford, "1820 Census Corrections," **Georgia Genealogical Magazine** (1969), #32, pp. 2222-3. Names omitted or misspelled in published statewide census index for Georgia census of 1820. PERIODICAL ROOM

† 1850 Federal Census. Folks Huxford, **1850 Census of Appling County, Ga.** (Jacksonville, 1964). G 975.8 Appling

Baker County

† 1850 Federal Census. Rhea Cumming Otto, **1850 Census of Georgia (Baker County)** (Savannah, 1976). G 975.8 Baker

Baldwin County

† 1810 Federal Census (substitute). Mrs. Robert L. Green, "Baldwin County 1810 Tax List," **Georgia Genealogical Magazine**, no. 71-2 (1979): 11-20 PERIODICAL ROOM

† 1820 & 1850 Federal Census. Mrs. George Heard Tunnell, "Baldwin County, Georgia Census," (typescript, DAR Collection, 1945). DAR Baldwin

Banks County

† 1860 & 1880 Federal Census. Jessie Julia Mize, **The History of Banks County, Georgia, 1858-1976** (Homer, 1977). The 1860 census is on pages 555-711; the 1880 on 733-47. G 975.8 Banks

† 1860 Federal Census (mortality schedule). "Banks County, Georgia, 1860 United States Mortality Schedule," **Georgia Genealogical Society Quarterly** vol. 15 (1979): 49. PERIODICAL ROOM

Bartow (Cass) County

† 1834 State Census. Robert S. Davis, Jr., "The 1834 State Census of Cass (Bartow) County," **Northwest Georgia Historical & Genealogical Society Quarterly** 12 (1980), no. 4, pp. 26-7. PERIODICAL ROOM

† 1840 Federal Census. Lucy Josephine Cunyas, **History of Bartow County, Formerly Cass** (rep. ed., Easley, 1971), 329-33. G 975.8 Bartow

† 1840 Federal Census (Index only). Homer H. Bradley, II, "The Georgia Cherokee Strip 1840 U.S. Census," **Georgia Genealogical Society Quarterly** 5 (1969): 1-82. DESK & PERIODICAL ROOM

† 1850 Federal Census (Index to Heads of Families). "Heads of Families — 1850 Census Cass County," **They Were Here**, vol. 3, no. 3 (1967): 544-7. PERIODICAL ROOM

Berrien County

† 1860 Federal Census. James W. Dupree, **1860 Census Berrien County, Georgia** (1976). G 975.8 Berrien

Bibb County

† 1850 Federal Census. Genealogical Enterprises, **1850 Bibb County, Georgia Census** (Morrow, 1968). G 975.8 Bibb

Brooks County

† 1860 Federal Census. Folks Huxford, "1860 Census of Brooks County, Georgia and Brooks County, Georgia, Public Records," (typescript, DAR Collection, 1947). DAR Brooks

Bryan County

† 1830 Federal Census. (Index Only). Alvaretta K. Register, "The 1830 Bryan County, Georgia Census," **Georgia Genealogical Magazine**, nos. 44-45 (1972): 120-4. PERIODICAL ROOM

† 1850 Federal Census. Rhea Cumming Otto, **1850 Census of Georgia (Bryan County)** (Savannah, 1975). G 975.8 Bryan. PERIODICAL ROOM

Bulloch County

† 1830, 1840, & 1850 Federal Census. Alvaretta Kenan Register, **Bulloch County, Georgia, Census 1830, 1840, 1850** (1966). G 975.8 Bulloch

† 1860 Federal Census. Alvaretta Kenan Register, **1860 Census of Bulloch County, Georgia** (Statesboro, n.d.) G 975.8 Bulloch

† 1866 State Census. Alvaretta K. Register, "1865 Census of Bulloch County, Georgia," **Georgia Genealogical Magazine**, no. 70 (Fall 1978): 247-56. PERIODICAL ROOM

† 1870 Federal Census. Alvaretta Kenan Register, **1870 Census Bulloch County** (Statesboro, n.d.). G 975.8 Bulloch

† 1880 Federal Census. Alvaretta Kenan Register, **United States Census of Bulloch County, Georgia, 1880** (Statesboro, n.d.). G 975.8 Bulloch

Burke County

† 1820 Federal Census (Index Only). Alvaretta Kenan Register, "Index to 1820 Burke County Census," **Georgia Genealogical Magazine** no. 75-76 (1980) 15-25.

† 1820, 1830, 1840, & 1850 Federal Census. Robert S. Davis, Jr., **The Families of Burke County, 1755-1855 a Census** (Easley, 1980). Includes the Mortality, Slave, Agriculture, and Social schedules of the 1850 census. G 975.8 Burke
  • The original of the 1840 federal census of Burke County has an error in the original document. The second page of information for each family is bound in such a way that these second pages always appear before the first ones. That is, when you see a head of a family listed on one page, the data on that family is not continued on the succeeding page but on the preceding page. This error in binding is, of course, duplicated in the microfilm copy of the 1840 federal census for Burke County. When using the 1840 census for other counties, researchers should check to make sure that this did not happen again.

† 1850 Federal Census. Rhea Cumming Otto, **1850 Census of Georgia (Burke County** (Savannah, 1975). G 975.8 Burke

Butts County

† 1830 Federal Census (Index Only). "Butts County 1830 Heads of Family," **They Were Here**, vol. 5, no. 4, (1969): 982-7. PERIODICAL ROOM

† 1850 Federal Census (Free Blacks Only), 1860 Federal Census (Free Blacks Only), and 1870 Federal Census (Blacks Only). Lois McMichael, **History of Butts County, Georgia, 1825-1976** (Atlanta, 1978). The 1830 census index is on pp. 28-33, the 1850 and 1860 censuses of free blacks are on p. 449, and the 1870 census of Negroes is on pp. 450-513. G 975.8 Butts

† 1850 Federal Census. Rhea Cumming Otto, **1850 Census of Georgia** (Butts County) (Savannah, 1974). G 975.8 Butts

Camden County

† 1850 Federal Census. Rhea Cumming Otto, **1850 Census of Georgia (Camden County)** (Savannah, 1974). G 975.8 Camden

Campbell County

† 1830 Federal Census (Index Only). "1830 Heads of Families Campbell County," **They Were Here**, vol. 6, no. 4 (1970): 1158-62. PERIODICAL ROOM

† 1850 Federal Census. Rhea Cumming Otto, **1850 Census of Georgia (Campbell County)** (Savannah, 1976). G 975.8 Campbell

† 1860 Federal Census. Mrs. Verona Robertson Mitchem, "1860 Census of Old Campbell County, Georgia," (typescript, n.d.). G 975.8 Campbell

Carroll County

† 1830 Federal Census. "1830 Heads of Families Carroll County," **They Were Here**, vol. 6, no. 3 (1970): 1092-7. PERIODICAL ROOM. (Index Only)

Chatham County

† 1845 State Census. Marilyn L. Adams, **Censuses for Georgia Counties** (Atlanta 1979).

† 1850 Federal Census. Rhea Cumming Otto, **1850 Census of Georgia (Chatham County)** (Savannah, 1975). G 975.8 Chatham

† 1860 Federal Census. Georgia Historical Society, **The 1860 Census of Chatham County, Georgia** (Easley, 1980). Available from the Southern Historical Press, Easley, S.C. G 975.8 Chatham

• In **Georgia Genealogist**, issue no. 28, pp. 18-19, under "State Records: Tax Digests," there is a fragment of the 1786 state census of the Little Ogeechee District, Chatham County.

Chattooga County

† 1840 Federal Census (Index Only). Homer H. Bradley, II, "The Georgia Cherokee Strip 1840 U.S. Census," **Georgia Genealogical Society Quarterly** 5 (1969): 1-82. DESK AND PERIODICAL ROOM

† 1850 Federal Census. Rhea Cumming Otto, **1850 Census of Georgia (Chattooga County)** (Savannah, 1980). Not yet available at the Ga. Archives.

Cherokee County

† 1834 State Census. To be published in the **Northwest Georgia Historical and Genealogical Quarterly**, after August 1980. PERIODICAL ROOM

† 1840 Federal Census. Homer H. Bradley, II, "The Georgia Cherokee Strip 1840 U.S. Census," **Georgia Genealogical Society Quarterly** 5 (1969): 1-82. DESK AND PERIODICAL ROOM. (Index Only)

† 1850 Federal Census. Rhea Cumming Otto, **1850 Census of Georgia (Cherokee County)** (Savannah, 1976). G 975.8 Cherokee

Clarke County

† 1810 Federal Census (substitute). Mrs. Robert L. Green, "Clarke County Georgia – 1810 Tax List," **Georgia Genealogical Magazine**, nos. 75-6 (1980): 65-77. PERIODICAL ROOM

† 1830 Federal Census (Index Only). "Clarke County, 1830, Heads of Family," **They Were Here**, vol. 6, no. 1 (1970): 1037-46. PERIODICAL ROOM

† 1850 Federal Census. "7th Census 1850 Clarke County, Georgia," (typescript, DAR Collection), in "Miscellaneous Genealogical Records," pp. 66-200. SN 1967 vol. 1 [no. 132] DAR

Clayton County

† 1860 Federal Census. Doris F. Curry, **Clayton County, Georgia, 1860 Census** (Riverdale, 1978). Not available at the Georgia Archives.

† 1870 Federal Census. Doris F. Curry, **Clayton County, Georgia 1870 Census** (Riverdale, 1978). Not available at the Georgia Archives.

Cobb County

† 1834 State Census. Robert S. Davis, Jr., "The 1834 State Census of Cobb County," **Northwest Georgia Historical and Genealogical Quarterly** 12 (1980), no. 4, pp. 30-1. PERIODICAL ROOM

† 1840 Federal Census. Mrs. George Moore, "Cobb County 1840 Census Records," **Georgia Pioneers**, vol. 10 (1973): 114-7, 174-7; vol. 11 (1974): 27-30, 81-4, 136-9. PERIODICAL ROOM

† 1840 Federal Census (Index Only). "Cobb County 1840 Census," **They Were Here**, vol. 8 (1978), pp. 31-8, 111-5. PERIODICAL ROOM

† 1840 Federal Census (Index Only). Homer H. Bradley, II, "The Georgia Cherokee Strip 1840 U.S. Census," **Georgia Genealogical Society Quarterly** 5 (1969): 1-82. DESK AND PERIODICAL ROOM

Coffee County

† 1860 Federal Census. Folks Huxford, "Coffee County, Georgia, The Census of 1860," (typescript, Homerville, 1947). G 975.8 Coffee

Colquitt County

† 1860 Federal Census (Index to Heads of Families). "Heads of Families — 1860 Colquitt County," **They Were Here**, vol. 5, no. 4 (1969): 954-6; vol. 6, no. 1, (1970): 1019-20. PERIODICAL ROOM

Columbia County

† 1820 Federal Census (substitute). Nancy Claymore Watson, "Missing Districts, 1820 Columbia County, Georgia Census," **National Genealogical Society Quarterly**, 59 (1971): 118-21. PERIODICAL ROOM

† 1850 Federal Census. Rhea Cumming Otto, **1850 Census of Georgia (Columbia County)** (Savannah, 1978). G 975.8 Columbia

† 1850 Federal Census. W.D. Thiem, **1850 U.S. Census Columbia County, Georgia** (San Angelo, Texas, 1969). G 975.8 Columbia

† 1859 State Census. Merita Rozier, Leoda Sherry, and Nesba Wright, "State Census Columbia County, Georgia, 1859," **Georgia Genealogical Society Quarterly**, 13 (1977): 254-73. PERIODICAL ROOM

Coweta County

† 1830 Federal Census (Index Only). "First Census of Coweta County, taken 13th of December, 1830." G 975.8 Coweta

† 1830 Federal Census (Index Only). "Coweta County – 1830 Heads of Family," **They Were Here**, vol. 5, nos. 1 & 2 (1969): 848-54. PERIODICAL ROOM

† 1840 & 1870 Federal Census. The Georgia Archives has some back issues of **Coweta Chatter** that include an index to the 1840 federal census in vol. I and the 1870 federal census in vols. III & IV. PERIODICAL ROOM

Crawford County

† 1850 Federal Census. Rhea Cumming Otto, **1850 Census of Georgia (Crawford County)** (Savannah, 1979). G 975.8 Crawford

† 1850 Federal Census. Mrs. E.T. Nottingham, "1850 United States Census of Crawford County, Georgia," (typescript, DAR Collection, 1945). DAR Crawford

Dade County

† 1840 & 1850 Federal Census. Paul R.L. Vance, **Dade County Pioneers 1840 & 1850 Census** (1970). G 975.8 Dade

† 1840 Federal Census (Index Only). Homer H. Bradley, II, "The Georgia Cherokee Strip 1840 U.S. Census," **Georgia Genealogical Society Quarterly** 5 (1969): 1-82. DESK AND PERIODICAL ROOM

Decatur County

† 1850 Federal Census. Floreda Duke Varick and Phyllis Rose Smith, **Decatur County, Georgia, 1850 Census** (Tallahassee, Fla., 1978). G 975.8 Decatur

DeKalb County

† 1830 Federal Census (Index Only). Leon S. Hollingsworth, "1830 Federal Census of DeKalb County, Georgia," (typescript, Atlanta, 1958). G 975.8 DeKalb

† 1850 Federal Census. Rhea Cumming Otto, **1850 Census of Georgia (DeKalb County)** (Savannah, 1979). G 975.8 DeKalb

† 1850 Federal Census (Atlanta Only). "Federal Census of Atlanta, 1850," **Atlanta Historical Bulletin**, 7 (1942): 16-82. PERIODICAL ROOM

Dooly County

† 1830 (Index Only), 1840 (Index Only), and 1850 Federal Census. Nora Powell and Watts Powell, **Historical and Genealogical Collections of Dooly County, Georgia** (Vienna, 1974), II. The index of the 1830 census is on pp. 98-101, index of the 1840 census is on pp. 102-5, and the 1850 census is on pp. 106-239. G 975.8 Dooly. May be at the desk.

† 1845 State Census. Brigid S. Townsend, **Indexes to Seven State Census Reports for Counties in Georgia, 1838-1845** (Atlanta, 1975). G 939.34 T74i

† 1850 Federal Census. Rhea Cumming Otto, **1850 Census of Georgia (Dooly County)** (Savannah, 1971). G 975.8 Dooly

Early County

† 1830 Federal Census. (Index Only). "Early County Index to 1830 Census," **They Were Here**, vol. 4, no. 4 (1968): 772-4. PERIODICAL ROOM

† 1850 Federal Census. Rhea Cumming Otto, **1850 Census of Ga. (Early Co.)** (Savannah, 1970). G 975.8 Early

Effingham

† 1820, 1830, 1840 Federal Census (Index Only). Milton D. Wilson, "Index to Heads of Families in U.S. Census of 1820, 1830, & 1840 of Effingham Co." G 975.8 Effingham (oversize)

† 1830 Federal Census (Index Only). Alvaretta K. Register, "1830 Census of Effingham County, Ga.," **Ga. Genealogical Magazine #44** (1972): 203-4. PERIODICAL ROOM

† 1850 Federal Census. Rhea Cumming Otto, **1850 Census of Ga. (Effingham County)** (Savannah, 1970). G 975.8 Effingham

Elbert

† 1790 Federal Census (substitute). Frank P. Hudson, **A 1790 Census of Elbert County, Ga.** (Atlanta, 1967). Com. from tax records. G 975.8 Elbert

† 1820 Federal Census. Ann C. Holloman, **Elbert County, Ga. 1820 Census** (Macon, 1963). G 975.8 Elbert

† 1820, 1830, 1840, 1850, & 1860 Federal Census. Irene S. Wilcox, **The 1820, 1830, 1840, 1850 & 1860 Census of Elbert County, Ga., and the 1850 Census of Wilkes County** (Easley, S.C.). Not available at Ga. Archives; can be purchased from Southern Historical Press, Easley, S.C.

† 1850 Federal Census. Rhea Cumming Otto, **1850 Census of Ga. (Elbert Co.)** (Savannah, 1970). G 975.8 Elbert

Emanuel County

† 1830 Federal Census (Index Only). "Emanuel County 1830 Heads of Families." **They Were Here**, vol. 3, #4 (1967): 604-7. PERIODICAL ROOM

† 1830 Federal Census (Index Only). Alvaretta K. Register, "1830 Census of Emanuel County," **Ga. Genealogical Magazine #46** (1972): 358-61. PERIODICAL ROOM

† 1850 Federal Census. Rhea Cumming Otto, **1850 Census of Ga. (Emanuel Co.)** (Savannah, 1970). G 975.8 Emanuel

† 1880 Federal Census. John E. Mosley, **1880 Census Emanuel County, Georgia** (Dunwoody, n.d.). G 975.8 Emanuel

Fayette County

† 1830 Federal Census (Index Only). "Heads of Family Fayette County 1830," **They Were Here**, vol. 5, no. 3 (1969): 904-11. PERIODICAL ROOM

† 1850 Federal Census. Rhea Cumming Otto, **1850 Census of Georgia (Fayette County)** (Savannah, 1973). G 975.8 Fayette

Floyd County

† 1840 Federal Census. Franklin MacArthur Blair, **1840 Census of Floyd County, Georgia** (Rome, 1974). G 975.8 Floyd

† 1840 Federal Census (Index Only). Homer H. Bradley, II, "The Georgia Cherokee Strip 1840 U.S. Census," **Georgia Genealogical Society Quarterly** 5 (1969): 1-82. PERIODICAL ROOM

† 1850 Federal Census. Rhea Cumming Otto, **1850 Census of Georgia (Floyd County)** (Savannah, 1973). G 975.8 Floyd

Forsyth County

† 1834 State Census. Robert S. Davis, Jr., "The 1834 State Census of Forsyth County," **Northwest Georgia Historical and Genealogical Society Quarterly**, 12 (1980), no. 4, pp. 32-3. PERIODICAL ROOM

† 1840 Federal Census. Kaaren D'Elia, **1840 Census Forsyth County, Georgia** (Palos Verdes Peninsula, Calif, n.d.). G 975.8 Forsyth

† 1840 Federal Census (Index Only). Homer H. Bradley, II, "The Georgia Cherokee Strip 1840 U.S. Census," **Georgia Genealogical Society Quarterly** 5 (1969): 1-82. PERIODICAL ROOM

† 1845 State Census. Brigid S. Townsend, **Indexes to Seven State Census Reports for Counties in Georgia, 1838-1845** (Atlanta, 1975). G 939.34 T74i

† 1850 Federal Census. Hazel Major Smith, "1850 Census Forsyth County, Georgia," (transcript, n.d.). G 975.8 Forsyth

† 1880 Federal Census (Index Only). Hazel Major Smith, **Surname Index 1880 Census Forsyth County, Georgia** (n.d.). G 975.8 Forsyth

Franklin County

† 1820 Federal Census (substitute). Mrs. William W. Watson, "Reconstruction of the 1820 Census of Franklin County, Georgia," **Georgia Genealogical Magazine**, no. 54 (Fall, 1974): 260-9. PERIODICAL ROOM

† 1830 Federal Census (Index Only). "Franklin County, Georgia, Heads of Families, 1830 Index," **They Were Here**, vol. 1, no. 1 (1965): 30-7. PERIODICAL ROOM

† 1850 Federal Census. Rhea Cumming Otto, **1850 Census of Georgia (Franklin County)** (Savannah, 1976). G 975.8 Franklin

† 1850 Federal Census. McCall Genealogical Fund, "Franklin County, Georgia, Census of 1850," (typescript, 1941). G 975.8 Franklin

Fulton County

† 1850 Federal Census (Atlanta Only). "Federal Census of Atlanta, 1850," **Atlanta Historical Bulletin**, vol. 7 (1942): 16-82. Fulton County was created in 1853. In 1850 all of Atlanta was in DeKalb County. PERIODICAL ROOM

Gilmer County

† 1834 State Census. Robert S. Davis, Jr., "The 1834 State Census of Gilmer County," **Northwest Georgia Historical and Genealogical Society Quarterly** 12 (1980), no. 4, p. 35. PERIODICAL ROOM

† 1840 Federal Census. Beulah Mae Scates, **1840 Census of Gilmer County, Georgia** (Ada, Okla., 1973). G 975.8 Gilmer

† 1840 Federal Census (Index Only). Homer H. Bradley, II, "The Georgia Cherokee Strip 1840 U.S. Census," **Georgia Genealogical Society Quarterly** 5 (1969): 1-82. DESK AND PERIODICAL ROOM

† 1850 Federal Census. John V. Haddock, Jr., **1850 Federal Census, Gilmer County, Georgia** (Atlanta, 1978). G 975.8 Gilmer

Glynn County

† 1850 Federal Census. Rhea Cumming Otto, **1850 Census of Georgia (Glynn County)** (Savannah, 1973), G 975.8 Glynn.

• In **Georgia Genealogist**, issue no. 28, pp. 11-2, under "State Records: Tax Digests," there is a fragment of the state census of Glynn County.

Gordon County

† 1850 Federal Census. Rhea Cumming Otto, **1850 Census of Georgia (Gordon County)** (Savannah, 1974). G 975.8 Gordon

Greene County

† 1850 Federal Census. Rhea Cumming Otto, **1850 Census of Georgia (Greene County)** (Savannah, 1974). G 975.8 Greene

† 1798 State Census. Frank Parker Hudson, "1798 Census of First Battalion, Greene County, Georgia," **Georgia Genealogical Society Quarterly** 4 (1968). pp. 649-54.

Habersham County

† 1820, 1830, & 1850 Federal Census. Herbert B. Kimzey, **Habersham County, Georgia, Genealogical Records** (Cornelia, 1969-1971). The 1820 census is in part 1, pp. 1-19; 1830 census (index) is in part 4, pp. 1-17; and the 1850 census is in part 5, pp. 1-72. G 975.8 Habersham

† 1830 Federal Census (Index Only). "Heads of Family 1830 Habersham County," **They Were Here**, vol. 6, no. 3 (1970): 1109-19. PERIODICAL ROOM

Hancock County

† 1850 Federal Census. Rhea Cumming Otto, **1850 Census of Georgia (Hancock County)** (Savannah, 1980). Not yet available at the Georgia Archives.

Harris County

† 1830 Federal Census (Index Only) & 1850 Federal Census. Louise Calhoun Barfield, **History of Harris County, 1827-1961** (Columbus, 1961): 113-211. G 975.8 Harris

† 1830 Federal Census (Index Only). "Heads of Families Harris County, 1830," **They Were Here,** vol. 5, nos. 1 & 2 (1969): 823-7. PERIODICAL ROOM

Hart County

† 1860 Federal Census. Ann C. Holloman, **Hart County, Georgia 1860 Census** (Albany, 1961). Includes slave and mortality schedules. G 975.8 Hart

Heard County

† 1850 Federal Census. Lynda S. Eller, **1850 Census Heard County, Georgia** (Lanett, Ala., 1976). G 975.8 Heard

† 1860 Federal Census. Lynda S. Eller, **1860 Census Heard County, Georgia** (Lanette, Ala., 1976). G 975.8 Heard

† 1870 Federal Census. Lynda S. Eller, **1870 Census Heard County, Georgia** (Lanette, Ala., 1977). G 975.8 Heard

† 1880 Federal Census. Lynda S. Eller, **1880 Census Heard County, Georgia** (Lanette, Ala., 1977). G 975.8 Heard

• Lynda S. Eller is currently preparing for publication the 1900 federal census of Heard County.

Henry County

† 1850 Federal Census. Rhea Cumming Otto, **1850 Census of Georgia (Henry County)** (Savannah, 1979). G 975.8 Henry

Houston County

† 1850 Federal Census. Rhea Cumming Otto, **1850 Census of Georgia (Houston County)** (Savannah, 1979). G 975.8 Houston

Irwin County

† 1820 Federal Census (corrections). Folks Huxford, "1820 Census Corrections," **Georgia Genealogical Magazine,** no. 32 (1969). pp. 2222-2223. Names omitted or misspelled in the published statewide census index for Georgia.

† 1850 Federal Census. Folks Huxford, "Irwin County, Georgia, 1850 Census," (typescript, Homerville, 1946). G 975.8 Irwin

Jackson County

† Elijah Clarke Chapter, DAR, "1850 Census of Jackson County, Georgia," (typescript, DAR Collection, 1969). DAR Jackson

Jasper County

† 1830 Federal Census (Index Only). "Jasper County 1830 Heads of Family," **They Were Here,** vol. 4, no. 3 (1968): 719-26. PERIODICAL ROOM

Jefferson County

† 1800 Federal Census (substitute). William H. Dumont, "Jefferson County,

Ga., Jury List, 1799," **National Genealogical Society Quarterly** 53 (1965): 209-13. PERIODICAL ROOM

† 1850 Federal Census. Rhea Cumming Otto, **1850 Census of Georgia (Jefferson County)** (Savannah, 1973). G 975.8 Jefferson

Johnson County

† 1880 Federal Census. John E. Mosley is currently preparing this census for publication.

Jones County

† 1820, 1830, 1840 Federal Census (list of names); 1850 & 1860 Federal Census. Frank M. Abbott, **History of Jones County (Macon, 1977), III**: "1820 through 1860 Census." Includes the 1850 and 1860 mortality schedules for Jones County. G 975.8 Jones

† 1850 Federal Census. Typescript, DAR Collection. DAR Jones

Laurens County

† 1830 Federal Census (Index Only). "Laurens County, 1830," **They Were Here**, vol. 2, no. 4 (1966): 385-90. PERIODICAL ROOM

† 1838 State Census (Index Only). Brigid S. Townsend, **Indexes to Seven State Census Reports for Counties in Georgia 1838-1845** (Atlanta, 1975). G 939.34 T74i

† 1850 Federal Census. Rhea Cumming Otto, **1850 Census of Georgia (Laurens County)** (Savannah, 1973). G 975.8 Laurens

Lee County

† 1830 Federal Census. Kate Harris, "Lee County, Georgia — 1830 Census Schedule," **Georgia Pioneers**, vol. 6 (1969): 163-5; vol. 7 (1970): 9-12. PERIODICAL ROOM

† 1850 Federal Census. Rhea Cumming Otto, **1850 Census of Georgia (Lee County)** (Savannah, 1973). G 975.8 Lee

Liberty County

† 1850 Federal Census. Rhea Cumming Otto, **1850 Census of Georgia (Liberty County)** (Savannah, 1971). G 975.8 Liberty

• In **Georgia Genealogist**, no. 28, p. 13, under "State Records: Tax Digests," there is a fragment of the 1786 state census of Sunbury in Liberty County.

Lincoln County

† 1800 Federal Census (substitute). Frank Parker Hudson, **An 1800 Census for Lincoln County, Georgia** (Atlanta, 1977). G 975.8 Lincoln

† 1830 Federal Census (Index Only). Heads of Family 1830 Lincoln County," **They Were Here**, vol. 2, no. 1 (1966): 236-40. PERIODICAL ROOM

† 1850 Federal Census. Rhea Cumming Otto, **1850 Census of Georgia (Lincoln County)** (Savannah, 1971). G 975.8 Lincoln

Lowndes County

† 1830 Federal Census (Index Only), 1840 Federal Census (Index Only), & 1850 Federal Census. General James Jackson Chapter DAR, **History of Lowndes County, Georgia 1825-1841** (Valdosta, 1943). The 1830 census index is on pp. 342-5; the 1840 index on pp. 345-51; and the 1850 census is on pp. 352-400. G 975.8 Lowndes

† 1850 Federal Census. Folks Huxford, "Lowndes County, Georgia U.S. Census of 1850," **Southern Genealogical Exchange** (1957-1958). G 975.8 Lowndes

Lumpkin County

† 1834 State Census. "1834 Census for the State of Georgia, Lumpkin County," **Northwest Georgia Historical and Genealogical Quarterly**, vol. 12, no. 3 (1980): 10-6. PERIODICAL ROOM

† 1838 State Census (fragment). Marilyn Adams, **Censuses for Georgia Counties** (Atlanta 1979).

† 1840 Federal Census (Index Only). Homer H. Bradley, II, "The Georgia Cherokee Strip 1840 U.S. Census," **Ga. Genealogical Society Quarterly** 5 (1969): 1-82. DESK & PERIODICAL ROOM

† 1850 Federal Census. Rhea Cumming Otto, **1850 Census of Ga. (Lumpkin County)** (Savannah, 1973). G 975.8 Lumpkin

McIntosh County

† 1850 Federal Census. Rhea Cumming Otto, **1850 Census of Georgia (McIntosh County)** (Savannah, 1974). G 975.8 McIntosh

Macon County

† 1850 Federal Census. Rhea Cumming Otto, **1850 Census of Georgia (Macon County)** (Savannah, 1973). G 975.8 Macon

Madison County

† 1850 Federal Census. John E. Ladson, Jr., "Madison County – 1850 Census Records," **Georgia Pioneers** Vols.: 8 (1971): 63-6, 119-22, 189-92; 9 (1972): 49-52, 105-6; 10 (1973): 17-21, 94-97, 126-129, 194-7; 11 (1974): 7-10, 89-92, 152-5, 197-200; 12 (1975): 32-5, 88-93, 140-1, 185-90; 13 (1976): 43-4, 94, 138-42.

† 1850 Federal Census. Elijah Clarke Chapter DAR, "1850 Census Madison County, Ga." (typescript, 1967, DAR Collection). DAR Madison or SN 1968 Madison

† 1850 Federal Census. Georgia Pioneers, **Madison-Upson Ga. Counties 1850 Census Records** (Albany: author, 1980). Not yet available at Ga. Archives.

Marion County

† 1850 Federal Census. Rhea Cumming Otto, **1850 Census of Georgia (Marion County)** (Savannah, 1974). G 975.8 Marion

Meriwether County

† 1830 Federal Census (Index Only). "1830 Heads of Family Meriwether County," **They Were Here,** vol. 7, #3-4, (1971): 2085-90. PERIODICAL ROOM

† 1830 Federal Census (Index Only). William H. Davidson, **Brooks of Honey and Butter, Plantations and People of Meriwether County, Georgia** (Alexander City, Ala., 1971), II, 417-20. G 975.8 Meriwether

† 1840 Federal Census (Index Only). Regina P. Pinkston, **Historical Account of Meriwether County, 1827-1974** (Greenville, Ga., 1974), 404-19. G 975.8 Meriwether

† 1850 Federal Census. "Meriwether County Census of 1850," (typescript, DAR Collection). DAR Meriwether

Miller County

† 1860 Federal Census (Index to Heads of Families). Ray B. Stephens, "1860 Miller County," **Georgia Genealogical Society Quarterly** 12 (1976): 13-5. PERIODICAL ROOM

Milton County

† 1860 Federal Census. Kaaren D'Elia, **1860 Census Milton County, Georgia** (Palos Verdes Peninsula, Calif., n.d.) G 975.8 Milton

Mitchell County

† 1860 Federal Census. Margaret Spence and Anna M. Fleming, **History of Mitchell County** (Camilla?, 1977?): 13-32. G 975.8 Mitchell

Monroe County

† 1850 Federal Census. Rhea Cumming Otto, **1850 Census of Georgia (Monroe County)** (Savannah, 1975). G 975.8 Monroe

Montgomery County

† 1850 Federal Census. Rhea Cumming Otto, **1850 Census of Georgia (Montgomery County)** (Savannah, 1975). G 975.8 Montgomery

† 1880 Federal Census. John E. Mosley, **1880 Census Montgomery County, Georgia** (Dunwoody, n.d.). G 975.8 Montgomery

Morgan County

† 1830 Federal Census (Index Only). "Morgan County Heads of Families 1830," **They Were Here,** vol. 4, no. 1 (1968): 627-36. PERIODICAL ROOM

† 1850 Federal Census. John E. Ladson, Jr., "Morgan County, Georgia — 1850 Census," **Georgia Pioneers,** vol. 6 (1969): 54-7, 113-6, 192-4; vol. 7 (1970): 38-41, 82-5, 151-4, 197-8; vol. 8 (1971): 37-40, 90-3, 145-8, 213-9; vol. 9 (1972): 41-4, 91-2, 138-41, 206-9; vol. 10 (1973): 30-3, 70-3, 154-7, 213-4. PERIODICAL ROOM

† 1850 Federal Census. Georgia Pioneers, **Early Georgia Marriage Book Four** (Albany: the author, 1980). This book is not yet available at the Georgia Archives.

Murray County

† 1834 State Census. Robert S. Davis, Jr., "The 1834 State Census of Murray County," **Northwest Georgia Genealogical Society Quarterly** 12 (1980), no. 4, pp. 34-5. PERIODICAL ROOM

† 1840 & 1850 Federal Census. Mrs. Raymond H. Whitehead, **Genealogical History of Original Murray County, Georgia** (Atlanta, Ga., 1972). The 1840 census is on pp. 88-124; 1850 on pp. 125-399. Both are in vol. 1. G 975.8 Murray

† 1840 Federal Census (Index Only). Homer H. Bradley, II, "The Georgia Cherokee Strip 1840 U.S. Census," **Georgia Genealogical Society Quarterly** 5 (1969): 1-82. DESK; PERIODICAL ROOM

Muscogee County

† 1850 Federal Census. Rhea Cumming Otto, **1850 Census of Georgia (Muscogee County)** (Savannah, 1977). G 975.8 Muscogee

Newton County

† 1838 State Census (Index Only). Brigid S. Townsend, **Indexes to Seven State Census Records for Counties in Georgia, 1838-1845** (Atlanta, 1975). G 939.34 T74i

† 1850 Federal Census. Theodore E. Davis, **The Complete 1850 Federal Census of Newton County, Georgia** (Oxford, Ga., 1978). G 975.8 Newton

Oglethorpe County

† 1800 Federal Census. Mary Bondurant Warren, **1800 Census of Oglethorpe County, Georgia, The Only Exant Census of 1800 Within the State of Georgia** (Athens, 1965). G 975.8 Oglethorpe.

† 1800 & 1880 Federal Census. Florrie Carter Smith, **Supplement to the History of Oglethorpe County** (Washington, Ga., 1972). The 1880 census only gives name, age, and sex. G 975.8 Oglethorpe.

† 1850 Federal Census. Elijah Clarke Chapter, DAR, "1850 U.S. Census Oglethorpe County, Georgia," (typescript, 1973, DAR Collection). DAR Oglethorpe

† 1860 Federal Census (Index to Heads of Households). Ray Stephens, "1860 Census, Oglethorpe County, Georgia," **Georgia Genealogical Society Quarterly** 12 (1976): 85-102. PERIODICAL ROOM

Paulding County

† 1838 State Census. Robert S. Davis, Jr., "The 1838 Paulding County State Census," **Northwest Georgia Genealogical Society Quarterly** 12 (1980), no. 4, pp. 36-7. PERIODICAL ROOM

† 1840 Federal Census (Index Only). Homer H. Bradley, II, "The Georgia Cherokee Strip 1840 U.S. Census," **Georgia Genealogical Magazine** 5 (1969): 1-82. DESK AND PERIODICAL ROOM

† 1850 Federal Census (Index to Heads of Families). David H. Young, Jr., "1850 Census of Paulding County, Georgia Family Index," **Georgia Genealogical Society Quarterly** 5 (1969): 284-95. PERIODICAL ROOM

† 1850 Federal Census. "Paulding County August — 1850 Census," **Georgia Genealogical Society Quarterly** 6 (1970): 1-113. PERIODICAL ROOM

Pickens County

† 1860 Federal Census. Luke E. Tate, **History of Pickens County** (rep. ed., Spartanburg, S.C., 1978): 93-199. G 975.8 Pickens

† 1860 Federal Census (Index to Heads of Families). "Pickens County Heads of Families — 1860," **They Were Here**, vol. 5, nos. 1-2, (1969): 881-5, no. 3: 935-8. PERIODICAL ROOM

Pierce County

† 1840 & 1850 Federal Census (Index Only) and 1860 Federal Census. Dean Broome, **History of Pierce County, Georgia** (Blackshear, 1973). Pierce County was created in 1857, but this volume includes a name index of the 1840 and 1850 federal censuses for the areas that became Pierce County (pp. 188-92) and the 1860 federal census of Pierce County (pp. 225-49). G 975.8 Pierce

Pike County

† 1830 Federal Census (Heads of Families). Historical Committee, **Sesquicentennial, 1822-1972, Pike County, Georgia** (Zebulon: the authors, 1972), pp. 86-8

† 1850 Federal Census. Rhea Cumming Otto, **1850 Census of Georgia (Pike County)** (Savannah, 1977). G 975.8 Pike

• Barbara J. Smith is currently preparing for publication the 1850 federal census of Pike County.

Pulaski County

† 1830 Federal Census (Index Only), 1840 Federal Census (Index Only), 1850 and 1860 federal censuses. Victor R. Myrick, **Census Records 1830 Through 1860 Pulaski and Bleckly Counties** (Cochran, 1976). The 1830 index is on pp. 1-4; 1840, pp. 5-8; 1850, pp. 9-49; and 1860, pp. 55-110. G 975.8 Pulaski

† 1850 Federal Census. Rhea Cumming Otto, **1850 Census of Georgia (Pulaski County)** (Savannah, 1978). G 975.8 Pulaski

Putnam County

† 1850 Federal Census. Rhea Cumming Otto, **1850 Census of Georgia (Putnam County)** (Savannah, 1979). G 975.8 Putnam.

• The W. Dennis Reid Collection in the Archives Microfilm Library has information from the now-lost 1810 federal census of Putnam County.

Rabun County

† 1830 Federal Census (Index Only). "1830 Census Rabun County," **They Were Here,** vol. 1, no. 3 (1965): 111-3. PERIODICAL ROOM

† 1830 Federal Census (Index Only). "Rabun County, Georgia 1830 Census," **Georgia Genealogical Magazine** 43 (1972); 28-32. PERIODICAL ROOM

† 1830 Federal Census (Index Only). Herbert B. Kimzey, "1830 Heads of Family Rabun County," **They Were Here** vol. 7 (1971): 2037-40. PERIODICAL ROOM

† 1850 Federal Census (Index to Heads of Families). Herbert Kimzey, "1850 Census — Rabun County," **They Were Here,** vol. 7 (1971): 2041-6, 2121-6. PERIODICAL ROOM

Randolph County

† 1830 Federal Census (Index Only). "Randolph County — 1830 Heads of Families," **They Were Here,** vol. 3, no. 1 (1967): 454-6. PERIODICAL ROOM

† 1850 Federal Census. Rhea Cumming Otto, **1850 Census of Georgia (Randolph County)** (Savannah, 1976). G 975.8 Randolph

Richmond County

† 1850 Federal Census. Genealogical Enterprises, **1850 Richmond County, Georgia Census** (Morrow, n.d.). G 975.8 Richmond

Screven County

† 1830 Federal Census. Alvaretta Kenan Register, **The Fifth Census of the United States 1830 Screven County, Georgia** (Norfolk, 1970). G 975.8 Screven

† 1850 Federal Census. Rhea Cumming Otto, **1850 Census of Georgia (Screven County)** (Savannah, 1975). G 975.8 Screven

• The Archives has typescripts of the 1820 and 1850 federal censuses of Screven County on microfilm reel 70-79.

Stewart County

† 1830 Federal Census (Partial List of Families). Helen Eliza Terrill, **History of Stewart County, Georgia** 2 vols. (Columbus, 1958), p. 72. G 975.8 Stewart

† 1850 Federal Census. Rhea Cumming Otto, **1850 Census of Georgia (Stewart County)** (Savannah, 1977). G 975.8 Stewart

† 1850 Federal Census. Folks Huxford, "Thomas County, Georgia; the 1850 Census with Index." MICROFILM LIBRARY, REEL 181-56.

Sumter County

† 1850 Federal Census. Rhea Cumming Otto, **1850 Census of Georgia (Sumter County)** (Savannah, 1977). G 975.8 Sumter

Talbot County

† 1850 Federal Census. Rhea Cumming Otto, **1850 Census of Georgia (Talbot County)** (Savannah, 1974). G 975.8 Talbot

Taliaferro County

† 1827 State Census. Marilyn L. Adams, **Censuses for Georgia Counties** (Atlanta, 1979).

† 1827 State Census. Alvin Mell Lunceford, Jr., **Early Records of Taliaferro County, Georgia** (Crawfordville, 1956); 1-10. Lunceford incorrectly identifies this census as a "Roster of Militiamen 1827." G 975.8 Taliaferro

† 1850 Federal Census. Rhea Cumming Otto, **1850 Census of Georgia (Taliaferro County, Georgia)** (Savannah, 1980). Not yet available at the Georgia Archives.

Tattnall County

† 1810 Federal Census (Substitute). Folks Huxford, "1810 Jury List, Tattnall County, Georgia," **National Genealogical Society Quarterly** 39 (1951): 89-91. PERIODICAL ROOM

† 1830 Federal Census (Index Only), "1830 Census – 1831 Tax Digest With Index of Tattnall County, Georgia," **Georgia Genealogical Society Quarterly** 5 (1969): 186-91. PERIODICAL ROOM

† 1838 State Census (Index Only). Brigid S. Townsend, **Indexes to Seven State Census Reports for Counties in Georgia, 1838-1845** (Atlanta, 1975). G 939.34 T74i

† 1850 Federal Census. Rhea Cumming Otto, **1850 Census of Georgia (Tattnall County)** (Savannah, 1971). G 975.8 Tattnall

† 1820, 1830, 1840, 1860, 1870, & 1880 Federal Census. John E. Mosley is currently preparing these census records for publication.

Telfair County

† 1830 Federal Census (Index Only). "Telfair County Heads of Families – 1830," **They Were Here**, vol. 3, no. 2, (1967): 502-4. PERIODICAL ROOM

† 1850 Federal Census. Rhea Cumming Otto, **1850 Census of Georgia (Telfair County)** (Savannah, 1970). G 975.8 Telfair.

Thomas County

† 1830 Federal Census (Index Only). "Thomas County 1830 Census Index," **They Were Here**, vol. 4, no. 4 (1968): 768-71. PERIODICAL ROOM

† 1840 Federal Census (Heads of Family). E.H. Hays, "1840 Thomas County, Georgia, U.S. Census; Alphabetically Arranged and Submitted by

E.H. Hayes," **Southern Genealogists Exchange Quarterly** 2 (11) (1959), pp. 19-23.

† 1850 Federal Census. Floreda Duke Varick and Phyllis Rose Smith, **Thomas County, Georgia, 1850 Census** (Cairo, Ga., 1950). G 975.8 Thomas

Troup County

† 1830 Federal Census (Index Only). "Troup County 1830 Heads of Families," **They Were Here**, vol. 1, no. 4 (1965): 190-4. PERIODICAL ROOM

† 1850 Federal Census. Rhea Cumming Otto, **1850 Census of Georgia (Troup County)** (Savannah, 1978). G 975.8 Troup

Twiggs County

† 1820 Federal Census (Substitute). "Twiggs County, Georgia, 1818 Tax Digest," **Georgia Genealogical Society Quarterly** 11 (1975), pp. 121-9. The 1820 federal census for Twiggs County is lost.

† 1850 Federal Census. Rhea Cumming Otto, **1850 Census of Georgia (Twiggs County)** (Savannah, 1980). Not yet available at the Georgia Archives.

Union County

† 1834 State Census. Bob Davis, "Georgia County Records Files in the Telamon Cuyler Collection," **Northwest Georgia Historical and Genealogical Society Quarterly** vol. 12, no. 2 (1980): 11-2. PERIODICAL ROOM

† 1834 State Census. Robert S. Davis, Jr., "Georgia County Records Files in the Telamon Cuyler Collection," **Georgia Genealogical Magazine**, no. 73 (1979): 214-5. PERIODICAL ROOM

† 1840 Federal Census (Index Only). Homer H. Bradley, II, "The Georgia Cherokee Strip 1840 U.S. Census," **Georgia Genealogical Society Quarterly** 5 (1969): 1-82. DESK AND PERIODICAL ROOM

† 1850 Federal Census. Rhea Cumming Otto, **1850 Federal Census of Georgia (Union County)** (Savannah, 1980). Not yet available at the Georgia Archives.

Upson County

† 1850 Federal Census, "Upson County, Georgia — 1850 Census," **Georgia Pioneers**, vol. 4 (1967): 95-7, 137-9; vol. 5 (1968): 24-7, 58-61, 106-8; 152-4; vol. 6 (1969): 38-42, 85-8, 141-4, 171-3; vol. 7 (1970): 45-9, 60-3, 144-7, 207-8; vol. 8 (1971): 45-8, 105-8, 127-30, 197-200; vol. 9 (1972): 14-7, 97-100, 160-3, 215-20. PERIODICAL ROOM

† 1850 Federal Census. Carolyn Walker Nottingham and Evelyn Hannah, **History of Upson County, Georgia** (Macon, 1930): 509-601. G 975.8 Upson .

† 1850 Federal Census. Georgia Pioneers, **Madison-Upson Counties 1850 Census Records** (Albany: Georgia Pioneers, 1980). Not yet available at the Georgia Archives.

Walker County

† 1840 Federal Census (Index Only). Homer H. Bradley, II, "The Georgia Cherokee Strip 1840 U.S. Census," **Georgia Genealogical Society Quarterly** 5 (1969): 1-82. DESK AND PERIODICAL ROOM

† 1850 Federal Census. Ethel B. Shaw and Linda L. Criswell, **1850 Census of Walker County, Georgia** (Orange, Calif., 1971). G 975.8 Walker

Walton County

† 1820, 1830, 1840, 1850 & 1860 Federal Census (Index Only). Anita B. Sams, **Wayfarers in Walton, a History of Walton County, Georgia, 1818-1967** (Monroe, 1967). The 1820 census index is on pp. 521-5; 1830, pp. 526-35; 1840, pp. 535-43; 1850, pp. 543-53; and the 1860, pp. 553-61. G 975.8 Walton

Warren County

† 1845 State Census (Index Only). Brigid S. Townsend, **Indexes to Seven State Census Reports for Counties in Georgia, 1838-1845** (Atlanta, 1975). G 939.34 T74i

† 1850 Federal Census. Rhea Cumming Otto, **1850 Census of Georgia (Warren County)** (Savannah, 1974). G 975.8 Warren

Washington County

† 1820, 1830 & 1850 Federal Census (Index to Heads of Families). Frances Wynd, **Washington County, Georgia Records** (Albany, n.d.). G 975.8 Washington

† 1880 Federal Census. John E. Mosley is currently preparing this census for publication.

Wayne County

† 1820 Federal Census (Corrections). Folks Huxford, "1820 Census Corrections," **Georgia Genealogical Magazine** (1969) no. 32, pp. 2222-3. Names omited or misspelled in the published statewide census index for Georgia. PERIODICAL ROOM

† 1850 Federal Census (Index to Heads of Families). "Heads of Family 1850 Census Wayne County," **They Were Here**, vol. 3, no. 3 (1967): 542-4. PERIODICAL ROOM

† 1860 Federal Census (Index to Heads of Households). Ray B. Stephens, "1860 Wayne County," **Georgia Genealogical Society Quarterly** 12 (1976): 16-8. PERIODICAL ROOM

White County

† 1860 Federal Census (Index to Heads of Families). "1860 White County, Georgia Census Index," **Georgia Genealogical Society Quarterly**, vol. 11 (1975): 102-6. PERIODICAL ROOM

Wilcox County

† 1860 Federal Census. Mrs. Henry Mashburn, "Wilcox County, Georgia Records," vol. III: 1-38 (typescript, DAR Collection, 1942-1943). DAR Wilcox

Wilkes County

† 1830 Federal Census (Index Only). "Wilkes County, Georgia – 1830 Heads of Family," **They Were Here**, vol. 2, no. 2 (1966): 274-80. PERIODICAL ROOM

† 1850 Federal Census (Index to Heads of Families). Mrs. Mildred Watkins and Miss Gloria Monk, "Index to 1850 Census Wilkes County, Georgia," **They Were Here**, vol. 3, no. 1 (1967): 433-41. PERIODICAL ROOM

† 1850 Federal Census. Irene Stilwell Wilcox, **The 1820, 1830, 1840, 1850 & 1860 Census of Elbert Co., Georgia, and the 1850 Census of Wilkes Co., Georgia** (Easley, 1979). Not at the Georgia Archives, but available from the Southern Historical Press, Easley, South Carolina.

Wilkinson County

† 1820, 1830, 1840, 1850 & 1860 Federal Census (Index to Heads of Families). Joseph T. Maddox, **United States Census Records With Related Information, 1820 Through 1860, Wilkinson County, Georgia** (Irwinton, 1969). G 975.8 Wilkinson

† 1850 Federal Census (Mortality Schedule). "United States Bureau of the Census Mortality Schedule, 1850 Wilkinson County, Georgia," **Georgia Genealogical Society Quarterly**, vol. 15 (1979): 41-2. PERIODICAL ROOM

9

COLONIAL BOOKS OF RECORD AND TAX DIGESTS
ON MICROFILM

COLONIAL BOOKS OF RECORD

During the periods that Georgia functioned as a royal colony — 1755 to 1777 and 1779 to 1782 — all of the province was essentially one county; with deed, mortgage, estate, and other books of record maintained at Savannah for the entire colony. The parishes in colonial Georgia were used as election and tax districts, as a means of locating land grants, and as areas of jurisdiction for minor courts held outside Savannah. **However, parishes did not function as county governments and kept no governmental books of record.**

Reproduced in this section is a list of the colonial books of record that have survived for Georgia, with their Georgia Archives Microfilm Library reel numbers. An asterisk indicates that the book of record is indexed; in the case of loose papers, the asterisk means that the documents are arranged alphabetically. The author would like to express his thanks to the R.J. Taylor, Jr., Foundation for their help in putting this list together.

Some information from the colonial books of record has been published, including abstracts of six of these books plus abstracts of what the compilers considered the most genealogically significant material in other books. The R.J. Taylor, Jr., Foundation is currently preparing a comprehensive index to the colonial conveyance (deed) books and hopes to some day publish a comprehensive index to the colonial estate books.

The following abbreviations are used on the list of colonial books of records to indicate which books have been published, in what form, and to what extent:

Beckemeyer — Frances H. Beckemeyer, **Abstracts of Colonial Conveyance Book C-1, 1750-1761** (Atlanta: R.J. Taylor, Jr., Foundation, 1975).

Bryan — Mary Givens Bryan, **Abstracts of Colonial Wills of the State of Ga., 1733-1777** (Atlanta: Town Committee of the National Society of the Colonial Dames of America, 1962).

Davidson — Grace G. Davidson, **Early Records of Ga. Wilkes County** 2 vols. (1936; Easley, S.C.: Southern Historical Press, 1968), vol. I, pp. 2-29. Davidson published a copy of the journal of the land court held in the Ceded Lands (after 1777 Wilkes County) from 1773 to 1775. The land court recorded the former place of residence and family composition of almost every family that moved into Ceded Lands. The original of this journal is now lost. For a history of this document and abstracts of related records, see Robert S. Davis, Jr., **The Wilkes County Papers, 1773-1833** (Easley, S.C.: Southern Historical Press, 1979), pp. 3-21.

Dumont — William H. Dumont, **Colonial Ga. Genealogical Data, 1748-1783** (Washington, D.C.: Special Publications of the National Genealogical Society, #36, 1971). Abstracts of only the items the compiler considered genealogically significant.

GGM — **Georgia Genealogical Magazine.** Abstracts of only the items the compiler (Folks Huxford) considered genealogically significant. These are specific issues in which the records appeared: Book CC — #4, pp. 171-8; #6, pp. 293-302; #7, pp. 357-66; #8, pp. 425-40; #10, pp. 559-68. Book DD — #11, pp. 627-36; #12, pp. 697-704; #13, pp. 763-72. Book S — #22, pp. 1468-72; #23, pp. 1533-8; #25, pp. 1663-70; #26, pp. 1779-1784. Book U — #26, pp. 1784-8; #27, pp. 1817-28; #28, p. 1887. Book V — #28, pp. 1888-96; #29, pp. 1971-8; #30, pp. 2035-42. Book U-3 — #42, pp. 389-96; #44-5, pp. 165-74. Book J — #16, pp. 988-94; #17, pp. 1059-68; #18, pp. 1129-34; #19, pp. 1205-9. Book O — #19, pp. 1209-12; #20, pp. 1281-8; #21, pp. 1357-64; #22, pp. 1465-8. Book CCC — #14, pp. 835-44; #15, pp. 907-14. Book DDD — #15, pp. 914-8; #16, pp. 983-7.

LeFar — Mabel F. LeFar & Caroline P. Wilson, **Abstracts of Wills Chatham County, Ga.** (Washington, D.C.: National Genealogical Society, 1936). A corrected copy of this book is at the Ga. Historical Society Library.

Surveyor General — Pat Bryant, **Entry of Claims for Ga. Landholders, 1733-1755** (Atlanta: Surveyor General Department, 1975). These claims were filed when Ga. went from being a trusteeship to a royal colony in 1755, for lands given to settlers by the trustees (1733-1755). Entries give names of claimants, original owners, and descriptions of land. This is known as Book M or U-3. Available from the Ga. Surveyor General Department.

Taylor — R.J. Taylor, Jr., Foundation. They are preparing for publication an index to the colonial conveyance books.

Walker — George F. Walker, **Abstracts of Colonial Book J, 1755-1762** (Atlanta: R.J. Taylor, Jr. Foundation, 1977).

MICROFILM REEL LIST

Reel 40-19 — Book C-1*, Conveyances (Deeds); Beckemeyer, Taylor; 1750-1761

Reel 40-19 — Book C2*, Conveyances (Deeds); Taylor; 1761-1766

Reel 40-20 — Book S*, Conveyances (Deeds); Taylor, GGM; 1766-1769

Reel 40-21 — Book U*, Conveyances (Deeds); Taylor, GGM; 1769

Reel 40-21 — Book V*, Conveyances (Deeds); Taylor, GGM; 1769-1771

Reel 40-22 — Book X-1*, Conveyances (Deeds); Taylor; 1771-1772

Reel 40-22 — Book X-2*, Conveyances (Deeds); Taylor; 1772-1774

Reel 40-23 — Book CC-1*, Conveyances (Deeds); Taylor, GGM, 1774-1775

Reel 40-23 — Book CC-2*, Conveyances (Deeds); Taylor, GGM; 1775-1778 and 1784-1798

Reel 40-25 — Book DD*, Conveyances (Deeds); Taylor, GGM; 1775-1778 and 1784-1798

Reel 40-25 — Book BBB* (B-3), Conveyances (Deeds); Taylor; 1783-1804. This book also includes records of confiscated Loyalist estates.

Reel 40-26 — Book E, Mortgages; 1755-1763. Microfilm Library has a special index to this volume.

Reel 40-26 — Book P, Mortgages; 1762-1765

Reel 40-27 — Book Q, Mortgages; 1765-1770

Reel 40-27 — Book W, Mortgages; 1770-1775 and 1778-1785

Reel 40-28 — Book EE, Mortgages; 1776-1778 and 1785-1822. Microfilm Library has a special index to this volume.

Reel 40-29 — Book A, Wills; Bryan; 1754-1772

Reel 223-1 — Book A, Wills (same as above); Bryan; 1754-1772

Reel 17-24 — Book B*, Wills; LeFar; 1777-1778. This volume is now Chatham County Will Book B.

Reel 40-30 — Book AA, Wills: Bryan; 1772-1777

Reel 81-5 — Book G, Appraisements and Administrations; 1777-1778

Reel 40-33 — Book F* (D), Inventories; 1754-1771

Reel 40-32 — Book FF*, Inventories; 1776-1777

Reel 40-32 — Book GG*, Inventories; 1777-1778

Reel 40-31 — Book D*, Letters of Administration; Dumont; 1755-1771

Reel 40-31 — Book Z*, Letters of Administration; Dumont; 1771-1775

Reel 40-31 — Book N*, Letters of Guardianship; Dumont; 1757-1775 and 1776-1777

Reel 40-34 — Book J*, Misc. Bonds, Deeds of Gift, etc.; Dumont, GGM, Walker; 1755-1762

Reel 40-34 — Book O*, Misc. Bonds, Deeds of Gift, etc.; Dumont, GGM; 1762-1765

Reel 40-35 — Book R*, Misc. Bonds, Deeds of Gift, etc.; Dumont; 1765-1772

Reel 40-36 — Book Y-1*, Misc. Bonds, Deeds of Gift, etc.; Dumont; 1772-1774

Reel 40-36 — Book Y-2*, Misc. Bonds, Deeds of Gift, etc.; Dumont; 1774-1775 and 1776-1777

Reel 40-37 — Book HH*, Misc. Bonds, Deeds of Gift, etc.; Dumont; 1777-1787 and 1798-1829

Reel 40-37 — Book JJ, Misc. Bonds, Deeds of Gift, etc.; Dumont; 1779-1780

Reel 40-37 — Book KK-1, Misc. Bonds, Deeds of Gift, etc.; Dumont; 1780-1781

Reel 40-37 — Book KK-2, Misc. Bonds, Deeds of Gift, etc.; Dumont; 1781-1782

Reel 40-38 — Book CCC, Misc. Bonds, Deeds of Gift, etc.; GGM; 1783-1792

Reel 40-38 — Book DDD, Misc. Bonds, Deeds of Gift, etc.; GGM; 1792-1813

Reel 40-39 — Book B-1*, Commissions; 1754-1776 and 1777-1778

Reel 40-39 — Book B-2*, Commissions; 1789-1827

Reel 40-40 — Book H, Proclamations; 1754-1794

Reel 40-41 — Book AAA*, Proclamations; 1782-1823

Reel 40-42 — Book K (Y3), Marks and Brands; Dumont; 1755-1778 and 1785-1793

Reel 40-43 — Book M* (U3), Entry of Claims; Dumont, GGM, Surveyor General; 1755-1757

Reel 40-44 — Book L, Fiats for Grants; Dumont; 1755-1767

Reel 40-44 — Book T, Fiats for Grants; 1767-1771

Reel 40-44 — Book BB, Fiats for Grants; 1772-1776

Reel 21-46 — Quit Rents*; 1758-1772

Reel 68-77 — Quit Rents*; 1772-1776

Reel 81-12 — Land Court Minutes; 1761-1766

Reel 154-65 — Land Court Minutes for the Ceded Lands area;* Davidson; 1773-1775

Reel 230-2 — Loose Estate Papers (A-E)*; 1776-1794

Reel 230-21 — Loose Estate Papers (F-M);* 1776-1794

Reel 230-22 — Loose Estate Papers (W-Z)*; 1776-1794

Reel 230-23 — Loose Estate Papers (oversized documents A-L)*; 1776-1794

Reel 230-24 — Loose Estate Papers (oversized documents L-W)*; 1776-1794

Reel 230-23 — Loose Land Settlement Papers; 1751-1775

Reel 230-33 — Loose Estate and Misc. Papers (A-L)*; 1776-1794

Reel 230-34 — Loose Estate and Misc. Papers (L-W and oversized)*; 1776-1794

Reel 231-43 — Loose Wills (A-H)*; Bryan; 1733-1777

Reel 231-44 — Loose Wills (H-Z)*; Bryan; 1733-1777

• Before the creation of the Georgia Department of Archives and History, loose colonial records were badly scattered. Today, the largest collections of these loose papers are in the Telamon Cuyler Collection, Special Collections, University of Georgia libraries, Athens; and the Manuscript Division, William R. Perkins Library, Duke University, Durham. Smaller collections can be found in such libraries as the New York Public Library and the New York Historical Society Library. Also, the Georgia Historical Society Library in Savannah and the Perkins Library have business papers of the colonial Georgia firm of Telfair and Company. The American Jewish Historical Society, 2 Thornton Road, Waltham, Massachusetts 02154, has the loose accounts of the Sheftall family, dealing primarily with their activities in supplying American troops during the American Revolution.

TAX DIGESTS

Tax records are valuable to genealogists because they provide clues as to age, year of death or migration, relationships to other families, and even to year of marriage. Many of Georgia's early tax digests have been published in Ruth Blair's book, **Some Early Tax Digests of Georgia** (1926; rep. ed., Easley, S.C.: Southern Historical Press, 1971). Records included are partial tax digests for Glynn County (1790); complete digest for Glynn County (1794); partial digests for Wilkes County (1792-1794); and complete digests for Camden (1794, 1809), Chatham (1806), Hancock (1812), Lincoln (1818), Montgomery (1797, 1798, 1805, 1806), Pulaski (1818), Richmond (1818), and Warren (1794, 1805, 1818) Counties.

The following is a list of pre-1800 tax digests in the Microfilm Library of the Georgia Archives. State copies of most county tax digests after 1872 have survived, although many are not on microfilm. These should be requested from the Government Records Office of the Archives through the Historical Research Advisor in Central Research.

Other Georgia tax digests are also not on microfilm. A few of the oldest are in such bad condition that even their year and county cannot be identified. Those records, because of their fragility, will not be available for use by researchers until proper restoration can be done. Tax digests that are fragmentary or not completely identified, but have been microfilmed, are not included on this list. Dates shown on the list were given by Microfilm Library personnel.

A few early tax digests are believed to still be in Georgia courthouses. Hopefully, the Archives will also be able to have them microfilmed before any more are lost to fire, neglect, or age. Federal Internal Revenue Assessment Lists for Georgia for 1865-1886 (Record Group 58, no. M-762) are available on microfilm at the Atlanta Federal Archives and Records Center, 1557 St. Joseph Avenue, East Point, Ga. 30344.

The following background information on Georgia tax laws is provided through the courtesy of Kenneth H. Thomas, Jr., of the Historic Preservation Section, Georgia Department of Natural Resources:

Ga. Tax Laws & Digests

Before 1805, a new tax law was passed each year, with evaluations similar to those used after 1805 except the values assigned changed frequently.

1805-

The Act of 1804 included new tax laws for Georgia, with rates being established as follows:

Poll

For free, white males, 21 years or older (if over age 60, exempted after 1825) — 31¼¢

Slave

Over 21 and under 60 (no mention of sex) — 31¼¢ ea.

For Every $100 Value of Town Lot and Buildings

Evaluation was left up to the owner to declare. Land has to be within city limits — 31¼¢

Professional

Lawyers, doctors, etc. — $4.00 ea.

Carriages

Four-wheel — $1.00 ea.
Two-wheel — 50¢ ea.

Land (acres)

Land was evaluated in relation to the rivers of Georgia. Perhaps the most confusing part of the tax laws, an example of land evaluations in the Piedmont:

"All Other Oak & Hickory Land":

Per Acre

Quality 1: 4¼ mills ($.00425)
Quality 2: 2½ mills ($.0025)
Quality 3: 1¼ mills ($.00125)

"All Other Pine Land":

3/4 mills ($.00075)

The land was itemized as to the county where it was situated; the waters on which it was situated; whose land it bordered; and in earlier days, to whom it was granted. In 1825, taxes were reduced by 25%; and in 1832, they were reduced by 50%. The tax was increased by 25% in 1842 and the poll tax reduced to 25¢ in 1850. The easiest way to tell if a reduction was in effect is to find a person only paying poll tax.

A tax digest can indicate: (1) amount of taxes a person was to pay (not what he paid), (2) lack of land and slaves and thus no estate to be probated, (3) age of person — when he first appears paying poll tax or is "exempt" due to old age, (4) ownership of land. If one paid taxes on land, usually that means ownership and thus a deed should be of record, and (5) land in other counties — when was it sold?

**1805 Tax Digest, Captain Wilson's Militia District,
Warren County, Georgia**

Thomas Ansley, Sr. — Poll, 1; Slaves, 7; Land, 136 (3), 1400 (P); Water, Upson's; Adjoins, Landrum.

Computation of Ansley's Taxes:

1 poll	.3125
7 slaves	2.1875
136 (3) = (136) x (.00125)	.17
1400 (P) = (1400) x (.00075)	1.05
	$3.7200

Tax: $3.72

Changes: 1852-Present

The tax laws changed with the Act of 1852 which established the "Ad Valorem" system still used today. The property was evaluated and the governor and the comptroller-general selected a percentage for statewide taxation to provide the state with enough money for the coming year. In 1852, the ceiling for the amount to be collected was placed at $375,000 and the percentage for taxation was 1/12 of 1%. This new system also exempted from taxation the following: all plantation and mechanical tools, furniture under $300 value, all libraries, all poultry, $200 exemption of the value of "all other property," all annual crops, all firearms and instruments, munitions of war and all wearing apparel. This system with minor variations is still in effect.

Nicholas C. Bacon
Ga. Militia Dist. 152; Warren Co., Ga.

	1854	1854
Poll	1	
Poll Tax		.25
Slaves	18	
Value of Slaves		$8,800
Acres of Land & Quality	(3)587	
Value of Land		5,800
Value of Money & Accounts		250
Value of Other Property		1,090
Total of Values		$15,940

PRE-1800 TAX DIGESTS ON MICROFILM (By County)

Appling
   1851, 1872-
Baker
   1845, 1874-
Baldwin
   1807-1811, 1813-1828, 1831-1842, 1844-1867, 1870-1871, 1874-1879
Banks
   1874
Bartow
   1871
Berrien
   1867, 1872-
Bibb
   1835-1836, 1845, 1871, 1874-
Brooks
   1866-1869, 1871-
Bryan
   1861, 1871, 1874-
Bulloch
   1854, 1866, 1868, 1874-

Burke
1798, 1855-1860, 1863, 1874-
Butts
1831 (nothing else until 1900)
Calhoun
none
Camden
1794, 1809, 1819-1863, 1866, 1869, 1874-
Campbell
1855-1859, 1861-1863, 1866, 1868-1869
Carroll
1832, 1841, 1842, 1844, 1847, 1852
Catoosa
none
Charlton
1855, 1871
Chatham
1793, 1798-1799, 1806, 1821-1827, 1831-1835, 1842-1843, 1846, 1848,
1855, 1866, 1868-1869, 1875-1876, 1878, 1881, 1883-1884, 1893, 1895,
1897
Chattahoochee
1854-1864, 1866-1867, 1869-1872
Chattooga
1871
Cherokee
1849-1871
Clarke
1802-
Clay
1855, 1864
Clayton
1861-1869
Clinch
1868-
Cobb
1848-1849, 1851
Coffee
1869, 1871-1872
Colquitt
1857, 1869
Columbia
1805-1806, 1808, 1812, 1821, 1823, 1825, 1827, 1829-1830, 1832-1867,
1872, 1876-
Coweta
1845-1848, 1854-1857, 1860-1861, 1864, 1867, 1872-1879
Crawford
1840-1842, 1845, 1851, 1856, 1858, 1868, 1871
Dade
none

Dawson
none
Decatur
1824-1862
DeKalb
1846-1847 (partial), 1848-1850, 1855
Dodge
1871-1877, 1880
Dooly
1851
Dougherty
none
Douglas
none
Early
1820, 1840, 1842, 1850
Echols
1867
Effingham
1855-1858, 1860-1864, 1866-1867, 1869-1879
Elbert
1848, 1849, 1851, 1860
Emanuel
1841, 1851
Fannin
1863, 1866
Fayette
1823-1824, 1826, 1829, 1831-1836, 1839-1841, 1843, 1845-1852, 1854-1859, 1861-1864, 1866-1869
Floyd
1852
Forsyth
1853
Franklin
1798, 1800-1803, 1805-1808, 1810-1811, 1818-1823, 1825-1839, 1842, 1844-1845, 1847, 1849-1850, 1852, 1854-1856, 1858, 1861, 1867
Fulton
1854-1857, 1862, 1864, 1866, 1868-1869, 1873-1874, 1876-
Gilmer
1855, 1864-1869
Glascock
1858, 1860-1864, 1866-1880
Glynn
1792-1794
Gordon
1851-1863
Greene
1788-1789, 1793, 1796-1799, 1801-1815, 1822, 1824-1825, 1827-1830, 1834, 1837, 1853-1854, 1859

Gwinnett
  1866, 1872
Habersham
  1850
Hall
  1852-1853
Hancock
  1794-1796, 1804, 1812, 1829-1849, 1851-1858, 1860-1870, 1882
Haralson
  1866
Harris
  1831, 1836, 1841-1843, 1845
Hart
  1867
Heard
  1871-1872
Henry
  1831, 1837, 1852, 1854-1855, 1857-1859, 1864-1869
Houston
  1829, 1831-1835, 1837-1839, 1841-1850, 1853, 1856-1860, 1863-1864,
  1869
Irwin
  1830-1832, 1839-1842, 1846-1858, 1870
Jackson
  1797-1799?, 1799, 1802-1811, 1820-1832, 1834-1847, 1849-1851, 1854,
  1856-1859, 1861-1862, 1866
Jasper
  1866, 1868, 1871-
Jefferson
  1796-1863, 1866-1879
Johnson
  1864, 1866, 1872
Jones
  1811, 1813-1814, 1816-1821, 1823, 1825-1827, 1830-1848, 1850, 1854-
  1861, 1863, 1866-1879
Laurens
  1841, 1850-1851, 1857-1859, 1866, 1871-1872
Lee
  1852
Liberty
  1800-1801, 1806-1809, 1812-1815, 1821, 1827, 1829-1830, 1832, 1835,
  1838, 1841, 1843-1844, 1846-1848, 1851, 1861-1863, 1867-1869, 1871-
Lincoln
  1801, 1802-1869
Lowndes
  1830, 1834-1835, 1838, 1840, 1844, 1869-1872, 1874-1876
Lumpkin
  1836, 1866

McDuffie
1871
McIntosh
1825, 1837, 1862
Macon
1838, 1852
Madison
1813, 1817, 1820-1821, 1824-1825, 1828, 1830, 1832-1833, 1838, 1840, 1843, 1848-1850, 1852-1855, 1857, 1859-1861
Marion
1848, 1850, 1852-1864, 1866, 1868, 1877
Meriwether
1863
Miller
1871-1872
Milton
1866, 1868
Mitchell
none
Monroe
1828, 1834, 1841, 1843-1844, 1847, 1849, 1851, 1853-1861, 1863-
Montgomery
1797-1798, 1805-1806, 1811-1812, 1828-1826, 1839-1842, 1846, 1849-1850, 1854, 1859-1861, 1867-1871
Morgan
1808-1810, 1812, 1817-1818, 1820, 1822-1824, 1826, 1829-1830, 1832, 1838-1840, 1842-1848, 1852, 1858-1863, 1869, 1871
Murray
1868-1869, 1874-1878
Muscogee
1838, 1845, 1847, 1867, 1869
Newton
1848-1849, 1851
Oconee
none
Oglethorpe
1795-1866, 1871
Paulding
1868-1869
Pickens
1867
Pierce
1864, 1868-1870, 1871
Pike
1825-1827, 1829, 1831, 1834-1839, 1843, 1845, 1848, 1850-1859, 1864, 1866, 1868, 1871-1872
Polk
1870

Pulaski
  1809-1811, 1816-1818, 1822-1824, 1827, 1829, 1839-1843, 1845-1847, 1850-1855, 1857-1859, 1861-1862, 1866-1870, 1876-1878
Putnam
  1812-1813, 1815, 1817, 1820, 1822-1828, 1830, 1833, 1836-1839, 1844, 1852, 1860-1862, 1866
Quitman
  none
Rabun
  1836, 1861-1862, 1869
Randolph
  1848-1849
Richmond
  1789, 1795, 1800, 1807, 1809-1810, 1816, 1818-1820, 1822-1864, 1866-
Rockdale
  1871
Schley
  1858, 1866, 1870
Screven
  1852, 1864
Spalding
  1852-1853, 1861-1864, 1866, 1871-1872, 1876-1880
Stewart
  1841, 1853, 1855-1864, 1866-1868, 1871
Sumter
  1844, 1852, 1864, 1871
Talbot
  1852, 1856
Taliaferro
  1826-1870
Tattnall
  1802-1839, 1841-1878
Taylor
  1852-1863, 1866-1870, 1873
Telfair
  1853-1854, 1856, 1867, 1870
Terrell
  1856-1857, 1859-1864, 1866-1871
Thomas
  1854, 1870-1871
Towns
  1869-1870
Troup
  1850-1851, 1861-1862, 1866-1867
Twiggs
  1818, 1826, 1830, 1833, 1853, 1863, 1870, 1872-1877, 1878-1880 (partial)
Union
  1849-1851, 1855, 1857, 1859

Upson
  1825-1834, 1836-1859, 1863-1867, 1869, 1871
Walker
  none
Walton
  1819, 1826, 1831, 1834, 1849-1853, 1859-1860, 1862, 1868-1869
Ware
  1862, 1867-1869
Warren
  1794, 1798, 1801, 1805, 1817-1818, 1849-1850, 1854-1864, 1867-1872
Washington
  1825-1826, 1828, 1830, 1836-1838, 1848-1851, 1855-1856, 1869-1870
Wayne
  1844, 1853, 1862-1879
Webster
  1856-1858, 1860-1864
White
  1858-1870
Whitfield
  1852, 1854, 1856, 1858-1859, 1863, 1869-1870
Wilkes
  (incomplete digests for 1787, 1790, 1791-1794, 1801) 1805-1807, 1809,
  1811-1814, 1816-1857, 1859, 1861, 1864, 1867
Wilkinson
  none
Worth
  1874-1887 (only partial for some years)

10

LAND LOTTERY RECORDS
AND REVISED LIST OF QUALIFICATIONS

In 1805, 1807, 1820, 1821, 1827, and twice in 1832, the state of Georgia gave away, in land lots, former Indian lands by means of state lotteries. Individuals and also families of orphans registered for draws (chances) in their respective counties. Winning, or fortunate, draws were made at random by state officials until all the lots were given away. Unlike modern state lotteries, Georgia's land lotteries had nothing to do with raising money for the state or gambling, but only with disposing of newly-acquired state lands.

With a few exceptions, described elsewhere in this section, only citizens of Georgia could qualify for draws in the land lotteries. However, in many instances, the winning Georgians sold their lots to land speculators who, in turn, sold the land to new families that were moving into the newly-acquired land from outside the state. The 1850 federal census, for example, shows that most of the families that settled the lands granted through the 1832 land lotteries (present-day northwest Georgia) were non-Georgians who had moved into the area and bought lots from the land lottery winners and land speculators.

The Georgia land lottery records are a goldmine of genealogical information. The names of almost every Georgia head of a family in 1802-1803 is included in the published 1805 land lottery, making it a substitute for the lost 1800 federal census of Georgia. This book does not give the designations of the lots that were won, but the information is available from the Georgia Surveyor General Department. The published books of the later land lotteries, 1807-1832, only provide the names of the winners, but they do include the lot numbers of the lots they won. These books are very useful as a means of learning in what counties a family was living during the various lotteries. Also, the published land lottery books sometimes provide information about a participant's marital status, children, and Revolutionary War service. Some county records on microfilm at the Archives provide local lists of all the participants in the land lotteries after 1805 for certain counties (see chapter 7). Following this introduction is a list of the qualifications for draws in each of the land lotteries, showing the type of genealogical information provided by the published land lottery books.

Below is a list of the published land lottery books, all of which can be purchased from the Southern Historical Press, P.O. Box 738, Easley, South Carolina 29640. A list of the Revolutionary War veterans identified in the lists of

Land Lottery Winners can be purchased from the Georgia Surveyor General Department, 330 Capitol Ave., S.E., Atlanta, Georgia 30334:Alex M. Hitz, **Authentic List of All Land Lottery Grants Made to Veterans of the Revolutionary War by the State of Georgia** (Atlanta: Secretary of State, 1966).

Virginia S. and Ralph V. Wood, **The 1805 Land Lottery of Ga.** (Cambridge: The Greenwood Press, 1964. Sold exclusively by Southern Historical Press.)

Silas E. Lucas, Jr., **The 1807 Land Lottery of Ga.** (Easley, S.C.: Southern Historical Press, 1968)

Silas E. Lucas, Jr., **The 1820 & 1821 Land Lotteries of Ga.** (Easley, S.C.: Southern Historical Press, 1973)

Martha Lou Houston, **The 1827 Land Lottery of Ga.** (1928; rep. ed. Easley, S.C.: Southern Historical Press, 1975)

James F. Smith, **The 1832 (Cherokee) Land Lottery** (1838 rep. ed. Easley, S.C.: Southern Historical Press, 1968)

Silas E. Lucas, Jr., **The 1832 Gold Lottery of Ga.** (Easley, S.C.: Southern Historical Press, 1976)

Robert S. Davis, Jr., & Silas E. Lucas, Jr., **The Ga. Land Lottery Papers, 1805-1914** (Easley, S.C.: Southern Historical Press, 1979). Claims filed by heirs of winners in the land lotteries.

• Also see Kenneth H. Thomas, Jr., "Corrections to the 1827 Land Lottery of Ga.," **Georgia Genealogical Society Quarterly** 16 (1980), p. 116.

The Manuscript Department, William R. Perkins Library, Duke University, has some loose land lottery papers (see above) not available at the Georgia Surveyor General Department. These are in the Georgia Papers Collection and have not been published. The Georgia Surveyor General Department has land lottery fraud court case papers.

REVISED QUALIFICATIONS FOR DRAWS IN THE GA. LAND LOTTERIES

A long time ago, someone sat down and compiled a summary of the qualifications for drawing chances in Georgia's seven land lotteries. This summary has been reprinted many times and is currently given to visitors at the Georgia Archives as part of a pamphlet on the records of the Surveyor General Department.

The problem with this summary is that it is filled with errors and oversimplifications, has serious omissions, and for the 1832 Cherokee Land Lottery gives qualifications for draws that were not given in the acts and amendments dealing with the lottery. For most researchers, these problems are not important, as the information they have obtained from the published lists of land lottery drawers and/or winners has no value to them beyond what is exactly given on the lottery list. For example, an entry in the 1832 Cherokee Land Lottery for an individual receiving a lot as a Revolutionary War soldier would probably not provide the researcher with any more or less useful information about that individual whether the researcher is using the summary described above or the actual acts relating to the lottery. However, some exceptions do exist, and the problems with the summary have confused many researchers over why their ancestors appear or do not appear in some lotteries and why some winners in the lotteries were successfully sued by "informants" (individuals who were entitled to a portion of a lot if they could prove the winner had received a draw or draws fraudulently).

I have summarized the qualifications for a draw or draws in each of the land lotteries, as I interpreted them; using the actual acts, supplements, and amendments. However, some of the acts are poorly put together, and the meanings of certain passages (particularly in the 1827 Land Lottery and the 1832 Cherokee Land Lottery) are not clear. In such instances, I have pointed out the problems and suggested what I feel are the intended meanings.

1805 Land Lottery

Each participant in the lottery was allowed to qualify for a draw or draws in no more than one of the following categories:

1. Every free white male, age 21 years or older, a United States citizen, and an inhabitant of the State of Georgia for twelve months immediately prior to the Act of 11 May 1803 (or had paid a tax towards the support of the state government of Georgia*) was entitled to one draw.**

2. Every free white male, meeting the same qualifications as above, but with a wife and/or legitimate child or children (at least one of the children under the age of 21 years) was entitled to two draws.

3. Every widow having a legitimate child or children under the age of 21 years and who has been an inhabitant of the State of Georgia for twelve months immediately prior to the Act of 11 May 1803,*** was entitled to two draws.

4. Every family of orphans, under the age of 21 years and having either both parents dead or the father dead and the mother remarried, was entitled to one draw.

Sources: Act of 11 May 1803 and 1803 Supplementary, no. 107, 10 Dec. 1803, in Augustin Smith Clayton, **A Compilation of the Laws of the State of Georgia** . . . (Augusta: Adams and Duyckinck, 1813), pp. 103-4, 131.

Notes: * Presumably, although the act does not so clearly state, this tax had to have been paid in the twelve months immediately prior to the Act of 11 May 1803.

** Time spent outside of the State of Georgia on lawful business counted towards meeting the residency requirements if the individual was otherwise an inhabitant of the state during that period.

*** The act does not state that widows qualified for the lottery if they had paid a state tax prior to 11 May 1803, unlike the qualifications for single or married male (see no. 1 above).

1807 Land Lottery

1. Individuals or families of orphans who won lots in the previous land lottery were not allowed to participate in the land lottery of 1807. Presumably, an individual who was a member of a family of orphans who won a lot in 1805 could qualify for a draw or draws as an individual in the 1807 land lottery, if the individual was now old enough and met the other qualifications given below. The act giving the qualifications of the 1807 land lottery is silent on this point.

2. Each participant in the 1807 land lottery had to be:

  a. A citizen of the United States and
  b. An inhabitant of the State of Georgia for three years immediately prior to the Act of 26 June 1806. Time spent outside of the State of Georgia on lawful business counted towards meeting this residency requirement if the individual was otherwise living in Georgia during the specified period.

3. Each participant in the 1807 land lottery could qualify for a draw or draws in only one of the following categories:

  a. Every free white male, 21 years old or older, was entitled to one draw.
  b. Every free white male, 21 years old or older, with a wife and/or legitimate child or children under the age of 21 years, was entitled to two draws.
  c. Every widow was entitled to one draw.
  d. Every free white female, unmarried and 21 years old or older, was entitled to one draw.
  e. Every family of orphans under the age of 21 years, whose father was dead, was entitled to one draw.
  f. Every family of two or more orphans, whose mother and father were both dead, was entitled to two draws. They were to be registered in the county and district where the eldest orphan lived.
  g. Every family of one orphan under the age of 21 years, whose father and mother were both dead, was entitled to only one draw.

Source: Act of 26 June 1806 in Augustin Smith Clayton, **A Compilation of the Laws of the State of Georgia** ... (Augusta: Adams and Duyckinck, 1813). pp. 292-4.

1820 Land Lottery

1. No one who fell into any of the following categories was allowed to qualify for draws in the 1820 land lottery.

  a. Any person or family of orphans who won in any of the previous land lotteries could not participate in the 1820 lottery. [However, an individual who won a lot as a member of a family of orphans in a previous lottery possibly could have qualified to draw in the 1820 lottery as an individual if they were old enough and met the other qualifications for a draw or draws. The act for the 1820 land lottery is silent on this point.] The act, however, does give two exceptions to the above restrictions against winners in the previous land lotteries. Any indigent or invalid Revolutionary War soldier who had won a lot in a previous lottery was entitled to one draw in the 1820 lottery, provided that he had served on the side of the United States during the Revolution. Any family of more than one orphan that had won a lot in a previous land lottery was also entitled to one draw in the 1820 land lottery.

b. Any person who was legally drafted in the "late war" with Great Britain [the War of 1812; however, the verbal oath described in the act says any of the wars with Great Britain or the Indians] who refused to serve or to hire a substitute to serve in his place during a tour of duty could not participate in the 1820 land lottery.

c. Any person who evaded the draft by leaving the state or the country could not participate in the 1820 land lottery.

2. Each participant in the 1820 land lottery had to meet all of the qualifications:

a. A citizen of the United States and

b. An inhabitant of the State of Georgia for three years immediately prior to the Act of 15 Dec. 1818. Time spent outside of the state on lawful business counted towards meeting these residency requirements if the individual was otherwise a resident of Georgia for the specified three-year period.

or

The act giving the qualifications for the 1820 land lottery provides an exception to the above residency requirement. Any person who served as a draftee or as a volunteer "in the late Indian war" and had become a citizen of Georgia and had lived in the state continuously since their military service had ended, was entitled to participate in the 1820 land lottery even though they may not have been an inhabitant of the State of Georgia for the three years immediately prior to 15 December 1818.

3. Each participant in the 1820 land lottery could receive a draw or draws in only one of the following categories:

a. Every white male, 18 years old or older, was entitled to one draw.

b. Every male, "of like description," with a wife and/or legitimate male child or children under the age of 18 years or unmarried female child or children was entitled to two draws.

c. Every widow was entitled to one draw.

d. Every family of orphans, under the age of 21 years, "except such as may be entitled in their own right to a draw or draws," whose father was dead, was entitled to one draw.

e. Every family of three or more orphans, with neither parent living, was entitled to two draws. They were to apply for their draws in the county and district where the eldest orphan or the eldest orphan's guardian lived.

f. Every family of one or two orphans, with neither parent living, was entitled to only one draw, to be applied for in the county or district where the oldest orphan or the oldest orphan's guardian lived.

g. Every family of more than one orphan that had won a lot in a previous land lottery was entitled to one draw.

h. Every Revolutionary War veteran, invalid or indigent, who had served in the forces of the United States and had won a lot in a previous land lottery was entitled to one draw.

4. Participants (except 3.g and 3.h above) in the 1820 land lottery who qualified for draws above could also qualify for additional draws under one of the following categories:

a. Every officer or soldier of the American Revolution who served in the forces of the United States and was invalid or indigent was entitled to two extra draws.

b. Every widow or family of orphans whose husband or father was killed "in the late wars" with Great Britain or the Indians was entitled to one extra draw above what they would normally receive as widows or orphans.

Sources: Act of 15 December 1818 in Lucius Q. Lamar, **A Compilation of the Laws of the State of Georgia** . . . (Augusta: T.S. Hannon, 1821), pp. 420-3.

1821 Land Lottery

1. No one who fell into any of the following categories could qualify for draws in the 1821 land lottery:

a. Anyone who had won a lot in an earlier land lottery could not receive a draw or draws in the 1821 land lottery. [However, an individual who won a lot previously as a member of a family of orphans possibly could have qualified to apply for a lot as an individual, if old enough and meeting the other qualifications. The act giving the qualifications for the 1821 land lottery is silent on this point.]

h. A citizen who was legally drafted in the wars with Great Britain or the Indians but refused to serve or hire a substitute was not entitled to a draw or draws in the lottery.

c. A person who deserted from the military forces of the State of Georgia or the United States was also disqualified from the 1821 lottery.

d. Anyone who illegally evaded the draft by removing from Georgia or the United States was disqualified from the lottery.

e. An individual who has moved beyond the boundaries of the State of Georgia to escape the laws of the state; who absconded for debt; or has not paid all of their taxes could not legally apply for a draw or draws in the lottery for themselves.

f. A convict in the penitentiary could not apply for draws in the land lottery. Children of such a convict were to be treated as if they were orphans with regards to the 1821 land lottery.

2. Each participant in the 1821 land lottery had to meet all of the following qualifications:

a. A United States citizen for three years and

b. An inhabitant of the State of Georgia for three years immediately prior to the Act of 15 May 1821. Time spent outside of the state on lawful business counted towards meeting this requirement if the individual otherwise was a resident of Georgia during the specified three-year period.

3. Each participant in the 1821 land lottery could apply for a draw or draws in only one of the following categories:

a. Every white male, 18 years old or older, was entitled to one draw.
b. Every male, "of like description," having a wife and/or legitimate male child or children under the age of 18 years or an unmarried female child or children, was entitled to two draws.
c. Every widow was entitled to one draw.
d. Every family of orphans under the age of 21 years, except those who qualified for a draw or draws individually, whose father was dead, was entitled to one draw.
e. Every family of 3 or more orphans, with neither parent living, was entitled to two draws. They were to register for their draws in the county and district where the oldest orphan resides or the guardian of the eldest orphan lived. If the eldest orphan or the eldest orphan's guardian lived in the newly acquired territory, the draws were to be applied for in the nearest organized Georgia county.
f. Every family of one or two orphans, with neither parent living, was entitled to only one draw, to be applied for in the same manner as in 3.c above.

Note: Anyone who qualified for a draw or draws in the land lottery who was an idiot or a lunatic had to be represented by their guardian. An individual who lost a judgment over debt could have the lot they won in the lottery seized to pay their creditor and the grant for the lot made to the creditor.

4. Some persons who received a draw or draws above, could also apply for an extra draw [draws in some instances?] in the following categories:

a. Every widow whose husband was killed in the wars with Great Britain or the Indians was entitled to one extra draw.
b. Every family of orphans whose father was killed in the late wars with Great Britain or the Indians was entitled to one extra draw.

Sources: Act of 15 May 1821 in Arthur Foster, **A Digest of the Laws of the State of Georgia** . . . (Philadelphia: J. Towar and D.M. Hogan, 1831), pp. 203-11.

1827 Land Lottery

1. All participants in the 1827 land lottery had to be:

a. A citizen of the United States and
b. An inhabitant of the State of Georgia for three years immediately prior to 1 January 1827 (see 5. Special Exceptions). Time spent outside of the state on lawful business during the specified period

counted towards meeting this residency requirement, provided that the individual was in every other way a resident during that time.

2. The following were reasons that a person could not legally qualify for draws in the 1827 land lottery:

    a. A winner in a previous land lottery could not receive draws in this lottery (however, see 5. Special Exceptions).

    b. No one who had refused to serve a tour of duty after having volunteered or having been drafted, during the previous war, or was a deserter could receive a draw or draws in the land lottery.

    c. No convict in the penitentiary could participate in the 1827 land lottery (see 5. Special Exceptions).

    d. Anyone who moved out of the state to evade Georgia laws; who absconded for debt; or had not paid all of their taxes was not entitled to participate in this lottery.

3. Everyone who met the above requirements could qualify for draws in only one of the following categories:

    a. Every white male, 18 years old or older, was entitled to one draw.

    b. Every white male of like description, with a wife and/or legitimate male child or children under the age of 18 years or unmarried female child or children, was entitled to two draws.

    c. Every widow was entitled to one draw.

    d. Every family of orphans under the age of 18 years and whose father was dead, who met the general residency requirements or had lived in Georgia continuously since their birth, was entitled to one draw.

    e. Every family of more than three orphans was entitled to two draws. They were to apply for their draws in the county and district of the eldest orphan or the eldest orphan's guardian, if in Georgia. [Apparently, the reference here is to orphans who lost bost parents, although the wording is not specific.]

    f. Every family of one or two orphans was entitled to one draw, to be applied for in the county and district where the eldest orphan or the eldest orphan's guardian lives. [Apparently, the reference here is to orphans who had lost both parents, although the wording is not specific.]

    g. Every male or unmarried female who was an idiot, a lunatic, insane, blind, or deaf and dumb and ten years old or older, but under the age of 18 years, was entitled to one draw.

4. Some individuals who qualified for draws above, also qualified for an additional draw in one of the categories below (also see 5. Special Exceptions):

    a. Every widow whose husband was killed or died in military service or on a return march in the wars against Great Britain or the Indians was entitled to one extra draw.

    b. Every orphan [family of orphans?] whose father was killed or died in the wars with Great Britain or the Indians or on the return march, was entitled to one extra draw.

    c. Every man who was disabled in the wars with Great Britain or the Indians was entitled to one extra draw.

    d. See 5. Special Exceptions.

5. Special Exceptions (to the qualifications and restrictions above):

    a. Every Revolutionary War veteran who had not drawn a lot for his Revolutionary War service in the previous lottery was entitled to two extra draws, even if he had won a lot under other qualifications in a previous lottery.

    b. Every Revolutionary War veteran who had drawn a lot for his Revolutionary War service in the previous lottery was entitled to one draw in the 1827 land lottery, even if he had been a winner in other lotteries.

    c. Every widow of a Revolutionary War veteran was entitled to one extra draw [even if they had won in an earlier lottery?].

    d. Every person who had previously won a lot as a member of a family of orphans but was eighteen years old or older on 1 January 1827 was entitled to one draw and any other members of the orphan family, under 18 years old, were entitled to one draw as a family.

    e. The children of a convict were treated as if they were a family of orphans for purposes of the 1827 land lottery.

    f. Illegitimate children were treated as orphans for purposes of the 1827 land lottery.

    g. The wife and/or children of a man who was absent from Georgia for three years or more were treated as a widow and orphans for purposes of the 1827 land lottery and title to any lots they won was permanently vested in them.

    h. Every man who served a three-month tour of duty in the previous war with Great Britain or the Indians was entitled to one extra draw in the 1827 lottery even if he had won a lot in the previous lottery. Men who served as substitutes in all their tours of duty they claimed in the war were not entitled to this extra draw.

Note: The original act giving the qualifications for draws in the 1827 lottery gave the date for determining age and residency requirements as 9 June 1825. The act was later amended to change this date to 1 Sept. 1826 but the date was finally changed to 1 January 1827.

Sources: Act of 9 June 1825, Amendatory of 24 December 1825, Amendatory of 14 December 1826, and Supplemental of 27 December 1826 (all in reference to the Act of 9 June 1825) in Arthur Foster, **A Digest of the Laws of the State of Georgia** . . . (Philadelphia: J. Towar and D.M. Hogan, 1831), pp. 220, 224-5, 233-7.

1832 Cherokee Land Lottery

1. Everyone who participated in the 1832 Cherokee land lottery had to be:

    a. A citizen of the United States and

    b. An inhabitant of the organized areas of Georgia for three years immediately prior to 1 January 1832, or born in Georgia and had lived in the state continuously, prior to 1 January 1832. Time spent outside of the state on legal business counted towards meeting the residency requirement if the individual was an inhabitant of the state during the specified period in all other ways.

2. No one who fell into one of the following categories was allowed by law to participate in the lottery:

a. No one was entitled to a draw or draws in the lottery whose immediate family did not meet the general residency requirements above, except officers of the United States army or navy or others employed by the United States.

b. Winners in the previous land lotteries were not allowed to participate in the 1832 Cherokee land lottery, with the exception of orphans and soldiers, as explained below. Any individual who had won a lot in a previous lottery as a member of a family of orphans was but turned 18 years old since the previous lottery was entitled to one draw in the 1832 Cherokee lottery and any other members of the family of orphans who were still under 18 years of age were entitled to one draw as a family in the 1832 Cherokee land lottery. Anyone who had won a lot for having served a tour of duty in the military of Georgia or the United States was also exempt from the restriction against persons who had won in previous lotteries.

c. Anyone who volunteered or was legally drafted in the previous war with Great Britain or the Indians but refused to serve and to hire a substitute to serve in his place or deserted was not allowed to participate in the land lottery.

d. No individual "either directly or indirectly concerned or interested with a certain horde of Thieves known as the Pony Club, shall be entitled to the provisions of this act."

e. No person who had been convicted of a felony in a Georgia court, was involved, by himself or through his agents, in mining gold, silver, or other metals in the new territory since 1 January 1830; was living in the new territory; or a convict in the penitentiary was allowed to draw for a lot or lots in the land lottery. Anyone who had left Georgia to escape the laws of the state was also excluded from the lottery.

3. Each participant in the lottery could qualify in only one of the following categories for a draw or draws:

a. Every deaf and dumb or blind person, who had not drawn a lot in a previous lottery, was entitled to one draw, unless provided for elsewhere as an orphan.

b. Every white male, 18 years old or older, was entitled to one draw.

c. Every male of like description with a wife and/or legitimate male child or children under the age of 18 years or unmarried female child or children was entitled to two draws.

d. Every widow was entitled to one draw.

e. Every unmarried female, 18 years old or older, whose father was killed in the wars with Great Britain or the Indians or upon the return march was entitled to one draw.

f. The wife and/or children of any man who has been absent from the state for three years or more shall be treated as a widow and orphans for purposes of the lottery and title to any lots they won were to be vested in them permanently and not in the absent husband or father.

g. Every family of orphans, under the age of 18 years, was entitled to one draw. [The act does not define "orphans" but presumably in this reference the term means someone who had lost their father.] See the qualifications for the 1807, 1820 and 1821 lotteries.

h. Every family of 3 or more orphans was entitled to two draws. [The act does not define what is meant by "orphans" here but the qualifications for the 1807, 1820 and 1821 lotteries suggest that in this reference, orphans were people who had lost both parents.]

i. Every family of one or two orphans was entitled to one draw. [See 3.h above for the most likely definition for "orphans" in this instance.]

j. Orphans were to apply for their draw or draws in the county and district where the eldest orphan or eldest orphan's guardian lived. If they had no guardian, then in the county or district where their mother or next friend lived.

k. Every family of children of a convict in the penitentiary were to be treated as orphans for the purposes of the land lottery.

l. Every idiot, lunatic, deaf and dumb person, or blind person who qualified for a draw or draws in the land lottery were to have their draw or draws applied for through their guardian, in their name.

m. See 2.b above for draws for families of orphans who had won in a previous lottery.

4. Some individuals who qualified for a draw or draws in one of the above categories, also qualified for an additional draw or draws in the categories below:

a. Every widow whose husband was killed or died in the military service of the United States or the State of Georgia during the war with Great Britain or the Indians or upon the return march was entitled to one extra draw.

b. Every family of orphans whose father was killed or died in the military service of the State of Georgia or the United States in the wars with Great Britain or the Indians or upon the return march was entitled to one extra draw. Such a family of orphans could qualify for this draw or extra draw even if they did not meet the general residency requirements of this act by having been moved from the state, provided that they had returned and were now living in Georgia.

c. Every widow of a Revolutionary War soldier was entitled to one extra draw.

d. Every Revolutionary War soldier, who had not won a lot in a previous lottery as a Revolutionary War soldier, was entitled to two extra draws. [The verbal oath described elsewhere in the act specified that no Revolutionary War soldier could qualify for these draws if they had served as an enemy or a spy against the United States.]

e. Every man who served as a soldier of the State of Georgia at any time during the Indian Wars from 1784 to 1797 was entitled to one extra draw. No one could qualify for this draw who was receiving extra draws for being a Revolutionary War veteran or who accepted protection from the British or Tories during the American Revolution. Every person who qualified for this extra draw also had to have been an inhabitant of the state at the time of their service and a citizen of Georgia on 1 January 1832.

f. Every widow of a person who would have been entitled to a draw in 4. e above was entitled to one draw, provided she was not also qualifying for a draw as the widow of a Revolutionary War soldier.

g. Every family of orphans of a person who would have qualified for a draw in 4. e above was entitled to one extra draw.

h. Every citizen of the State of Georgia who served in the military of Georgia or the United States for at least two months in the previous war with Great Britain or the Indians [the War of 1812] was entitled to one draw, provided that the service in which the draw is claimed was not done as a substitute. However, the man who paid for the substitute could qualify for such a draw.

Sources: Act of 21 December 1830 in **Acts of the General Assembly of the State of Georgia . . . In October, November and December, 1830.** (Milledgeville: Camak and Ragland, 1831), pp. 132-43; and Amendment of 26 December 1831 in **Acts of the General Assembly of the State of Georgia . . . In November and December, 1831.** (Milledgeville: Prince and Ragland, 1832), pp. 141-3.

1832 Gold Lottery

1. To participate in the 1832 Gold land lottery, a participant had to be:

a. A citizen of the United States and

b. An inhabitant of organized areas of the State of Georgia for three years immediately prior to 1 January 1832. Time spent outside of the state on lawful business counted towards meeting the above residency requirements if the individual was in every other way a resident of the state for the specified period.

2. No one could participate in the lottery who:

a. Had a family who did not meet the general residency requirements above except for officers of the United States army or navy or

b. Who had evaded military service to the State of Georgia or the United States during the American Revolution or the other wars with Great Britain or the Indians. [This restriction is given in the oath described in the act and not in the qualifications described in the act.]

3. Everyone who satisfied the above requirements was entitled to a draw or draws in only one of the following categories:

a. Every white male, 18 years old or older, was entitled to one draw.

b. Every head of a family was entitled to one draw or one extra draw for their family.

c. Every widow was entitled to one draw.

d. Every family of orphans, except those who qualify for a draw or draws elsewhere in the 1832 Gold Lottery, was entitled to one draw.

Sources: Act of 24 December 1831 in **Acts of the General Assembly of the State of Georgia . . . In November and December, 1831.** (Milledgeville: Prince and Ragland, 1832), pp. 165-6.

11

COUNTY HISTORIES
AND OTHER GENEALOGICALLY SIGNIFICANT BOOKS

Books that are solely census records or indexes to census records and tax records that are substitutes for census records are listed in Chapter 8. Georgia Land Lottery books are given in Chapter 10.

Although this book includes citations to more than 1,000 books, far from every work on Georgia is cited. Generally, historical works are not included, although some do include background or other information of interest to genealogists. Family histories are also not included. For all the books on a specific Georgia county or topic of interest, see the list of Georgia bibliographies in this section or write to local libraries in the geographical areas of your interest. Almost all public libraries have directories of public libraries in Georgia and elsewhere. Published, nationwide bibliographies of family and county histories also exist.

In compiling the following bibliography, a number of arbitrary decisions had to be made as to what was or was not a genealogically significant work. No library in Georgia has a complete collection of such works to check and no complete bibliography of such works exists. For these reasons, some books that probably would have been included here had the compiler known of them were unintentionally overlooked. The compiler apologizes for these omissions. A few articles from genealogical periodicals are included here because they cover all of Georgia or a large area of the state. However, because of space limitations, most are not.

Many of the books listed in this chapter are not on the shelves at the Archives Library. However, if you are unable to find the one you are interested in as listed in their card catalogue or on the shelves, ask a staff member for help. Some of their books are kept behind the main desk in the rare book room, which is closed to the public, or on a special shelf by the window.

GENERAL WORKS

BIBLIOGRAPHIES AND GUIDES (County Boundary Changes, Locations, and Maps)

American Guide Series, Federal Writers Project, Ga. — **A Guide to Its Towns & Countryside** (1940; rev. ed., Atlanta: Tupper & Love Publishers, 1954).

Janice G. Blake, **Pre-19th Century Maps in the Collections of the Ga. Surveyor General Dept.** (Atlanta: State Printing Office, 1975). [A second catalogue, for 1800-1850, is currently being prepared for publication.]

James C. Bonner, **Atlas for Ga. History** (Milledgeville, 1969).

Pat Bryant, **Ga. Counties: Their Changing Boundaries** (Atlanta: State Printing Office, 1977).

"Church & Campground Incorporations, 1833," **Ga. Genealogical Society Quarterly** 7 (1971), pp. 101-2.

Ga. Historical Quarterly, **The Counties of the State of Ga.** (Savannah: The Society, 1974). [Provides information on persons for whom Ga. counties were named.]

John H. Goff, **Placenames in Ga.**, eds. Frances L. Utley & Marion R. Hemperley (Athens: University of Ga. Press, 1975).

Marion R. Hemperley, **Cities, Towns, & Communities of Ga. Between 1847-1962** (Easley, S.C., Southern Historical Press, 1980). [Locations of 8,500 places shown on maps in the Surveyor General Dept.]

Marion R. Hemperley, **Handbook of Ga. Counties** (Atlanta: Ga. Surveyor General Dept., 1980). [Valuable, accurate, inexpensive little guide to the creation & changes of Ga. counties.]

Marion R. Hemperley, **The John H. Goff Collection** (Atlanta: Ga. Surveyor General Dept. Descriptive Inventory no. 2, 1971). [Guide to the Goff Collection of files on early Ga. forts, ferries, and roads.]

Historical Records Survey, **Classified Inventory of Ga. Maps** (East Point: the author, 1941).

Arnold Richardson, "Ga. Acts Incorporating Towns, 1800-1900," **Ga. Genealogical Society Quarterly** 7 (1971), pp. 176-90.

Carroll P. Scruggs, **Ga. Historical Markers** (Helen: Bay Tree Grove Publishers, 1973).

Adiel Sherwood, **A Gazetteer of the State of Ga.** (various printers, 1827, 1829, 1837, and 1860). [Reprints — include data on Ga. counties & placenames.]

George White, **Historical Collections of the State of Ga.** (1852; rep. ed. Danielsville: Heritage Papers, 1968). [Heritage has also published an index to this book.]

George White, **Statistics of the State of Ga.** (1849; rep. ed. Spartanburg: The Reprint Company, 1972).

• The Ga. Dept. of Archives & History publishes **Ga.'s Official & Statistical Register,** which includes county-by-county population figures for Ga. from 1790 to the most recent census. More detailed census statistics compilations for the entire U.S. are available in the Government Documents Center, Woodruff Library, Emory University.

BIBLIOGRAPHIES AND GUIDES (County History)

Azalea Clizbee, **Catalogue of the Wymberly Jones DeRenne Ga. Library at Wormsloe, Isle of Hope,** 3 vols. (Savannah: Privately Printed, 1931).

P. William Filby, **American & British Genealogy and Heraldry** (Chicago: American Library Association, 1975).

Carroll Hart, **Supplement to Yenawine's Checklist of Source Materials for the Counties of Ga.** (Atlanta: Ga. Dept. of Archives & History, 1967).

Hazel Purdie, **Ga. Bibliography: County History** (Atlanta, Ga. Dept. of Education, 1979). [Limited only to books available through interlibrary loan from Reader's Services, Div. of Public Library Services. Can be ordered from Dept. of Education, Reader's Services, 156 Trinity Ave., SW, Atlanta, Ga. 30303.]

A. Ray Rowland & James E. Dorsey, **A Bibliography of the Writings on Ga. History, 1900-1970** (Spartanburg, S.C.: The Reprint Co., 1978).

John E. Simpson, **Ga. History: A Bibliography** (Metuchen, N.J.: The Scarecrow Press, 1976).

J. Steven Storey, **Resource Index: A Guide to Natural Resource Information of Ga.** (Atlanta: Ga. Dept. of Natural Resources, 1977). [Includes a large Ga. county histories section. Can be ordered from National Technical Information Service, 5285 Port Royal Rd., Springfield, Va. 22161. It is item #PB 268 943.]

Mary Warren, **Ga. Genealogical Bibliography** (Danielsville: Heritage Papers, 1969).

Wayne S. Yenawine, "A Checklist of Source Materials for Counties in Ga.," **Ga. Historical Quarterly** 32 (1948), pp. 179-229. [Outdated, but includes publications not mentioned in more recent bibliographies.]

• The Ga. Dept. of Archives & History has the Martin Stiles Collection, 1915-1961, of newspapers commemorating centennial or anniversary celebrations for Ga. towns, cities, counties, and newspapers — available in the Microfilm Library, on microfilm.

BIBLIOGRAPHIES AND GUIDES (Georgia Genealogy)

Mary G. Bryan, **Catalogue of the Ga. Society, DAR Library in the Ga. Dept. of Archives & History** (Atlanta: Ga. Dept. of Archives & History, 1956).

Mildred Crane, **Genealogical Sources: A Selected List** (Athens: University of Ga. Libraries, 1979). [Order from publisher, Athens, Ga. 30602.]

Diane Dieterle, **Easy Genealogy** (Mableton: Roots Publishing Co., 1978). [Order from publisher, Box 476, Mableton, Ga. 30059.]

Wallace R. Draughon and William Perry Johnson, **North Carolina Genealogical Reference: A Research Guide for all Genealogists, Both Amateur and Professional** 2nd ed. (Durham: Seeman Printery, 1966). [A valuable guide to genealogical references to Georgia and South Carolina families as well as North Carolinians.]

Lynda S. Eller, **In the Beginning — How to Trace Your Family Tree** (Lanett, Al.: the author, 1977). [Order from author, Box 249, Lanett, Al. 36863.]

Leon S. Hollingsworth, "Work Shop Issue," **Ga. Genealogical Society Quarterly** 4 (1968), #2. [A "how-to" manual on Ga. genealogy; available from publisher, Box 38066, Atlanta, Ga. 30334.]

Helen F.M. Leary and Maurice R. Stirewalt, **North Carolina Research Genealogy and Local History** (Raleigh: North Carolina Genealogical Society, 1980). [Includes valuable information on doing genealogical research anywhere.]

Silas E. Lucas, Jr., **Master Index to the Ga. Genealogical Magazine Numbers 1-46 (1961-1972)** (Easley, S.C.: Southern Historical Press, 1973).

Mary Warren, **Ga. Bibliography of Articles in Print in Genealogical Magazines Thru Aug. 1967** (Danielsville: Heritage Papers, 1967).

• Guides to specific research libraries are given in Chapter 4.

BIOGRAPHICAL SKETCHES

Compilations of biographical sketches are rich in genealogical information. Even those of persons living in the late 1800s and early 1900s sometimes contain family data going back to the American Revolution. Such books often included anyone willing to pay to have their biography included or willing to buy a copy of the book. As a result, even sketches of persons of only very local prominence were published. Because of the amount of family information in these works, researchers may find useful genealogical material in sketches of distant cousins, as well as in biographies of direct ancestors.

The following is a list of some of the more famous compilations of biographical sketches. For more complete listings, see Kenneth H. Thomas, Jr., "Biographical Sketches for Georgians," **Ga. Life** 5 (Summer 1978), pp. 38-9, and Division of Librarianship, Emory University, **Sources of Ga. Biography** (Emory: the author, 1975). The latter only deals with compilations in Atlanta area libraries. County histories also often contain biographical and family sketches. Special Collections, Atlanta Public Library, 1 Margaret Mitchell Square, Atlanta, Ga. 30303, has a card index to published biographical sketches of Georgians and a separate card index to articles and biographies of black Americans. The Ga. Dept. of Archives & History is currently preparing a similar card index to biographical sketches in print in their department. The Georgia Room, University of Georgia libraries, Athens, has biographical files on important Georgians. Most college and university libraries have alumni files. Also, most nationwide compilations of biographies for special professions (such as doctors, lawyers, etc.) include Georgians.

The Georgia Archives has autobiographical questionnaires of prominent Georgians. These were first sent out in the 1920s, but some were filled out for persons who died as early as 1859 by their descendants. These questionnaires contain a great deal of genealogical information. The earliest of these records are on microfilm. The Archives Central Research Library also has index cards with individual public service records for Georgians.

• **The Directory of Georgia Biography,** a compilation of sketches of deceased persons judged by a committee of scholars to have been important to the history of Georgia, is currently being prepared for publication during Georgia's

250th birthday (1983). Each sketch will include the name of the subject's parents, spouse, children, and other genealogical information when known.

Jack N. Averitt, **Ga.'s Coastal Plain** 3 vols. (New York: Lewis Historical Pub- lihsing Co., 1964). [#3 includes family & personal information.]

Biographical Souvenir of the States of Ga. & Fla. (1889; rep. ed. Easley, S.C.: Southern Historical Press, 1976.)

Samuel Boykin, **History of the Baptist Denomination in Ga. with Biographical Compendium & Portrait Gallery of Baptist Ministers & Ga. Baptists** (1881; rep. ed. Easley, S.C.: Southern Historical Press, 1976). [Sketches of 628 Ga. Baptists.]

Sarah H. Butts, **The Mothers of Some Distinguished Georgians of the Last Half of the Century** (New York: J.J. Little & Co., 1902).

Allen D. Candler & Clement A. Evans, **Ga. Comprising Sketches of Counties, Towns, Events, Institutions, & Persons, Arranged in Cyclopedic Form**, 4 vols. (1906; rep. ed. Spartanburg: The Reprint Co., 1972). [Also known as "Cyclopedia of Ga."]

Absalom H. Chappell, **Miscellanies of Ga.; Historical, Biographical, Descrip- tive, etc.** (Columbus: Gilbert Printing Co., 1974). [On Ga. leaders of the early years of the state – rep. ed.]

Dixie Council of Authors and Journalists, **Georgia Authors** (Lithonia: the authors, 1970). [Index to 5,200 titles of 2,700 native authors, 1732-1968.]

Franklin M. Garrett, **Atlanta & Environs. A Chronicle of Its People & Events**, 3 vols. (New York: Lewis Publishing Co., 1954). [#3, not by Garrett, is a compilation of biographical sketches by & of Atlanta area people.]

George R. Gilmer, **Sketches of Some of the First Settlers of Upper Ga.** (1926; rep. ed. Baltimore: Genealogical Publishing Co., 1965). [Has sketches of families on the northern frontiers of Ga. during the decades immediately after the Amer. Revolution. Information is extremely unreliable.]

Warren Grice, **Ga. Thru Two Centuries** 3 vols. (New York: Lewis Publishing Co., 1965).

Lucian L. Knight, **A Standard History of Ga. & Georgians** 6 vols. (New York: Lewis Publishing Co., 1917).

Lucian L. Knight, **Encyclopedia of Ga. Biography** (Atlanta: A.H. Cawston, 1931).

Lucian L. Knight, **Ga.'s Bicentennial Memoirs & Memories** 2 vols. (Atlanta: the author, 1932).

Lucian L. Knight, **Reminiscences of Famous Georgians** 2 vols. (Atlanta: Franklin-Turner, 1907-1908).

Stephen E. Miller, **The Bench & Bar of Georgia** 2 vols. (Philadelphia: Lippin- cott, 1858).

Robert M. Myers, **The Children of Pride: A True Story of Ga. & the Civil War** (New Haven, Conn.: 1972).

William J. Northen, **Men of Mark in Ga.** 7 vols. (1906-1912; rep. ed. Spartanburg, S.C.: The Reprint Co., 1974). [Biographical sketches of Georgians from colonial times to early 1900s.]

Adiel Sherwood, **A Gazeteer of the State of Georgia** (Philadelphia: J.W. Martin & W.K. Boden, 1929; Washington, D.C.: P. Force, 1837; Macon: S. Boykin, 1860). [These editions of Sherwood include brief biographical sketches of the persons for whom Ga.'s counties & major towns & cities were named.]

Southern Historical Assoc., **Memoirs of Ga., Historical & Biographical** 2 vols. 1895; rep. ed. Easley, S.C.: Southern Historical Press, 1976.

NEWSPAPER ABSTRACTS – STATEWIDE

Mrs. T.F. DePourcq & Mrs. William L. Martin, Jr., "The Gospel Messenger, 1899," **Ga. Genealogical Society Quarterly** 2 (1965), pp. 221-6. [The **Gospel Messenger** was a Primitive Baptist newspaper pub. in Wilmington, N.C.]

Brent Holcomb, **Marriage & Death Notices From the Southern Christian Advocate**, vol. 1, 1837-1860 (Easley, S.C.: Southern Historical Press, 1979). [From a leading Methodist newspaper, although some Lutheran marriage & death notices are also included. Vol. II covers the years 1861-1867.]

Brent Holcomb, **Marriage & Death Notices From the Charleston Observer, 1827-1845** (Greenville, S.C.: A Press, 1980). [From a leading Presbyterian newspaper.]

Brent Holcomb, **Marriage & Death Notices From the Lutheran Observer, 1831-1861, and the Southern Lutheran, 1861-1865** (Easley, S.C.: Southern Historical Press, 1979).

Brent Holcomb has also published several books of S.C. newspaper abstracts that also cover prominent persons in Ga. For a list of these, write Southern Historical Press, Box 738, Easley, S.C. 29640.

Elizabeth T. LeMaster, **Abstracts of Ga. Death Notices From the Southern Recorder, 1830-1855** (Orange, Calif.: Orange County Genealogical Society, 1968). [Does not include 1835, although newspapers for that year were abstracted in **Ga. Genealogical Magazine**. The **Southern Recorder** was a Milledgeville, Baldwin County newspaper. Copies of this book & the one below can be ordered from Orange County Genealogical Society, Orange, Calif. 92668.]

Elizabeth T. LeMaster, **Abstracts of Marriage Notices From the Southern Recorder, 1830-1855** (Orange, Calif.: Orange County Genealogical Society, 1971).

Mary Overby & Jewell M. Lancaster, **Marriages Published in the Christian Index, 1828-1855: Abstracts** (Macon, Ga. Baptist Historical Society, 1971). [A leading Baptist newspaper.]

Mary Overby, **Obituaries Published in the Christian Index, 1822-1879** (Macon: Ga. Baptist Historical Society).

Kenneth H. Thomas, Jr., "Obituaries Abstracted From the **Masonic Journal,** 1849-1852," **Ga. Genealogical Society Quarterly** 15 (1979), pp. 129-34.

Mary B. Warren, **Marriages & Deaths, 1763-1820, Abstracted From Extant Ga. Newspapers** (Danielsville: Heritage Papers, 1968). [End with 1819.]

Mary B. Warren, **Marriages & Deaths, 1820-1830, Abstracted From Extant Ga. Newspapers** (Danielsville: Heritage Papers, 1972). [End with 1829.]

• Abstracts of marriage, death, & legal notices from several newspapers have been published in **Ga. Genealogical Magazine.** These are being edited & consolidated into a 3-vol. series to come out in late 1981.

STATE RECORDS (Also see Land Records and Tax Digests, Military Records, and Migrations)

Marilyn Adams, **A Preliminary Guide to 18th Century Records Held by the Ga. Dept. of Archives & History** (Atlanta: Ga. Dept. of Archives & History, 1976).

Robert S. Davis, Jr., "Georgia Murders, Murderers, & Murder Victims, 1823-1840," **Ga. Genealogical Society Quarterly** 15 (1979), pp. 103-15. [From governors proclamation books at the Archives, providing physical descriptions of murderers & victims' date of death.]

William H. Dumont, "Extracts From Ga. Court Records," **National Genealogical Society Quarterly** 52 (1964), pp. 199-204. [Examples of genealogical data found in 2 early vols. of Ga. superior court cases **(Ga. Decisions)** & state supreme court cases in **Ga. Reports.** Actual court case papers for the state supreme court, beginning in 1846, are at the Archives.

Carroll Hart, "Genealogical Information Found in Legislative Acts – Divorces," **Ga. Genealogical Society Quarterly** 1 (1965), pp. 9-19. [Covers 1798 to 1847. Ga. divorces could be obtained on county level after 1847, but some couples preferred obtaining divorces from the legislature for many years after.]

[John Moseley] , **Name Changes in Legislative Acts of Ga., 1800-1856** (Atlanta? 1979?).

Arthur R. Rowland, "Names Changed Legally in Ga., 1800-1856," **National Genealogical Society Quarterly** 55 (1967), pp. 177-210.

R.J. Taylor, Jr., Foundation, **Censuses for Ga. Counties** (Atlanta: R.J. Taylor, Jr., Foundation, 1979). [Includes state census returns for Chatham, Lumpkin, & Taliaferro Counties.]

R.J. Taylor, Jr. Foundation, **Index to Ga. Poor School & Academy Records, 1826-1850** (Atlanta: R.J. Taylor, Jr. Foundation, 1980). NOT INCLUDED IN THIS INDEX are poor school records in the Archives in microfilmed county records, in the loose county records, in county files – file II – Archives' Central Research, or any after 1850. Poor school and academy records often include names of students, their ages, names of parents or guardians (which sometimes include information on 2nd marriages by mothers).]

Brigid S. Townsend, **Indexes to 7 State Census Reports for Counties in Ga., 1838-1845** (Atlanta: R.J. Taylor, Jr. Foundation, 1975). [Indexes to Dooly, Forsyth, Laurens, Newton, Tattnall, & Warren Counties.]

BLACK GENEALOGY

Charles L. Brockson & Ron Fry, **Black Genealogy: How to Discover Your Own Family's Roots** (New York: Prentice-Hall, 1977).

Arthur B. Caldwell, **History of the American Negro: Ga. Edition** (Atlanta: the author, 1908). [Different editions of this book are available at the University of Ga. libraries, Athens, and Atlanta University Library.]

Microfilm Records: Black History (Atlanta: Ga. Dept. of Archives & History, 1977). [A bibliography of material on microfilm at the Archives. Researchers should also check the Negro History box, file II, in Central Research and the various catalogues to manuscript collections around the Archives.]

George P. Rawick, **The American Slave: A Composite Autobiography** 10 vols. (Westport, Conn.: Greenwood Publishing Co., 1972-1973). [#12 & 13 have Ga. slave narratives; other vols. have narratives from other states.]

Kenneth H. Thomas, "A Note on the Pitfalls of Black Genealogy: Origins of Black Surnames," **Ga. Archive** 6 (1978), pp. 22ff.

James D. Walker, **Black Genealogy: How to Begin** (Athens: University of Ga. Independent Study/WGTV, 1977).

• A Ga. organization devoted to black genealogy is the African-American Family History Assoc., c/o Carole Merritt, 2077 Bent Creek Way, SW, Atlanta, Ga. 30311.

CEMETERY, CHURCH, & BIBLE RECORDS (Statewide)

Pearl R. Baker, **'Neath Ga. Sod Cemetery Inscriptions** (Albany: Ga. Pioneers, 1970). [Includes those in Columbia, Glascock, Jefferson, Lincoln, McDuffie, Richmond, & Wilkes Counties.]

Georgia Chapters DAR, **Historical Collections** 5 vols. (1932; rep. ed. Easley, S.C.: Southern Historical Press, 1969), vol. 4. [Bible records.]

Historical Records Survey, **Inventory of Church & Synagogue Archives of Ga.** 2 vols. (Atlanta: Atlanta Association of Baptists, 1941).

Charles O. Walker, **History of the Holiness Baptist Assoc. of Ga.** (Jasper: the author, 1968). [The Holiness Assoc. has churches in Atkinson, Berrien, Coffee, Colquitt, Cook, Crisp, Decatur, Dodge, Irwin, Jeff Davis, Johnson, Lowndes, Miller, Mitchell, Pulaski, Telfair, Tift, Toombs, Treutlen, Turner, Ware, Wheeler, Wilcox, & Worth Counties.]

Caroline Wilson, **Annals of Ga.: Important Early Records of the State** 3 vols. (Savannah: Braid Hutton, 1928-1933), vol. III. [Includes cemetery records from Camden, Chatham, Effingham, Liberty, McIntosh, & some S.C. counties.]

• Central Research Library, Ga. Archives has 5 vols. of typescripts of cemetery records by Lawrence M. Edwards including cemeteries from Bryant, Bulloch,

Candler, Effingham, Emanuel, Evans, Jenkins, Liberty, Screven & Tattnall Counties.

Ga. genealogical quarterlies often publish local cemetery & Bible records. Researchers should consult back issues. The **Ga. Genealogical Society Quarterly** has devoted considerable space, sometimes entire issues, to publishing rural cemetery records. **Ga. Genealogist** has published many Bible records.

COLONIAL RECORDS (1733-1777)

Marilyn Adams, **A Preliminary Guide to 18th Century Records Held by the Ga. Dept. of Archives & History** (Atlanta: Ga. Historical Society, 1976).

Frances H. Beckemeyer, **Abstracts of Ga. Colonial Conveyance Book C-1, 1750-1761** (Atlanta: R.J. Taylor, Jr. Foundation, 1975).

Mary G. Bryan, **Abstracts of Colonial Wills of the State of Ga., 1733-1777** (Atlanta: Atlanta Town Committee of the National Society of the Colonial Dames of America, 1962).

Pat Bryant, **Entry of Claim for Ga. Land Holders, 1733-1755** (Atlanta: Ga. Surveyor General Dept., 1975).

Allen D. Candler, **The Colonial Records of the State of Ga.** 26 vols. (Atlanta: various state publishers, 1904-1916). [Ga. Archives has unpublished vols. of this series & a comprehensive index to the published vols.]

E. Merton Coulter & Albert Saye, **A List of Early Settlers of Ga.** (Athens: University of Ga. Press, 1949).

Robert S. Davis, Jr. "Lost Colonial Ga. Land Plats," **Ga. Genealogical Magazine** 75-6 (1980), pp. 78-82. [1764 list of now-lost original land surveys for which grants were not issued.]

Robert S. Davis, Jr., "Lost Ga. Land Grants, 1775 & 1778," to be published in **Ga. Genealogical Magazine**. [List of receipts for land grant fees paid for grants that were never issued.]

Robert S. Davis, Jr., **The Wilkes County Papers, 1773-1833** (Easley, S.C.: Southern Historical Press, 1979). [Includes rosters of Captain Edward Barnard's co. of provincial Ga. rangers, 1773-1775.]

William H. Dumont, **Colonial Ga. Genealogical Data, 1748-1783** (Washington, D.C.: Special Publications of the National Genealogical Society #36). [Abstracts from colonial Ga. books of reocrd.]

Georgia Surveyor General Dept., **English Crown Grants** 10 vols. (Atlanta: State Printing Office, 1972-1976). [Typescript index to all but the last vol. of this series available at Ga. Archives.]

Sarah B. Gober Temple & Kenneth Coleman, **Ga. Journeys Being An Account of the Lives of Ga.'s Original Settlers & Many Other Early Settlers . . .** (Athens: University of Ga. Press, 1961).

George F. Walker, **Abstracts of Ga. Colonial Book J, 1755-1762** (Atlanta: R.J. Taylor, Jr. Foundation, 1977).

• William L. Clements Library, University of Mich., has rosters of Ga. provincial rangers from the French & Indian War.

DOCTORS

"Board of Physicians' Minute Book, 1826-1861," **Ga. Genealogical Society Quarterly** 2 (1965), pp. 67-70. [A photostatic, indexed copy of the original record is available in the Central Research Library (shelf #G 610 G35r.)]

Medical Assoc. of Ga., **Transactions of the Medical Assoc. of Ga. 51st Session 1900** (Atlanta: the authors, 1900) [On pp. 400-21 is a list of members, residence, & years they were admitted as drs. On pp. 409-10 is a list of deceased members with information on admission. Some later vols. also carry such membership lists.]

• Ga. Archives has the original manuscript & an indexed Xerox copy in the Central Research Library of "Board of Physicians Registry of Applicants, 1826-1881" on shelf #G 610 G35r. Includes information on persons attempting to be certified by the state of Ga. as doctors, surgeons, druggists, etc. This manuscript will be published in the **Ga. Genealogical Society Quarterly**.

Emory University's medical library has copies of published proceedings of early Ga. medical associations.

GEORGIA HISTORIES (General)

Kenneth Coleman, et al., **A History of Ga.** (Athens: University of Ga. Press, 1977).

E. Merton Coulter, Ga., **A Short History** (Chapel Hill: University of N.C. Press, 1947).

Harold H. Martin, Ga., **A Bicentennial History** (New York: W.W. Norton & Co., Inc., 1977). Basic, lively, & general history of Ga.

GOLDMINERS

Marilyn Adams, **Censuses for Ga. Counties** (Atlanta: R.J. Taylor, Jr. Foundation, 1979). [Contains a fragment of the 1838 state census of Lumpkin Co.]

Mary Dean Allsworth, **Gleanings From Alta, California: Marriages and Deaths Reported in the First Newspaper Published in California, 1846-1850** (Rancho Cordova, Calif.: Dean Pub. Co., 1980). [Includes obituaries of many men who went to California during the Gold Rush and committed suicide there.]

E. Merton Coulter, **Auraria: Story of a Ga. Gold Mining Town** (Athens: University of Ga. Press, 1956).

Carroll Hart & Betty Willis, "California Census of 1852," **Ga. Genealogical Society Quarterly** 4 (1968), #6, and 10 (1974), #2. [Census of Georgians in Calif. during the gold rush. Ga. Archives has a microfilm copy of the original census.]

"1834 Census for the State of Georgia, Lumpkin Co.," **NW Ga. Historical & Genealogical Society Quarterly** 12 (1980), #3, pp. 10-6.

Gold Placers of the Vicinity of Dahlonega, Ga. (Boston: n.p., 1859). Available on microfilm reel 186-41, Ga. Archives.

INDIAN RECORDS

"Cherokee Biographies," **Ga. Genealogical Society Quarterly** 9 (1973), pp. 95-6. [From **Macon Telegraph** 2/18/1832, p. 2.]

"Cherokee Indian Land Reserves, 1817," **Ga. Genealogical Society Quarterly** 9 (1973), p. 237.

"Ga. Cherokee Indian Citizenship Act, 1838," **Ga. Genealogical Society Quarterly** 8 (1972), p. 260. [Cherokees made citizens of the state of Ga.]

David K. Hampton, **Cherokee Reserves,** (Oklahoma City: Baker Publishing Co., 1980). [Census-like information on Cherokees who settled in Oklahoma under the treaties of 1817 & 1818.]

James Puckett, "Cherokee Indian Agency Persons Baptized by Evan C. Jones in the Cherokee Nation," **Ga. Genealogical Society Quarterly** 5 (1969), p. 225.

James Puckett, "1832 Creek Census of the Lower Towns — Abbott," **Ga. Genealogical Society Quarterly** 8 (1972), pp. 177-205.

James Puckett, "1832 Creek Census of the Upper Towns — Parsons," **Ga. Genealogical Society Quarterly** 8 (1972), pp. 111-53.

Ga. Genealogical Society Quarterly 3 (1967), #3. Special issue by James M. Puckett on the Creeks & Cherokees. [Includes census of white men with Indian families (1830), census of Creeks (1833), & census of Cherokees (1835).]

David W. Siler, **The Eastern Cherokees: A Census of the Cherokee Nation in N.C., Tenn., Ala., & Ga. in 1851** (Cottonport: Polyanthos Press, 1972).

Emmet Starr, **Old Cherokee Families** (Norman: University of Okla. Foundation, 1968).

Mary Warren, **Marriages & Deaths, 1820-1830, Abstracted From Extant Ga. Newspapers** (Danielsville: Heritage Papers, 1972). [Includes genealogical data from the **Cherokee Phoenix** up to & incl. 1829. More information from this paper was pub. in Mary Warren's **Ga. Genealogist** #9 (winter 1972), pp. 1-4.]

Mrs. Raymond H. Whitehead, **Genealogical History of Original Murray Co., Ga.** 2 vols. (Atlanta: the author, 1972). [In #1, pp. 79-82 is "Whites Living Among the Indians, 1838."]

• Office of Indian Affairs, Ga. Archives, is currently preparing a list of Indian sources available at the Archives.

Articles on the history of Cherokees are published in **Journal of Cherokee Studies,** Museum Complex, Box 770-A, Cherokee, N.C. 28719.

LAND RECORDS & TAX DIGESTS (Also see Colonial Records)

Ruth Blair, **Some Early Tax Digests of Ga.** (1926; rep. ed. Easley, S.C.: Southern Historical Press, 1971). [Includes early digests for Camden, Chatham,

Glynn, Hancock, Lincoln, Montgomery, Pulaski, Richmond, Warren, & Wilkes Counties. Complete transcripts of information.]

Silas E. Lucas, Jr., **Index to the Headright and Bounty Grants of Ga., 1756-1909** (Easley, S.C.: Southern Historical Press, 1970).

Douglas C. Wilms, "Ga.'s Land Lottery of 1832," **Chronicles of Oklahoma** 52 (1974), pp. 52-60.

• Books on Ga. land lottery records are listed in Chapter 10.

LOYALISTS

Allen D. Candler, **The Revolutionary Records of the State of Ga.** 3 vols. (Atlanta: Franklin-Turner, 1908). [Archives has typescript comprehensive index to this series.]

Murtie June Clark, **Loyalists in the Southern Campaign,** 1 vol. to date (Baltimore: Genealogical Publishing Co., 1980).

Peter Wilson Coldham, **American Loyalist Claims** (Washington, D.C.: National Genealogical Society, Special Publications, no. 45, 1980), vol. 1. First in a series of books of abstracts of Loyalist claims for all of the original thirteen colonies.

Robert S. Davis, Jr., **Ga. Citizens & Soldiers of the Amer. Revolution** (Easley, S.C.: Southern Historical Press, 1979).

John B. Ellis, "List of Loyalists from Ga. Who Settled in Jamaica," **New England Historical & Genealogical Register** 52 (1908), pp. 300-1.

Ga. Genealogist, #3, pp. 1-4; #4, pp. 5-8; #5, p. 9-14; #7, pp. 15-22. [Includes list of Loyalists who moved to British E. Florida from Ga.]

Beatrice Lang, "The 1783 Spanish Census of Fla.," **Ga. Genealogical Magazine** (1971) #39, pp. 49-76; #40, pp. 177-90; #41, pp. 315-26; #42, pp. 449-56. [Census that provides name, place of birth, occupation & other information on Loyalists living in Fla. after Spanish takeover in 1783.]

Lydia Austin Parrish, "Records of Some Southern Loyalists," **Ga. Genealogical Society Quarterly** 8 (1972), pp. 272-3. [List of 80 Loyalists who settled in the Bahamas after the Amer. Revolution. The unfinished Parrish dissertation, to which this list serves as an index, is available on microfilm reel 12-1 at the Ga. Archives.]

Meckler Publishing, 654 Madison Ave., New York, N.Y. 10021, has announced that they will be publishing in 1981 Bibliography of Loyalist Source Material in the United States, Canada, and Great Britain and Greg Palmer, **Biographical Sketches of American Loyalists.**

• The Archives has a microfilm copy of a few pages from each Ga. Loyalist claim. More complete copies may be requested for interlibrary loan from the Public Archives of Canada.

Heard Robertson of Augusta is currently preparing for publication a book on the Loyalists of frontier Ga., and the R.J. Taylor, Jr. Foundation is preparing an index to the Loyalist confiscation records in Conveyance Book BBB & elsewhere at the Archives.

Many compilations of Loyalist materials for all of the colonies are currently being prepared for publication. Researchers should consult lists of books in print available at major libraries.

An international organization of descendants of Loyalists is the United Empire Loyalists Assoc., 23 Prince Arthur Ave., Toronto, Canada M5R 1B2.

MARRIAGE & ESTATE RECORDS FROM COUNTY RECORDS

Ted O. Brooke, **In the Name of God, Amen: Ga. Wills, 1733-1860: An Index** (Marietta: the author, 1976). [Author planning 2nd vol. for period up to 1900.]

Mary Carter, **Early Ga. Marriages, Book 4** (Albany: **Ga. Pioneers,** 1980). [Covers Carroll, Cherokee, Clayton, Floyd, Marion, Morgan, Murray, Tattnall, Wayne, & Wilkes Counties.]

Joseph T. Maddox & Mary Carter, **37,000 Early Ga. Marriages** (Albany: the authors, 1975). [From Baldwin, Bulloch, Bartow (Cass), Columbia, Crawford, Emanuel, Fayette, Franklin, Gilmer, Henry, Jackson, Jones, Lincoln, Madison, Monroe, Montgomery, Muscogee, Pike, Putnam, Screven, Talbot, Taliaferro, Troup, Union & Warren Counties.]

Joseph T. Maddox & Mary Carter, **40,000 Early Ga. Marriage Records** (Albany: the authors, 1976). [From Bibb, Butts, Clarke, Coweta, Crawford, Decatur, DeKalb, Elbert, Greene, Hancock, Harris, Laurens, Liberty, Newton, Oglethorpe, Pulaski, Richmond, Telfair, Warren (earlier marriages than in the other vol.), Washington, & Wilkinson Counties and of the early Saltzburgers.]

Joseph T. Maddox & Mary Carter, **Early Ga. Marriage Roundup** (Albany: the authors, 1977). [From Brooks, Camden, Chatham, Crawford, Dooly, Forsyth, Glynn, Hall, Houston, Irwin, Johnson, Lumpkin, Macon, Randolph, Stewart, Sumter, & Walton Counties.]

• Mary Warren published **Ga. marriages for 1800 thru 1810** in issues #13-24 of **Ga. Genealogist.**

MIGRATIONS

Howard Askew, "1850 Census of Texas Persons Born in Ga.," **Ga. Genealogical Society Quarterly** 8 (1972), pp. 1-62.

Jane A. Beard, **Births, Deaths and Marriages From El Paso Newspapers** (Easley: Southern Historical Press, 1981). [Includes death notices of many people who went West in 1880-1900 for their health and died there.

Mary G. Bryan, "Camden County Archives," **Nat'l. Genealogical Society Quarterly** 43 (1955), pp. 11-4. [Includes list of persons in "Affidavits made by owners bringing slaves into the state, 1818-1847."]

Mary G. Bryan, **Passports Issued by Ga. Governors, 1785-1809** (Washington, D.C.: Nat'l. Genealogical Society, 1959) and **Passports Issued by Ga. Governors, 1810-1820** (same publisher, 1964). [Publication of typescript in Ga. Archives by Louise F. Hays, but published by Mary G. Bryan. These records show migrations of Georgians to other parts of the country. Originals are in the Archives.]

Caroline Cunningham, **Migrations Actual & Implied**, vol. 1 (Raleigh: the author, 1968). [Information on migrations from N.C. to Ga.]

Robert S. Davis, Jr., "Birth States of Federal Employees in Ga., 1816 & 1820," to be published in **Ga. Genealogical Magazine.** [Taken from the **Official Register** of federal employees & includes local postmasters.]

William H. Dumont, "Through Richmond Co., Ga., Importers of Slaves," **Nat'l. Genealogical Society Quarterly** 58 (1970), pp. 31-51.

Genealogical Enterprises, **Immigrants From Great Britain to the Ga. Colony** (Morrow: author, 1970).

"Indentured Servants," **Ga. Genealogical Society Quarterly** 7 (1971), pp. 118-119. [Thomas Brown's indentured servants from the Orkney Islands of Scotland & their settlement in Ceded Lands of Ga.]

"Whitfield Co. Emigrations — 1870," **Ga. Genealogical Society Quarterly** 7 (1971), pp. 109-11. [Petition signed by foreign born persons living in Whitfield, giving places of birth.]

Charles H. Hamlin, **They Went Thataway** (Baltimore: Genealogical Pub. Co., 1974). [Information on migrations from Va. to Ga.]

James M. Puckett, Jr., "Colonel William Wofford's Report on the Wofford Settlement," **Ga. Genealogical Society Quarterly** 2 (1965), pp. 65-6.

Jean Stephenson, **Scotch-Irish Migration to S.C. Rev. William Martin & His 5 Shiploads of Immigrants** (Washington, D.C.: the author, 1971).

William C. Stewart, **Gone to Ga.: Jackson & Gwinnett Counties & Their Neighbors in the Western Migration** (Washington, D.C.: Nat'l. Genealogical Society, 1965).

• Records of migrations to Ga. from other states are regularly published in **Ga. Genealogical Magazine, Va. Genealogist, & N.C. Carolina Genealogical Society Journal.** Researchers should consult back issues. The Southern Historical Press publishes late 19th & early 20th century compilations of biographical sketches for Texas, Ark., Tenn. & other states that contain family information on migrations from Ga.

MILITARY RECORDS – COLONIAL (See Colonial Records)

MILITARY RECORDS – REVOLUTIONARY WAR

Ruth Blair, **Revolutionary War Soldiers Receipts for Ga. Bounty Grants** (Atlanta: Foote & Davies, 1928). [Original manuscript from which this book was compiled is now in the Ga. Surveyor General Dept.]

Allen D. Candler, **The Revolutionary Records of the State of Ga.** 3 vols. (Atlanta: Franklin Turner Co., 1908). [Archives has a typescript comprehensive index to this series.]

Mary Carter, **Ga. Revolutionary Soldiers, Sailors, Patriots & Descendants** 2 vols. (Albany: Ga. Pioneers, 1976).

Robert S. Davis, Jr., **Ga. Citizens & Soldiers of the Amer. Revolution** (Easley, S.C.: Southern Historical Press, 1979). [Includes detailed guide to sources in Ga. for information on Revolutionary War service.]

William H. Dumont, "Some Revolutionary Soldiers & Their Heirs," **New England Historical & Genealogical Register** 64 (1960), pp. 191-3. [Heirs of continental soldiers who served in Ga. & S.C. units; similar list for N.C. was pub. in **The North Carolinian**, vol. 4 #4, pp. 484-6; list for Va. continentals is in **The Va. Genealogist**, vol. 2, pp. 147-56 and vol. 2, pp. 28-32.]

Alex M. Hitz, **Authentic List of All Land Lottery Grants Made to Vets. of Revol. War by Ga.** (Atlanta: Secty./State, 1966).

Wanda Hoffer, "Marked Graves of Revolutionary Soldiers & Patriots Buried in Ga. (NSDAR)," **Ga. Genealogical Society Quarterly** 8 (1972), pp. 211-22.

Mrs. J.M. Julich, **A Roster of Revolutionary Soldiers & Patriots in Ala.** (Decatur, Ala.: the author, 1979).

Lucian L. Knight, **Georgia's Roster of the Revolution** (1920 rep. ed. Baltimore: Genealogical Pub. Co., 1970). [Many of the original certificates used in this book have since been lost.]

Hugh McCall, **The History of Ga., 1811-1816;** (rep. ed. Covington: Cherokee Pub. Co., 1968).

Philip W. McMullin, **Grassroots of America: A Computerized Index to the American State Papers: Land Grants & Claims (1789-1837) With Other Aids to Research** (Salt Lake City: Gendex Corp., 1972). [The **American State Papers** contain considerable information on federal bounty grants given to continental soldiers. The Archives has all the land claims books of this series except vols. 2 & 5, which they may soon receive from the State Library of Ga. The only complete set in Ga. is at the Government Documents Center, Woodruff Library, Emory Univ.]

National Genealogical Society, **Index of Revolutionary War Pension Applicants in the Nat'l. Archives** (2nd ed., Washington, D.C.: National Genealogical Society, 1976).

Gwen B. Neumann & Helen M. Lu, **Revolutionary War Period Bible, Family & Marriage Records, Gleaned From Pension Applications** (Dallas: the authors, 1980), vol. 1.

John Pierce, **Pierce's Register; Register of Certificates Issued by John Pierce, Esquire, Paymaster General & Commissioner of any Accounts for the U.S. to Officers & Soldiers of the Continental Army Under Act of July 4, 1783** (1915; rep. ed. Baltimore: Genealogical Pub. Co., 1973).

Caroline P. Wilson, **Annals of Ga.; Important Early Records of the State** 2 vols. (1928-1933; rep. ed. (Easley, S.C.: Southern Historical Press, 1968). [Vol. 1 includes a Ga. Revolutionary War public accounts list.]

MILITARY RECORDS – LATER WARS

Irwin R. Berent, "Georgians Crewed the Virginia," **Ga. Genealogical Society Quarterly** 15 (1979), pp. 123-7. [Georgians who served on the Civil War ironclad **CSS Virginia** (formerly the **USS Merrimac**).]

Bert E. Boss, **The Ga. State Memorial Book** (Atlanta: Amer. Memorial pub. Co., 1921). [Photos and data, by county, of Georgians killed in WWI.]

Southern Historical Press, **Ga. State Civil War Pension Index** 5 vols. (Easley, S.C.: Southern Historical Press, 1981). [List of Confederate pensioners in Ga. to be published in late 1981.]

Franklin County Chapter, Ohio Genealogical Society, **Confederate Cemeteries in Ohio** (Columbus, Ohio: the authors, 1980), vol. 1.

James E. Garman, "Materials for the Writing of Histories of Ga. Confederate Regiments," (Masters Thesis, Emory University, 1961).

"List of Ga. Pensioners on the U.S. Rolls, Jan. 1, 1883," **Ga. Genealogical Society Quarterly** 15 (1979), pp. 169-200. [Includes pensioners for the War of 1812, Mexican War, Indian Wars, & Union forces during the Civil War.]

"Index to Names in Capt. William Jones' Letters & Orderly Book, 1812-1821," **Ga. Genealogical Society Quarterly** 15 (1979), pp. 166-8. [Ga. Archives has the original Jones records, which include name, place of birth, age, occupation & other information on some recruits from Chatham, Elbert & Richmond Counties.]

Lillian Henderson, **Roster of the Confederate Soldiers of Ga., 1861-1865** 6 vols. (Atlanta: State Printing Office, 1959-1964). [Only includes rosters for volunteer infantry units.]

Lucy K. McGhee, **Ga. Pension List of All Wars From the Revolution Down to 1883** (Washington, D.C.: the author, 1962).

Joseph M. Toomey, **Ga.'s Participation in the World War & the History of the Dept. of Ga., the Amer. Legion** (Macon: J.W. Burke Co., 1936). [Information on Georgians in World War I.]

June Hart Wester, "List of Volunteer Union Soldiers of Ga.," **Ga. Genealogical Society Quarterly** 15 (1979), pp. 83-6. [List of north Georgians in the Ga. Battalion, U.S. Army, during the Civil War.]

• Ga.'s genealogical periodicals often publish rosters of local military units for the Civil War or earlier plus individual pension & service records. Researchers should consult back issues.

The Nat'l. Archives has the "Register of Enlistments in the U.S. Army, 1798-1913" providing name, place of birth, place of enlistment, age, & other information on volunteers. Although these records have been for sale, on microfilm, from the Nat'l. Archives, no set of this microfilm is available in Ga. See Jean Stephenson, "1812 Enlistment Records As Source for Age and Birthplace," **National Genealogical Society Quarterly** 51 (1963), pp. 108-9.

For other military records from the Nat'l. Archives, pre-WWI compiled service records & pensions, write to Military Service Records (NNCC), Washington, D.C. 20408. For information on WWI or later military service, write to National Personnel Service Records Center, GSA, (Military Records), 9700 Page Blvd., St. Louis, Mo. 63132. Some such records on the county level are available in the Archives' Microfilm Library.

MISCELLANEOUS

A list of Masonic officers in Ga. from 1733-1859 was published in **Ga. Genealogist**, #14, pp. 332-46.

Historical Records Survey, **Guide to Public Vital Statistics Records in Ga.** (Atlanta: the author, 1941).

The Office & Duty of a Justice of the Peace (Milledgeville, Ga., 1819). [Includes a county-by-county list of subscribers that includes many prominent Georgians. This list has been published by Mary Warren in **Ga. Genealogist** under "State Records." A copy of the original book is available at the University of Ga. libraries.]

Mrs. William W. Peel, **Historical Collections of the Joseph Habersham Chapter of the DAR** 3 vols. (1902-1910; rep. ed. Baltimore: Genealogical Pub. Co., 1967). [Vols. 1 & 2 are compilations of genealogical queries in early 20th century issues of **The Atlanta Constitution.**]

James M. Puckett, Jr., "Ga. Mail Contractors, 1839," **Ga. Genealogical Society Quarterly** 7 (1971), pp. 112.

Moses Waddel, **A Register of Marriages Celebrated and Solemnized by Moses Waddel in S.C. & Ga., 1795-1836** (Danielsville: Heritage Papers, 1967).

• Ga. Archives has a typescript by Kirby-Smith Anderson, "Taverns & Inns of early Ga." (1939).

NATURALIZATIONS

"Chatham County Naturalization Papers, 1828-1906," **Ga. Genealogical Society Quarterly** 9 (1973), pp. 205-17.

"Naturalization Records on Microfilm in the Ga. Dept. of Archives & History," and "Chatham County, Ga. Naturalization Papers (loose), 1828-1906," **Ga. Genealogical Society Quarterly** 15 (1979), pp. 69-82.

Marion R. Hemperley, "Federal Naturalization Oaths, Savannah, Ga., 1790-1860," **Ga. Historical Quarterly** 51 (1967), pp. 454-87.

June Hart Wester, "Naturalizations, Irwin, Co., Ga., 1827-1847," **Ga. Genealogical Society Quarterly** 15 (1979), pp. 117-22. [Naturalization oaths by Irishmen. From the superior court minutes.]

• Naturalizations have also been published in **Ga. Genealogist**. Ga. Archives has a typescript by Marion R. Hemperley, "Federal Naturalization Oaths, Charleston, S.C., 1790-1860."

COUNTY – SPECIFIC WORKS
Appling

Folks Huxford, **Pioneers of Wiregrass Ga.: A Biographical Account of . . .** the Original Counties of Irwin, Appling, Wayne, Camden, & Glynn 7 vols. (Adel: Patten Pub. Co., 1951-1975).

• A new Appling County history is being prepared for pub. by Taylor Pub. Co. Ga. Archives has H.J. Laurens, "Book of Genealogies, Appling Co.," on microfilm reel 21-3.

Bacon

Bonnie T. Baker, **Short History of Alma & Bacon County** (Alma: the author, 1977).

Bonnie T. Baker, **History of Camp Ground United Methodist Church** (Alma: Historical Society of Alma-Bacon County, 1979).

• A new Baker County history is being prepared for pub. by Taylor Pub. Co.

Baldwin

Leola Beeson, **Historical Sketch of the 1st Presbyterian Church of Milledge-ville, Ga.** (Milledgeville, 1955).

James C. Bonner, **Milledgeville, Ga.'s Antebellum Capitol** (Athens: Univ. of Ga. Press, 1978).

Anna Marie Cook, **History of Baldwin Co., Ga.** (1925; rep. ed., Spartanburg: Reprint Co., 1978).

Delwyn Associates, **Records of Baldwin Co., Ga.** (Albany: authors, 1975).

Ga. Chapters DAR, **Historical Collections**, 5 vols. (1926; rep. ed. Southern Historical Press, 1968). vol. I, pp. 1-10. [List of wills & marriage records.]

Nelle Hines, **Such Goings On** (Macon: J.W. Burke Co., 1958).

Walter M. Lee, **History of the 1st Baptist Church of Milledgeville, Ga.** (Milledge-ville: n.p.)

• On the oversize shelf of the county histories section of the Archives, there is a scrapbook of obituaries from the Milledgeville area, 1860-1890.

Banks

Jessie J. Mize, **History of Banks Co., Ga., 1858-1876** (Homer: Banks Co. Chamber of Commerce, 1977).

Barrow

Barrow County Historical Society, **Beadland to Barrow: A History of Barrow Co.** (Atlanta: Cherokee Pub. Co., 1978).

• A new pictorial history of Barrow Co. is being prepared for pub. by Taylor Pub. Co.

Bartow

Lucy J. Cunyus, **History of Bartow Co., Formerly Cass** (1933; rep. ed. Easley, S.C.: Southern Historical Press, 1976).

Cartersville Centennial Committee, **Cartersville Centennial, 1872-1972** (Cartersville: the authors, 1972).

Joseph B. Mahan, "A History of Old Cassville, 1833-1864," (Masters Thesis, Univ. of Ga., 1950).

James A. Sartain, **History of the Coosa Baptist Assoc.: at the 100th Session Held at Peavine Baptist Church near Rock Spring, Ga., on Aug. 5 & 6, 1936** (n.p., 1935?).

Ben Hill

Jay Shrader, **New Canaan! Fitzgerald & the Old Soldier Colony in Irwin Co., Ga., as Seen by an Outsider** (1896; Fitzgerald: Diamond Jubilee, 1971).

• Ga. Archives has copies of the series of articles "History of Ben Hill Co." by Isidor Gelders & Maud Gelders and a similar series on "History of Fitzgerald." These are bound & in the Central Research Library.

Berrien

Berrien Co. Historical Committee, **Historical Notes — Berrien Co., 1856-1956** (Adel: the authors, 1956).

Berrien Co. Chamber of Commerce, **History of Berrien Co.** (Nashville: Nashville Printing & Office Sply. Co., 1979).

Bibb

John C. Butler, **Historical Record of Macon & Central Ga., Containing Many Interesting & Valuable Reminiscences Connected With the Whole State** (1879; rep. ed. Macon: J.W. Burke Co., 1958).

Bessie L. Hart, **Pastors of Mulberry, 1826-1964** (Macon: Southern Press, 1965). [Methodist church.]

Oliver J. Hart, **The History of Christ Church Parish, Macon, Ga., March 5th, 1825-March 5th, 1925** (Macon: Lyon, Harris & Brooks, 1925). [Episcopal.]

Marion R. Hemperley, **Records of the Town of Macon & the Public Reserve at Macon** (Atlanta: Surveyor General Dept., 1971). [Guide to records in the Sur. Gen. Dept. relating to Macon and the Macon Reserve.]

William T. Jenkins, "Ante-Bellum Macon & Bibb Co., Ga.," (Ph.D. diss., Univ. of Ga., 1966).

Paul M. Johnson, "The Negro in Macon, Ga., 1865-1871," (Masters Thesis, Univ. of Ga., 1972).

Silas E. Lucas, Jr., **Some Ga. County Records** 3 vols. (Easley, S.C.: Southern Historical Press, 1978), vol. 3, pp. 1-29). [Marr. records & wills.]

C.B. McCook, **Remembering Lizella** (Lizella: the author, 1973).

Eleanor D. McSwain, **The Founding Fathers of Bibb & the Town of Macon, Ga., 1823, Short Biographical Sketches of the Men Involved** (Macon: Nat'l. Printing Co., 1977).

Jean S. Willingham & Berthenia C. Smith, **Bibb Co., Ga.: Early Wills & Cemetery Records** (Macon: the authors, 1961).

Ida Young et al., **History of Macon, Ga.** (Macon: Marshall & Brooks, 1950).

• Ga. Archives has a typescript by the Bartow, Fl. Chapter DAR, "Some Genealogical Notes Taken From Early Newspapers of Macon, Bibb Co., Ga.," (1955).

Bleckley

Bleckley Co. Elementary School, **Cemetery Survey of Bleckley Co., Ga.** (the author, 1977).

Cochran-Bleckley Centennial, **"Centi-Rama" Journal 1869-1969** (n.p., 1969).

Virginia S. Harris, **History of Pulaski & Bleckley Cos., Ga., 1808-1956** 2 vols. (Macon: J.W. Burke Co., 1957-1958).

• Ga. Archives has W.M. Lee, "Historical Sketch of Cochran, Ga., & the Baptists of Bleckley County," on microfilm reel 240-30.

Brooks

Folks Huxford, **History of Brooks Co., Ga.** (1948; rep. ed., Spartanburg, S.C.: The Reprint Co., 1978).

Folks Huxford, **Excerpts From the Quitman Reporter, 1874-1877** (Homerville: the author, 1947).

Alton J. Murray, **South Ga. Rebels: The True Wartime Experiences of the 26th Regiment, Ga. Vol. Inf.** (St. Mary's: the author, 1976).

Quitman Chapter, UDC, **Historic Treasures of Brooks Co.** (Quitman: Quitman Pub. Co., 1974).

Bryan

Mrs. William Lawson Peel, **Historical Collections of the Joseph Habersham Chapter DAR** 3 vols. (1913; rep. ed. Easley, S.C.: Southern Historical Press, 1968). [Vol. 3, pp. 7-13 includes list of jurors, 1795-1797 & deeds, 1793-1850.]

Caroline P. Wilson, **Abstracts of Court Records of Bryan Co., Ga.** (Savannah: Lachlan McIntosh Chapter, DAR, 1929). [Covers 1799 to 1805.]

• Ga. Archives has Ben Green Cooper, "History of Bryan Co., Ga." on microfilm reel 240-30.

Bulloch

Archibald Bulloch Chapter DAR, **Eastside Cemetery, Statesboro, Bulloch Co., Ga.** (Statesboro: the authors, 1976?).

Brooks & Leodel Coleman, **Story of Bulloch Co.** (Statesboro: Bulloch Co. Historical Society, 1973).

Leodel Coleman, **Statesboro: 1866-1966: A Century of Progress** (Statesboro: Bulloch Herald Pub. Co., 1969).

Ga. DAR, **Historical Collections** 4 vols. (1926; rep. ed. Easley, S.C.: Southern Historical Press, 1968) [Vol. 1, pp. 10-15 lists returns for administrators & guardians.]

Alvaretta K. Register, **Marriage Records of Bulloch Co., Ga., 1796 (Origin of Co.) thru 1875** (Norfolk: the author, 1971).

Statesboro Regional Library System, **Bulloch Co. Bibliography: A List of Materials Avail. at the Statesboro Reg. Lib., March 9, 1976** (Statesboro: the author, 1976).

Statesboro Regional Library System, **(Same as previous title, March 1, 1976)** (Statesboro, the author, 1976).

Caroline P. Wilson, **Annals of Ga.; Important Early Records of the State** 2 vols. (1933; rep. ed. Easley, S.C.: Southern Historical Press, 1969). [Vol. 2, pp. 159-70, includes signatures to deeds, 1797-1813; marriages, 1795-1842.]

Burke

Alden Associations, **Jefferson-Burke Co., Ga.: Early Records** (Albany: the authors, 1965).

Nell Baldwin & Robert H. Hillhouse, **An Intelligent Student's Guide to Burke Co. History** (Waynesboro: the authors, 1956). [Dr. Hillhouse is working on a greatly expanded ed. of this book.]

Pat Bryant, **English Crown Grants in St. Georgia Parish in Ga., 1755-1775** (Atlanta: State Printing Off., 1974).

Pat Bryant, **English Crown Grants for Islands in Ga., 1755-1775** (Atlanta: State Printing Off., 1972).

"The Burke County Sharpeshooters," **Confederate Veteran** 32 (1924), pp. 464-6.

Robert S. Davis, Jr., **The Families of Burke Co., 1755-1855, a Census** (Easley, S.C.: Southern Historical Press, 1980).

James E. Dorsey, **Midville, Ga., 1884-1900: A Collection of Newspaper Sources** (Swainsboro: Emanuel Community College Library, 1979).

Mrs. William L. Peel, **Historical Collections of the Joseph Habersham Chapter DAR** 3 vols. (1928; rep. ed. Easley S.C.: Southern Historical Press, 1968). [Vol. 3, pp. 13-5 lists wills, 1853-1870; and marr. contracts, 1843-1845.]

Lillian L. Powell, Dorothy C. Odom & Albert M. Hillhouse, **Grave Markers in Burke Co., Ga., with 39 Cemeteries in 4 Adjoining Counties** (Waynesboro: Chalker Pub. Co., 1974).

Butts

Silas E. Lucas, Jr., **Some Georgia Co. Records** 3 vols. (Easley, S.C.: Southern Historical Press, 1978). [Vol. 3, pp. 30-146, includes deeds, 1825-1828; wills & admin. of estates, 1826-1841; marr., 1826-1881.]

Lois McMichael, **History of Butts Co., Ga., 1825-1976** (Atlanta: Cherokee Pub. Co., 1978).

Camden

Pat Bryant, **English Crown Grants for Islands in Ga., 1755-1775** (Atlanta: State Printing Off., 1972).

Mamie L. Gross, **Early Baptist Churches of the 1800s of Camden Co.** (n.p., 1970).

Marion R. Hemperley, **English Crown Grants for Parishes of St. David, St. Patrick, St. Thomas, & St. Mary in Ga., 1755-1775** (Atlanta: State Printing Off., 1973).

Folks Huxford, **Pioneers of Wiregrass Ga. A Biographical Account of the Original Co. of Irwin, Appling, Wayne, Camden, & Glynn** 7 vols. (Adel: Patten Pub. Co., 1951-1975).

Alton J. Murray, **South Ga. Rebels: The True Wartime Experiences of the 26th Reg., Ga. Vol. Inf.** (St. Mary's: the author, 1976).

Mrs. William Lawson Peel, **Historical Collections of the Joseph Habersham Chapter DAR** 3 vols. (1928; rep. ed. Easley, S.C.: Southern Historical Press, 1968). [Vol. 3, pp. 15-24, includes lists of wills & admin., 1791-1827; jurors & inhabitants, 1794; marriages, 1796-1797 & 1819-1831.]

Marguerite Reddick, **Camden's Challenge: A History of Camden Co., Ga.** (Woodbine: Camden Co. Historical Comm., 1976).

Shirley J. Thompson, **History of Oak Grove Baptist Church, Camden Co., Ga.** (Jacksonville, Fl.: author, 1980). [List of marr. going back to 1841.]

James T. Vocelle, **History of Camden Co., Ga.** (Kingsland: SE Georgian, 1967).

Caroline P. Wilson, **Annals of Ga.: Important Early Records of the State** 2 vols. (1928-1933; rep. ed. Easley, S.C.: Southern Historical Press, 1969). [Vol. 2, pp. 172-3, lists early marr. Original edition of this work pub. by Braid & Hutton, 1928-1933, has cemetery records in vol. 3, pp. 270-7.]

Woodbine Women's Club, **Pen Portraits Stories of Camden Women & Their families, Also Other Autobiographies, Articles & Interesting Pictures** (Kingsland: SE Georgian, 1969).

• Ga. Archives has following typescripts: "St. Mary's, Camden Co., Ga. Oak Grove Cemetery Inscriptions" (1953); Folks Huxford, "Genealogical Extracts From Public Records of Camden Co., Ga." and "Camden Co. List of Free Persons of Color, 1818." Special Collections, Univ. of Ga. lib. has a 1792 Camden Co. voters list.

Campbell

Nancy Jones Cornell, **Campbell Co., Ga., Marriage Book A, 1829-1842** (Riverdale: the author, 1980). [Copies can be ordered from the author at 1661 Lauranceae Way, Riverdale, Ga. 30296.]

Carroll

Mary T. Anderson, **History of Villa Rica, City of Gold** (Villa Rica: author, 1976).

James C. Bonner, **Ga.'s Last Frontier: the Development of Carroll Co.** (Athens: Univ. of Ga. Press, 1971).

Private Joe Cobb, **Carroll Co. & Her People** (n.p., 1907).

Jessie B. Digby, **Bowden Has a Centennial** (Bowden: Bowden Bulletin, 1954).

Mr. & Mrs. Alton W. Earnest, **Mt. Zion United Methodist Church Cemetery** (Mt. Zion: the authors, 1980).

William Wyatt Givens, **Cen. History of Carrollton Baptist Assoc., 1873-1973** (Carrollton: Car. Bapt. Assoc., 1974).

Buell W. Holder et al., **Historical Sketch of Temple** (Carrollton: Thomason Print. Co., 1976).

Leon P. Mandeville, **History of Carroll Co. Ga.** (Carrollton, 1910?).

• Ga. Archives has vol. 1 (1968) of **The Carroll Historical Quarterly.**

Catoosa

William H.H. Clark, **History in Catoosa Co.** (n.p., 1972).

Susie B. McDaniel, **Official History of Catoosa Co., Ga., 1853-1953** (Dalton: Gregory Printing & Off. Sply., 1953).

Charlton

Charlton Co. Historical Commission, **Charlton Co., Ga.: Historical Notes, 1972** (n.p., 1972).

Alexander S. McQueen, **History of Charlton Co.** (1932; rep. ed. Spartanburg, S.C.: Reprint Co., 1978).

Lois B. Mays, **Settlers of the Okefenokee** (Folkston: Okefenokee Press, 1975).

Alton J. Murray, **S. Ga. Rebels: True Wartime Experiences of 26th Reg., Ga. Vol. Inf.** (St. Mary's: author, 1976).

Chatham

Lowry Axley, **Holding Aloft the Torch: A History of the Independent Presbyterian Church of Savannah, Ga.** (Savannah: author, 1958).

Pat Bryant, **English Crown Grants for Islands in Ga., 1755-1775** (Atlanta: State Print. Off., 1972).

Adelaide L. Fries, **Moravians in Ga., 1735-1740** (Raleigh, N.C.: Edwards & Broughton Printing, 1905).

Ga. Historical Society, **The 1860 Census of Chatham Co., Ga.** (Ealsey, S.C.: Southern Historical Press, 1980).

Pearl R. Gnann, **Ga. Salzburger & Allied Families** (1956; rep. ed. with additions, Southern Historical Press, 1976).

William Harden, **History of Savannah & S. Ga.** (Atlanta: Cherokee Pub. Co., 1969). [Reprint, vol. 1 of 1913 ed.]

Marion R. Hemperley, **English Crown Grants in Christ Church Parish in Ga., 1755-1775** (Atlanta: State Print. Off., 1973).

Marion R. Hemperley, **English Crown Grants in St. Philip Parish in Ga., 1755-1775** (Atlanta: State Print Off., 1972).

Historical Records Survey, **Inventory of County Archives of Ga. – Chatham Co. (Savannah)** (Atlanta: the author, 1940).

Mabel F. LaFar & Caroline P. Wilson, **Abstracts of Wills, Chatham Co., Ga.** (Washington, D.C.: National Genealogical Society, 1936). [Covers 1773 to 1817. Corrected copy available at Ga. Historical Society Library.]

Mabel F. LaFar, "Joining the Savannah Baptist Church in the Early 19th Century." **Ga. Historical Society Quarterly** 28 (1944), pp. 176-7. [Includes information on church minutes.]

Nat'l. Society of the Colonial Dames of America, Georgia, **Chatham County Map Portfolio . . . Early Ga. Plantations & the Township of Savannah, 1752-1871** (Athens: Univ. of Ga. Press, 1942).

Mrs. William Lawson Peel, **Historical Collections of the Joseph Habersham Chapter DAR** 3 vols. (1926; rep. ed. Southern Historical Press, 1968). [Vol. 3, pp. 24-39, lists wills & estates, 1783-1825.]

James M. Simms, **1st Colored Baptist Church in N. Amer., Constituted at Savannah, Ga., Jan. 20, A.D. 1788** (1888; rep. ed. New York: Greenwood Press, 1969).

Caroline Wilson, **Annals of Ga.: Important Early Records of the State** 3 vols. (Savannah: Braid & Hutton, 1928-1933). [Vol. 3, pp. 9-237 – Chatham Co. mortality records, 1803-1832.]

• A copy of **List of Registered Voters of Chatham Co., Ga.** (n.p., 1896) is available at the Univ. of Ga. Lib., Athens. Ga. Archives has typescripts of Chatham marr., 1805-1866; an index to Chatham estate records; Will Book F, 1817-1826; and lists of persons buried in Savannah's old colonial cemetery & Jewish cemetery.

Chattahoochee

N.K. Rogers, **History of Chattahoochee Co., Ga.** (1933; rep. ed. Easley, S.C.: Southern Historical Press, 1976).

Chattooga

John H. Cook, "History of Chattooga Co.," (Masters Thesis, Mercer Univ., 1931).

Cherokee

Glenn Hubbard, **The History of Bascomb United Methodist Church & Cemetery Listing** (Woodstock: the author, 1980). [This church is near Woodstock, Ga.; order from author, Box 193, Woodstock, Ga. 30188.]

Lloyd G. Marlin, **The History of Cherokee Co.** (Atlanta: Walter W. Brown Pub. Co., 1932).

Sybil McKay, **Sesquicentennial History of the Chattahoochee Baptist Assoc.** (n.p.).

• A new Cherokee Co. history is being prepared for publication.

Clarke

Robert P. Brooks, **A Brief History of the 1st Methodist Church, Athens, Ga.** (Athens: the author, 1924).

Emanuel Church, **100 Years of Life** (Athens, the author, 1943).

1st Presbyterian Church, **The Exercises Commemorating the Centennial of the 1st Presbyterian Church of Athens** (Athens: the author, 1920).

Ga. Chapters, **DAR Historical Collections** 5 vols. (1926; rep. ed. Easley, S.C.: Southern Historical Press, 1968). [Vol. 1, pp. 15-26, includes lists of names in the minutes of superior court, lists of jurors, wills, & marriages.]

Walter B. Hill, **Rural Survey of Clarke Co., Ga., With Special Reference to the Negroes** (Athens: Univ. of Ga. Press, 1916).

Augustus L. Hull, **Annals of Athens, Ga., 1801-1901** (1879; rep. ed. Danielsville: Heritage Papers, 1966).

Ernest C. Hynds, **Antebellum Athens & Clarke Co., Ga.** (Athens: Univ. of Ga. Press, 1974).

Elsa A. Johnson, **History of the Tuckston Methodist Church, Athens, Ga.** (Athens: the author, 1960).

Frances T. Long, **The Negroes of Clarke Co., Ga., During the Great War** (Athens: Univ. of Ga. Press, 1919).

Silas E. Lucas, **Some Ga. County Records** 3 vols. (Easley, S.C.: Southern Historical Press, 1977). [Vol. 2, pp. 1-41, includes wills, 1803-1842; administrators & Guardians bonds, 1801-1825; & marriages, 1807-1821.]

Charlotte T. Marshall, **Oconee Hill Cemetery: Tombstone Inscriptions** (Athens: Athens Historical Society, 1971).

Edward B. Mell, **A Short History of the Athens Baptist Church, Now the 1st Baptist Church of Athens, 1830-1953** (Athens: the author, 1954).

Sylvanus Morris et al., **History of Athens & Clarke Co.** (Athens: H.J. Rowe Pub. Co., 1923).

Frances W. Reid & Mary B. Warren, **Mars Hill Baptist Church** (constituted 1799) **Clarke-Oconee Co., Ga.** (Athens: Heritage Papers, 1966).

Peter E. Schinkel, "The Negro in Athens & Clarke Co., 1872-1900," (Masters Thesis, Univ. of Ga., 1971).

John F. Stegemen, **These Men She Gave: Civil War Diary of Athens, Ga.** (Athens: Univ. of Ga. Press, 1964).

Charles M. Straham, **Clarke Co., Ga., & the City of Athens** (Atlanta: Chas. P. Bird, 1893).

Mary Warren, **Marriage Book A (1805-1821) Clarke Co., Ga. Including Previously Unrecorded Marr. Licenses Found in the Office of the Ordinary** (Danielsville: Heritage Papers, 1966).

Mary Warren, **Jackson Street Cemetery, Original City Cemetery of Athens, Ga.: Tombstone Inscriptions & Obituaries** (Athens: Heritage Papers, 1966).

• The Athens Historical Society publishes papers on Athens history in their series **Papers of the Athens Historical Society**. Ga. Archives has "History of Clarke Co. by Its People" on microfilm reels 18-80, 18-59, 76-50, 18-71, & 18-72.

Clay

P.C. King, **Ft. Gaines and Environs** (Auburn, Ala.: Warren Enterprises, 1976).

Priscilla Neves Todd, **History of Clay Co.** (Ft. Gaines: Clay Co. Library Bd., 1976).

• Ga. Archives has an unpublished manuscript by E.A. Green entitled "History of Ft. Gaines & Clay Co., Ga." (no date).

Clayton

Ancestors Unlimited Gene. Soc., **All Known Cemeteries in Clayton Co., Ga.** (College Park: authors, 1980).

Doris F. Curry, **Clayton Co., Ga., Marr. Book A, 1850-1870** (Riverdale: author, 1978). [Also avail. from Ancestors Unlimited is Book B, 1870-1881.]

J. Ellis Mundy, **Around a Town Named for Jones** (Jonesboro: author, 1973).

• A Clayton Co. history is being prepared for publication by Ancestors Unlimited.

Clinch

"Early Settlers of Clinch County," **S. Ga. Historical & Genealogical Quarterly** 1 (1922), pp. 39-41.

Folks Huxford, **History of Clinch Co., Ga.** (Macon: J.W. Burke Co., 1916).

Historical Records Survey, **Inventory of the Co. Archives of Ga., Clinch Co. (Homerville)** (Atlanta: the author, 1940).

Alton J. Murray, **S. Ga. Rebels: The True Wartime Experiences of the 26th Regiment, Ga. Vol. Inf.** (St. Mary's: the author, 1976).

Cobb

Carrie Dyer Woman's Club, **Acworth, Ga. From Cherokee Co. to Suburbia** (Acworth: Star Printing Co., 1976).

Sarah B. Temple, **1st 100 Years, a Short History of Cobb Co.** (1935; rep. ed., Covington: Cherokee Pub. Co., 1980).

• Ga. Archives has L. Harold Glore, "History of Mableton," on microfilm reel 232-6. Mr. Glore, 960 Front St., SW, Mableton, Ga. 30059, has also compiled **Bicentennial History of S. Cobb Co.** (Mableton: the author, 1976) and "History Coxos (8P5th) District," avail. at S. Cobb Library, Mableton

Coffee

Warren P. Ward, **Ward's History of Coffee Co.** (1930; rep. ed., Spartanburg, S.C.: The Reprint Co., 1978).

Colquitt

Merle M. Baker, **Past & Present: A History of Funston, Ga.** (Moultrie: R.M. Printing Co., 1976).

William A. Covington, **History of Colquitt Co.** (1937; rep. ed., Spartanburg, S.C.: The Reprint Co., 1980).

Mattie Coyle, **History of Colquitt Co., Ga. & Her Builders** (Moultrie: Observer Press, 1925).

Ann G. Foshee et al., **Index to the History of Colquitt Co. by W.A. Covington, 1937** (Moultrie: Colquitt-Thomas Regional Library, 1976).

Columbia

Ga. Pioneers, **Century of Columbia Co., Ga., Wills, 1790-1890** (Albany: the author, 1966).

Ga. Pioneers, **Columbia Co., Ga.: Early Court Records** (Albany: the author, 1966).

Ga. Pioneers, **Columbia Co., Ga.: Early Marr. Records** (Albany: the author, 1966).

Ga. Pioneers, **Columbia Co., Ga. — Early Deeds & Will Abstracts** (Albany: the author, 1980).

Silas E. Lucas, Jr., **Some Ga. County Records** 3 vols. (Easley, S.C.: Southern Historical Press, 1977). [Vol. 1, pp. 1-77 — county deeds, 1791-1801.]

James D. Mosteller, **A History of Kiokee Baptist Church in Ga.** (Ann Arbor, Mich.: Edwards Bros., Inc., 1952).

Mrs. William Lawson Peel, **Historical Collection of the Joseph Habersham Chapter DAR** 3 vols. (1926; rep. ed., Easley, S.C.: Southern Historical Press, 1968). [Vol. 3, pp. 40-48, includes lists of wills, 1790-1839, and marriages, 1806-1812.]

Caroline P. Wilson, **Annals of Ga.: Important Early Records of the State** 2 vols. (1928-1932; rep. ed., Southern Historical Press, 1968). [Vol. 2, pp. 131-4, has marriages, 1806-1812.]

Cook

Historical Records Survey, **Inventory of the Co. & Town Archives of Ga. Cook Co. — Adel** (Atlanta: author, 1941).

June J. Parrish, **History of Cook Co. & Its Municipalities** (Adel: Adel News Pub. Co., 1968).

Coweta

U.W. Anderson, **History of Coweta Co. From 1825-1880** (Newnan-Coweta Historical Society, 1977).

Mary G. Jones & Lily Reynolds, **Coweta Co. Chronicles for 100 Years With an Account of the Indians From Whom the Land Was Acquired** (1928; rep. ed., Easley, S.C.: Southern Historical Press, 1976).

Newnan-Coweta Historical Society, **Coweta Co. Marr. (1827-1979)** (Newnan: the authors, 1980).

Crawford

Emmie C. Bankston, **History of Roberta & Crawford Co., Ga.** (Macon: Omni Press, 1976).

Commemorative Book Committee, **Crawford Co. Sesquicentennial** (Roberta, 1972).

Crisp

Cordele-Crisp Co. Historical Society, **Crisp Co.'s History in Pictures & Stories** (Atlanta: W.H. Wolfe Assoc., 1978).

William P. Fleming, **Crisp Co., Ga., Historical Sketches** (1932; rep. ed., Spartanburg: The Reprint Co., 1980).

Ft. Early Chapter, DAR, **History of Crisp Co.** (Cordele, n.p., 1916).

• Ga. Archives has on microfilm Ida Wade, "History of Pateville," reel 232-12.

Decatur

Ga. Pioneers, **Decatur Co., Ga., Early Marr. Records & Abstracts of Early Wills** (Albany: the author, 1970).

Frank S. Jones, **History of Decatur, Co., Ga.** (1971; rep. ed., Spartanburg, S.C.: The Reprint Co., 1980).

Lewis W. Rigsby, **Historic Ga. Families** (1925-1928; rep. ed., Baltimore: Genealogical Pub. Co., 1969).

DeKalb

Carolina M. Clarke, **The Story of Decatur, 1823-1899, Decatur Ga.** (Atlanta: Higgins McArthur, Logino & Porter Printers, 1973).

Elizabeth L. Davis & Ethel W. Spruil, **Story of Dunwoody: Its Heritage & Horizons, 1821-1975** (Atlanta: Williams Printing Co., 1975).

1st Baptist Church of Chamblee, **A Century in N. DeKalb: The Story of the 1st Baptist Church of Chamblee, 1875-1975** (Chamblee: the author, 1975).

The 1st County Directory of DeKalb Co., 1939 (Decatur: DeKalb Directory Co., 1939).

Franklin M. Garrett, **Atlanta & Environs: A Chronicle of Its People & Events** 3 vols. (New York: Lewis Historical Pub. Co., 1954). [Vol. 3, not by Mr. Garrett, is a compilation of biographical sketches.]

Franklin M. Garrett, "DeKalb Co. During the Cherokee Troubles," **Atlanta Historical Bulletin** 2 (1936), pp. 24-9. [Deals with the role played by the DeKalb Light Inf. during the Cherokee troubles of 1936.]

John D. Humphries, "Judges of the Superior Courts of Fulton & DeKalb Cos.," **Atlanta Historical Bulletin** 4 (1947), pp. 112-32. [Biographical sketches.]

John D. Humphries, "The Organization of DeKalb County," **Atlanta Historical Bulletin** 8 (1947), pp. 17-30.

Antoinette J. Matthews, **Oakdale Rd., Decatur, Ga., DeKalb History and Its People** (Atlanta: Atlanta Historical Society, 1972).

Maynard-Carter-Simmons, **Atlas of DeKalb Co.** (Decatur: Maynard & Simmons, 1915). [On Microfilm at Ga. Archives.]

William C. Stewart, **Gone to Ga.: Jackson & Gwinnett Cos. & Their Neighbors in the Western Migration** (Washington, D.C.: Nat'l. Genealogical Society, 1965).

Dodge

Addie D. Cobb, **History of Dodge Co.** (1932; rep. ed., Spartanburg, S.C.: The Reprint Co., 1979).

Dooly

Dooly County Historical Committee, **History of Dooly Co.** (Vienna?: Dooly Co. Sesquicentennial Corp., 1971).

Nora & Watts Powell, **Historical & Genealogical Collections of Dooly Co., Ga.** 3 vols. (Vienna: n.p., 1973).

Dougherty

Mary E. Bacon, **Albany on the Flint: Indians to Industry, 1836-1936** (Albany: Albany Town Committee of the Colonial Dames of America in the State of Ga., 1970).

Aaron Brown, **The Negro in Albany** (Albany: the author, 1946).

Ga. Historical Records Survey, **Inventory of the County Archives of Ga., #47: Dougherty Co. (Albany)** (Atlanta: the author, 1941).

Thronateeska Chapter DAR, **History & Reminiscences of Dougherty Co., Ga.** (1924; rep. ed., Spartanburg, S.C.: The Reprint Co., 1978).

Early

Early Co. Historical Society, **Collections of the Early Co. Historical Society** 2 vols. (Blakely: the authors, 1971-1979).

Joel W. Perry, **Some Pioneer History of Early County, 1818-1971** (Early Co. News, 1871).

Jack G. Standifer, **History of the Magnolia Lodge, #86, Free & Accepted Masons, 1844-1926** (Blakely, n.d.).

Echols

Echols Co. Centennial History Committee, **History of Echols Co., 1858-1958** (n.p., 1958).

• Ga. Historical Records Survey, **Inventory of the Co. Archives of Ga., #50: Echols County (Statenville)** (Atlanta: the author, 1940).

Effingham

Pat Bryant, **English Crown Grants for Islands in Ga., 1755-1775** (Atlanta: State Printing Off., 1972).

Adelaide L. Fries, **Moravians in Ga., 1735-1740** (Raleigh: Edwards & Broughton Press, 1905).

Ga. Pioneers, **Effingham Co., Ga., & Liberty Co., Ga.: Early Records** (Albany: Ga. Pioneers, 1976).

Pearl R. Gnann & Mrs. Charles LeBey, **Ga. Salzburgers & Allied Families** (1956; rep. ed., Easley, S.C.: Southern Historical Press, 1976).

Marion R. Hemperley, **Eng. Crown Grants St. Matthew Par., 1755-1775** (1972) **& St. Philip Par., 1755-1775** (1974). (Atlanta: State Print Off.).

C.A. Linn, **Ebenezer Record Book Containing Early Records of Jerusalem Evangelical Lutheran Church, Effingham, Ga. & More Commonly Known as Ebenezer Church** trans. by A.G. Voight (Savannah: Braid & Hutton, 1919.)

Mrs. William Lawson Peel, **Historical Collections of the Joseph Habersham Chapter DAR** 3 vols. (1910; rep. ed., Easley, S.C.: Southern Historical Press, 1968). [Vol. 3, pp. 48-9, has list of wills, 1791-1820.]

P.A. Strobel, **Salzburgers & Their Descendants** (1855; rep. ed. Easley, S.C.: Southern Historical Press, 1980).

Samuel Urlsberger, **Detailed Reports on the Salzburger Emigrants Who Settled in America** 3 vols. (Athens: Univ. of Ga. Press, 1968-1972).

Caroline P. Wilson, **Annals of Ga.; Important Early Records of the State** 2 vols. (1928-1933; rep. ed. Easley, S.C.: Southern Historical Press, 1969). [Vol. 2, pp. 7-129, contains abstracts of early county records, some of which reportedly no longer survive.]

Caroline P. Wilson, **Annals of Ga.; Important Early Records of the State** 3 vols. (Savannah: Braid & Hutton, 1828-1933). [Vol. 3, pp. 260-4, contains cemetery records.]

Caroline P. Wilson & Silas E. Lucas, Jr. **Records of Effingham Co., Ga.** (Easley, S.C.: Southern Historical Press, 1976).

Elbert

Alden Associates, **Early Marriage Records, Elbert Co., Ga.** (Albany: the authors, 1965).

E. Merton Coulter, **Old Petersburg & the Broad River Valley of Ga., Their Rise & Decline** (Athens: Univ. of Ga. Press, 1965).

Grace G. Davidson, **Historical Collections of the Ga. Chapters, DAR** 4 vols. (1926; rep. ed., Easley, S.C.: Southern Historical Press, 1968). [Vol. 3 devoted entirely to Elbert Co. records.]

Joyce H. Gossett & Blanche F. Sexton, **Elbert Co. Marriages, 1800-1850** (East Point: the author, 1980). [Order from author, 2453 Constance St., E. Point, Ga. 30344.]

William F. Jones, **Selections From "The Sons of Elbert Co., Ga., in the Great World War"** (Elberton: the author, 1922).

John H. McIntosh, **Official History of Elbert Co., 1790-1935. Supplement, 1935-1939** (1940; rep. ed. Atlanta: Cherokee Pub. Co., 1968).

Mrs. William L. Peel, **Historical Collections of the Joseph Habersham Chapter DAR** 3 vols. (1910; Easley, S.C.: Southern Historical Press, 1968). [Vol. 3, pp. 49-56, contains lists of wills & appraisements, 1790-1805; marr. licenses, 1808-1812; & wills, 1829-1860.]

Clara A. Stowers, **Coldwater Community in Elbert Co., 1770s-1970** (n.p., 1971?).

Emanuel

James E. Dorsey, **Emanuel Co. Legal Notices: Pre-1860 Notices Appearing in Selected Ga. Newspapers** (Swainsboro: Emanuel Historic Preservation Society, 1978).

James E. Dorsey, **Footprints Along the Hoopee: A History of Emanuel Co., 1812-1900** (Spartanburg, S.C.: The Reprint Co., 1978).

James E. Dorsey & John K. Derden, **Tombstone Registry of Emanuel Co.** (Swainsboro: the author, 1976).

W.C. Rogers, Sr., **Memories of Emanuel, 1776-1976** (Swainsboro: Forest-Blade Pub. Co., 1976).

Evans

Lucille Hodges, **History of Our Locale, Mainly Evans Co., Ga.** (Macon: Southern Printing, Inc., 1965).

Fannin

Kathy Thompson, **Touching Home – A Collection of History & Folklore From Copper Basin, Fannin Co. Area** (Orlando, Fla.: Daniels Pub., 1976).

• Ga. Archives has Lassie A.C. Brackett, "Scrapbook of Obituaries and Births, Fannin & Union Co., Ga.," which was compiled from the now-lost Fannin & Union Co. newspapers. •

Fayette

Fayette Co. Historical Society, **History of Fayette Co., 1821-1971** (Fayetteville: authors, 1977).

Silas E. Lucas, Jr. **Some Ga. County Records** 3 vols. (Easley, S.C.: Southern Historical Press, 1978). [Vol. 3, pp. 262-87, includes marriages, 1823-1832, Docket, Court of Ordinary; and index to Will Book A.]

Joel D. Wells & Donald R. Schultz, **All Known Cemeteries in Fayette Co., Ga.** (Hampton: Joel D. Willis, 1979).

Joel D. Wells, **Know Your Kin – A Compilation of Genealogy Columns Pub. in the Fayette Co. Sun & the Henry Sun During 1979** (Hampton: the author, 1980).

• Ga. Archives has the Mrs. H.P. Redwine Collection of newspaper clippings on the history of Fayette Co. (microfilm reel 17-80).

Floyd

George M. Battey, Jr., **History of Rome & Floyd Co., State of Ga., USA, Including Numerous Incidents of More Than Local Interest, 1540-1922** (1922; rep. ed., Covington: Cherokee Pub. Co., 1977).

Catherine C. Mann, **Marriage Record A, Floyd Co., Ga., 1834-1848** (Cedar Bluff, Ala.: the author, 1970).

Wiley C. Owen & Beatrice Millican, **An Index to George Magruder Battey's History of Rome & Floyd Co.** (Rome: Rome Heritage Foundation, 1976).

Hughes Reynolds, **Coosa River Valley From DeSoto to Hydroelectric Power** (Cynthiana, Ky.: The Hobson Book Press, 1944).

James A. Sartain, **History of the Coosa Baptist Assoc.: at the 100th Session Held at Peavine Baptist Church Near Rock Spring, Ga., on Aug. 5 & 6, 1936** (n.p.).

Forsyth

Garland C. Bagley, **History of Harris Grove School, 1880-1940** (Cumming: the author, 1971).

Sybil McRay, **Sesquicentennial History of the Chattahoochee Baptist Assoc. & Its Affiliated Churches** (n.p.).

Franklin

Martha W. Acker, **Deeds of Franklin Co., Ga., 1784-1826** (Easley, S.C.: Southern Historical Press, 1976).

Martha W. Acker, **Franklin Co., Ga., Tax Digests, Vol. 1, 1798-1807** (Birmingham, Ala.: the author, 1980).

Martha W. Acker, **Index to Deeds of Franklin Co., Ga., 1784-1860** (Birmingham, Ala.: the author, 1979).

Georgia Chapters DAR, **Historical Collections** 5 vols. (1926; rep. ed., Easley, S.C.: Southern Historical Press, 1968). [Vol. 1, pp. 136-354, includes early marriages, deeds, wills, & records of Revolutionary War soldiers.]

Mrs. William Lawson Peel, **Collections of the Joseph Habersham Chapter DAR** 3 vols. (1910; Easley, S.C.: Southern Historical Press, 1968). [Vol. 3, pp. 56-67, lists wills, 1786-1849; and marriages, 1805-1812.]

William C. Stewart, **Gone to Ga.: Jackson & Gwinnett Counties & Their Neighbors in the Western Migration** (Washington, D.C.: Nat'l. Genealogical Society, 1965).

Marie H. Williams, **Lavonia, Gem of the Piedmont, 1880-1977** (Lavonia: Lavonia Library Committee, 1977).

Frances Wynd, **Franklin Co., Ga. Records** (Albany: the author, 1969).

• Ga. Archives has 20 vols. of indexed typescripts of Franklin Co. records.

Fulton

(For other Atlanta material, see DeKalb.)

James L. Baggott, **Meet 1,000 Atlanta Baptist Ministers, 1843-1973** (Atlanta: the author, 1973).

Lois Coogle, **Sandy Springs — Past Tense** (Atlanta: Decor Master Co., 1971).

Walter G. Cooper, **Official History of Fulton Co.** (1934; rep. ed. Spartanburg, S.C.: The Reprint Co., 1978).

Barbara Crisp & Teresa Dougherty, **Palmetto, a Town & Its People** (Palmetto: Town & County Homemakers Club, 1980).

Elizabeth L. Davis & Ethel W. Spruill, **Story of Dunwoody, Its Heritage & Horizons, 1821-1975** (Atlanta: Williams Printing Co., 1975).

Franklin M. Garrett, **Atlanta & Environs: A Chronicle of Its People & Events** 3 vols. (New York: Lewis Historical Pub. Co., 1954). [Vol. 3, not by Garrett, is a compilation of biographical sketches.]

Alex M. Hitz, "Origins of Fulton Co.," **Atlanta Historical Society Bulletin** 9 (1951), pp. 3-25.

Lucian L. Knight, **History of Fulton Co., Ga., Narrative & Biographical** (Atlanta: A.H. Cawston, 1930).

Thomas H. Martin, **Atlanta & Its Builders, a Comprehensive History of the Gate City of the South** 2 vols. (Atlanta: Century Memorial Pub. Co., 1902).

Stephen Mitchell, "Original Grantees of Lots in the 14th Dist. of Originally Henry Co., now Fulton Co., Ga.," **Atlanta Historical Society Bulletin** 1 (1930), pp. 43-9.

"Names From the Fulton Co. Tax Digest of 1854," **Atlanta Historical Society Bulletin** 1 (1930), pp. 57-79.

Pioneer Citizens Society, **Pioneer Citizens History of Atlanta, 1833-1902** (Atlanta: Byrd Printing Co., 1902).

James C. Starbuck, **Historic Atlanta to 1930: An Indexed, Chronological Bibliography** (Monticello, Ill.: Council of Planning Librarians, 1974).

John S. Wilson, "Atlanta As It Is," **Atlanta Historical Bulletin** 6 (1941), #24. [A reprint of an 1871 publication on Atlanta's first settlers.]

• The preceding list includes only the Fulton County books of the most obvious genealogical value. For other sources, see the Ga. bibliographies given earlier in this chapter or visit the Atlanta Historical Society at 3009 Andrews Drive (P.O. Box 12423, Atlanta, Ga. 30355). Archives has Horace Sandiford Collec. of Fulton County history scrapbooks, 1921-1925 (reel 186-41).

Gilmer

Lawrence L. Stanley, **Little History of Gilmer Co.** (Ellijay: author, 1975).

George G. Ward, **Annals of Upper Ga.: Centered in Gilmer Co.** (Carrollton: Thompson Print. & Off. Equip., 1965).

Glynn

Pat Bryant, **English Crown Grants for Islands in Ga., 1755-1775** (Atlanta: State Print. Off., 1972).

Margaret D. Cate, **Our Todays & Yesterdays: a Story of Brunswick & the Coastal Islands** (1926; rep. ed., Spartanburg, S.C.: The Reprint Co., 1972).

Marion R. Hemperley, **English Crown Grants for Parishes of St. David, St. Patrick, St. Thomas, & St. Mary in Ga., 1755-1775** (Atlanta: State Printing Off., 1973).

Folks Huxford, **Pioneers of Wiregrass Ga.: a Biographical Account of the Original Counties of Irwin, Appling, Wayne, Camden, & Glynn** 7 vols. (Adel: Patten Pub. Co., 1951-1975).

Alton J. Murray, **S. Ga. Rebels: The True Wartime Experiences of the 26th Reg., Ga., Vol.** (St. Mary's: the author, 1976).

Mrs. William J. Peel, **Historical Collections of the Joseph Habersham Chapter DAR** 3 vols. (1910; rep. ed., Easley, S.C.: Southern Historical Press, 1968). [Vol. 3, pp. 67-74, includes lists of lost wills, 1793-1809; wills & administrations, 1810-1842; deeds, 1765-1800; and marriages, 1818-1850.]

Gordon

Burton J. Bell, **1976 Bicentennial History of Gordon Co., Ga., 1830-1976** (Calhoun: Gordon Co. Historical Society, 1976). [Includes a reprint of Lulie Pitts, **History of Gordon Co., Ga.**, (1933).]

Jewell B. Reeve, **Climb the Hills of Gordon. Stories of Gordon Co. & Calhoun, Ga.** (1962; rep. ed., Easley, S.C.: Southern Historical Press, 1979).

Grady

Yvonne Bruton, **Grady Co., Ga., Some of Its History, Folk Architecture & Families** (the author, 1979).

Lewis W. Rigsby, **Historical Ga. Families** (1925-1928; rep. ed., Baltimore: Genealogical Pub. Co., 1969).

• Ga. Archives has typescript index of Grady Co. cemetery inscriptions.

Greene

Ga. Chapters DAR, **Historical Collections** 5 vols. (Atlanta: various printers, 1926), vol. 5, pp. 7-148. [Greene Co. marriages, 1787-1875.]

Silas E. Lucas, Jr., **Some Ga. Co. Records** 3 vols. (Easley, S.C.: Southern Historical Press, 1977). [Vol. 2, pp. 162-365, includes wills, 1787-1810; deeds, 1785-1802; & marriages, 1787-1803.]

Mrs. William L. Peel, **Historical Collections of the Joseph Habersham Chapter DAR** 3 vols. (1910; rep. ed., Easley, S.C.: Southern Historical Press, 1968). [Vol. 3, pp. 74-85, includes lists of lost wills, 1793-1809; wills, 1810-1842; deeds, 1765-1890; & marriages, 1818-1850.]

Thaddeus B. Rice, **History of Greene Co., Ga., 1786-1886** (1961; rep. ed., Spartanburg, S.C.: The Reprint Co., 1979).

• Manuscripts Section, Ga. Archives, has the Thaddeus B. Rice Manuscript Collection, including his notes & materials for a history of Greene Co.

Gwinnett

James C. Flanigan, **Gwinnett Churches, a Complete History of Every Church in Gwinnett Co., Ga., With Short Biographical Sketches of Its Ministers** (Lawrenceville: the author, 1911).

James C. Flanigan, **History of Gwinnett Co., 1818-1960** 2 vols. (Hapeville: Tyler & Co.; Longino & Porter, Inc., 1943-1959).

Allen P. Francis, **A Compilation of Fact & Legend Pertaining to the History of Norcross in Gwinnett Co., Ga.** (Norcross: Harper Printing Co., 1967).

Sybil McRay, **Sesquicentennial History of the Chattahoochee Baptist Assoc. & Its Affiliated Churches** (n.p.).

William C. Stewart, **Gone to Ga.: Jackson & Gwinnett Counties & Their Neighbors in the Western Migration** (Washington, D.C.: National Genealogical Society, 1965).

• Gwinnett Historical Society, P.O. Box 261, Lawrenceville, Ga. 30246, is publishing **Gwinnett Families, 1818-1968,** through Cherokee Pub. Co.

Habersham

Mary L. Church, **Hills of Habersham** (Clarksville: the author, 1962).

Herbert B. Kimzey, **Habersham Co., Ga., Genealogical Records** 6 vols. (Cornelia: the author, 1969-1971). [Includes census, church, land lottery, & deed records.]

Sybil McRay, **Sesquicentennial History of the Chattahoochee Baptist Assembly & Its Affiliated Churches** (n.p.).

Hall

Sybil McRay:
**Book "A" Wills, 1837-1867, & Wills Recorded in Minute Book "A" —
Misc. "A", 1819-1939, Hall Co., Ga.** (1968).

1836 Hall Co. "Dragoons" (1970).

Hall Co., Ga., 1819-1839: Marriages (Book A) & Genealogical Notes (1968).

Hall Co., Ga., 1840-1870: Marriages (Book A, part II) (1969).

Misc. "D" 12 Month Support, Inventory & Appraisement, 1850-1869, Hall Co., Ga. (1969).

Sesquicentennial History of Chattahoochee Baptist Assoc. & Its Affiliated Churches (n.p.).

This 'N That: History of Hall Co., Ga., History, Genealogy, Personalities, Bible Records (1973). vol. 1.

Tombstone Inscriptions of Hall Co., Ga. (1971).

William C. Stewart, **Gone to Ga.: Jackson & Gwinnett Cos. & Their Neighbors in the Western Migration** (Washington, D.C.: Nat'l. Genealogical Society, 1965).

Hancock

Martha L. Houston, **Marriages of Hancock Co., Ga., 1806 to 1850** (Rep. ed., Baltimore: Genealogical Pub. Co., 1977). [Reprinted with the 1806 land lottery list of Hancock Co.]

Silas E. Lucas, Jr., **Some Ga. Co. Records** 3 vols. (Easley, S.C.: Southern Historical Press, 1977). [Vol. 1, pp. 78-121, includes wills & estate records, 1794-1804; & deeds, 1793-1795.]

Mrs. William L. Peel, **Collections of the Joseph Habersham Chapter DAR** 3 vols. (1910; rep. ed., Easley, S.C.: Southern Historical Press, 1968). [Vol. 3, pp. 85-92, contains lists of wills & estates, 1794-1850; & a few marriages, 1805-1810.]

Elizabeth W. Smith & Sara S. Carnes, **History of Hancock Co., Ga.** 2 vols. (Washington, Ga.: Wilkes Pub. Co., 1974).

Mary B. Warren, **Marriage Book A (1804-1821) Clarke Co., Ga.** (Athens: Heritage Papers, 1966), pp. 33-5. [Hancock Co. marriages.]

Haralson

Frances Greene, **The 1st Hundred Years of Tallapoosa, Ga.** (Tallapoosa: the author, 1972).

• A new history on Haralson Co. is being prepared by Taylor Pub. Co.

Harris

Louise C. Barfield, **History of Harris Co., Ga., 1827-1961** (Columbus: Coleman Office Sply. House, 1961). [Reprinted by W.H. Wolfe Assoc. in 1980.]

Chattahoochee Valley Historical Society, **West Point on the Chattahoochee** (West Point: the author, 1957).

William H. Davidson, **Pine Log & Greek Revival — Houses & People of 3 Counties in Ga. & Ala.** (Alexander City, Ala.: Chattahoochee Valley Historical Society, 1964).

William H. Davidson, **Valley Historical Scrapbook** (West Point: Chattahoochee Historical Society, 1970).

• On the oversize shelf of the co. histories section, Central Research Library, Ga. Archives, there is a scrapbook history of Harris Co. by Louise Calhoun Barfield.

Hart

John W. Baker, **History of Hart Co., 1933** (Atlanta: Foote & Davis, 1933).

Bobbie O. Martin, **Surname Index to History of Hart Co.** (Powder Springs: the author, 1980). [Can be ordered from author at 1420 Casteel Rd., Powder Springs, Ga. 30073.]

Travis Parker, **Hart Co., Ga., Will Book A, 1854-1894, Abstracts** (Atlanta: the author, 1980).

• Travis Parker, 889 Dewey St., NE, Atlanta, Ga. 30306, is currently preparing for publication booklets on Hart Co. records.

Heard

James C. Bonner, **A Short History of Heard Co.** (Milledgeville: Women's College of Ga., 1959).

Lynda S. Eller, **Heard Co. Cemeteries** (Lanett, Ala.: the author, 1977).

Stannye Wilkinson, **Our Town, Franklin, Ga.** (Franklin: the author, 1965).

• Lynda S. Eller is currently preparing for publication **Heard Co., Ga. — A History of Its People.**

Henry

Silas E. Lucas, Jr., **Some Ga. Co. Records** 3 vols. (Easley, S.C.: Southern Historical Press, 1978). [Vol. 3, pp. 147-210, includes deeds, 1822-1828 and index to wills.]

Stephens Mitchell, "Original Grantees of Lots in the 14th Dist. of Originally Henry Co., now Fulton Co., Ga." **Atlanta Historical Society Bulletin** 1 (1930), 43-9.

Vessie T. Rainer, **Henry Co., Ga., the Mother of Counties** (McDonough: Henry Co. Historical Found., 1971).

Vessie T. Rainer, **Henry Co., Ga., Family Cemeteries** (McDonough: the author, 1980).

Joel D. Wells, **Know Your Kin, A Compilation of Genealogy Cols. Pub. in Fayette Sun & Henry Sun During 1979** (Hampton: the author, 1979).

• Ga. Archives has a copy of Wiley A. Clements' unpublished "History of Henry Co., May 1821-1921" (microfilm reel 39-70).

Houston

Bobbie Smith Hickson, **A Land So Dedicated: Houston Co., Ga.** (Perry: Houston Co. Library Board, 1976).

John D. Wade, **Marshallville Methodist Church From Its Beginning to 1850** (Marshallville: the author, 1952).

• Ga. Archives has Warren Grice, "A History of Houston Co., Ga.," (1934) on microfilm reel 77-46; and Mrs. Walter M. Lee, "Historical Sketches of Houston Co. Baptists," (1923) on microfilm reel 76-44.

Irwin

James B. Clements, **History of Irwin Co.** (1932; rep. ed. Spartanburg, S.C.: Reprint Co., 1978).

Folks Huxford, **Pioneers of Wiregrass Ga., A Biographical Account of Some of . . . the Original Cos. of Irwin, Appling, Wayne, Camden & Glynn** 7 vols. (Adel: Patten Pub. Co., 1951-1975).

Jackson

Frary Elrod, **Historical Notes on Jackson Co., Ga.** (Jefferson: the author, 1967).

Ga. Chapters DAR, **Historical Collections** 5 vols. (1926; rep. ed., Easley, S.C.: The Southern Historical Press, 1968). [Vol. 1, pp. 27-35 & 103-9, has lists of wills, ministers, and justices of the peace.]

Georgia Pioneers, **Jackson Co. Ga. Misc. Records** (Albany: the author, 1980). [Includes wills, administrations, guardianships, etc.]

Thomas C. Hardman, **History of Harmony Grove — Commerce, Jackson Co., Ga., 1810-1949** (Athens: McGregor Co., 1949).

Sybil McRay, **Sesquicentennial History of the Chattahoochee Baptist Assoc. & Its Affiliated Churches** (n.p.).

William C. Stewart, **Gone to Ga.: Jackson & Gwinnett Counties & Their Neighbors in the Western Migration** (Washington, D.C.: Nat'l. Genealogical Society, 1965).

Gustavus J.N. Wilson, **The Writings of the Late G.J.N. Wilson . . . Early History of Jackson Co., Ga.** (Atlanta: Foote & Davies, 1914).

Gustavus J.N. Wilson, **Georgia Blood** (1914; rep. ed., Decatur: J & C Graphics, 1977). [Reprint of Wilson's **Early History of Jackson Co., Ga.**]

• A book of Jackson Co. cemetery records, 1811-1979, is currently being prepared for publication.

Jasper

Ga. Chapters DAR, **Historical Collections** 5 vols. (1926; rep. ed., Easley, S.C.: Southern Historical Press, 1968). [Vol. 1, pp. 35-43, contains lists of wills & appraisors, jurors, & marriages.]

Jewell M. Lancaster, **Jasper Co., Ga., Cemetery & Bible Records** (Shady Dale: the author, 1969).

Silas E. Lucas, Jr., **Some Ga. Co. Records** 3 vols. (Easley, S.C.: Southern Historical Press, 1977). [Vol. 2, pp. 42-82, includes misc. estate records, 1810-1815; & co. court minutes & wills, 1813-1822.]

William C. Stewart, **Gone to Ga.: Jackson & Gwinnett Cos. & Their Neighbors in the Western Migration** (Washington, D.C.: Nat'l. Genealogical Soc., 1965).

• Ga. Archives has on microfilm reel 82-24 Mrs. A.S. Thurmond, "A History of Jasper Co. & Monticello," (n.d.).

Jefferson

Alden Associates, **Jefferson-Burke Co., Ga.: Early Records** (Albany: the author, 1965).

Lois D. Cofer, **Queensborough or The Irish Town & Its Citizens** (Louisville: the author, 1977).

Ga. Chapters DAR, **Historical Collections** 5 vols. (1926; rep. ed., Easley, S.C.: Southern Historical Press, 1968). [Vol. 1, pp. 43-54, has lists of persons in the land lottery & tax digests.]

John Franklin Wren Ch. DAR, **Ebenezer A.R. Presbyterian Church Cemetery; Stone Family Cemetery; Misc. Bible Records of Families With Jefferson Co. Ga. Ties** (Augusta: the author, 1969).

James E. Dorsey, **Jefferson Co., Ga., 1871-1900: A Collection of Newspaper Sources** (Swainsboro: Emanuel Co. Jr. College Library, 1979).

Ga. Historical Records Survey, **Inventory of the Co. Archives of Ga., #81: Jefferson Co. (Louisville)** (Atlanta: the authors, 1940).

Silas E. Lucas, Jr., **Some Ga. Co. Records** 3 vols. (Easley, S.C.: Southern Historical Press, 1977). [Vol. 1, pp. 122-82, includes wills & estate records, 1771-1893; wills, 1796-1827; grand jurors, 1797; and petit jurors, 1799.]

Lillian L. Powell et al., **Grave Markers in Burke Co., Ga. With 39 Cemeteries in 4 Adjoining Cos.** (Waynesboro: Chalker Pub. Co., 1974).

Mrs. Z.V. Thomas, **History of Jefferson Co.** (1927; rep. ed., Spartanburg, S.C.: The Reprint Co., 1978).

Jenkins

James E. Dorsey, **Herndon & Lawtonville: A Collection of Newspaper Sources, 1883-1900** (Swainsboro: Emanuel Co. Jr. College, 1980).

James E. Dorsey, **Millen, Ga., 1883-1900: A Collection of Newspaper Sources** (Swainsboro: Emanuel Co. Jr. College Library, 1978).

Lillian L. Powell et al., **Grave Markers in Burke Co., Ga., With 39 Cemeteries in 4 Adjoining Cos.** (Waynesboro: Chalker Pub. Co., 1974).

Johnson

Mattie L.H. Meadows, **Searching for Our Ancestors Among the Gravestones: a Cemetery Record of Johnson Co., Ga.** (Wrightsville: Johnson Co. Historical Society, 1979).

Jones

Frank M. Abbott, **History of the People of Jones Co., Ga., 4 vols.** (Macon: Linage Unlimited, 1977). [Includes cemetery & census records.]

Ga. Chapters DAR, **Historical Collections** 5 vols. (1926; rep. ed., Easley, S.C.: Southern Historical Press, 1968). [Vol. 1, pp. 55-7, has a list of early wills.]

Margaret H. Stephens, **Index to the History of Jones Co., Ga.** (Macon: the author, 1980).

Carolyn Williams, **History of Jones Co., Ga., for 100 Years, Specif. 1807-1907** (1957; rep. ed., Macon: J.W. Burke Co., 1976).

Lamar

Augusta Lambdin, **History of Lamar Co.** (1932; Atlanta: William H. Wolfe, 1978).

Lanier

Lakeland-Lanier Co. Bicentennial History Committee, **Old Times There Are Not Forgotten, a Story in Picture & Words of the People of Lanier Co.** (Lakeland: Carey Cameron Pub., 1978).

"Burnt Church Cemetery Records, Lanier Co., Ga." **S. Ga. Historical 7 Genealogical Quarterly** 1 (1922), pp. 19-20.

Laurens

Ga. Chapters DAR, **Historical Collections** 5 vols. (1926; rep. ed., Easley, S.C.: Southern Historical Press, 1968). [Vol. 1, pp. 57-61, includes lists of marriages & wills.]

Bertha S. Hart, **Official History of Laurens Co., Ga., 1807-1941** (1941; rep. ed., Atlanta: Cherokee Pub. Co., 1972).

• James E. Dorsey of Emanuel Co. Jr. College is currently preparing small town histories of Laurens Co.

Lee

Ga. Historical Records Survey, **Inventory of the Co. Archives of Ga., #88: Lee Co. (Leesburg)** 2 vols. (Atlanta: the authors, 1942).

Liberty

Pat Bryant, **English Crown Grants for Islands of Ga., 1755-1775** (Atlanta: State Printing Off., 1972).

Pat Bryant, **English Crown Grants in St. Andrew Parish in Ga., 1755-1775** (Atlanta: State Printing Off., 1972).

Roger Durham, "A Study of the Civil War in Liberty Co., Ga." (Dept. of Natural Resources Report, Feb. 27, 1974).

Virginia F. Evans, **Liberty Co.: A Pictorial History** (Statesville, N.C.: Brady Printing Co., 1979).

Georgia Pioneers, **Effingham Co., Ga., & Liberty Co., Ga.: Early Records** (Albany: the authors, 1976).

Roland M. Harper, "A Statistical Study of the Midway Cemetery, With Notes on Members of the Same Community Buried Elsewhere," **Ga. Historical Quarterly** 21 (1937), pp. 265-73.

Marion R. Hemperley, **English Crown Grants in St. John Parish in Ga., 1755-1775** (Atlanta: State Printing Off., 1972).

James T. Lambright, **History of the Liberty Independent Troop During the Civil War, 1862-1865** (Brunswick: Glover Bros., 1910).

Paul McIlvaine, **The Dead Town of Sunbury, Ga.** (Hendersonville, N.C.: the author, 1971).

Mrs. William L. Peel, **Historical Collections of the Joseph Habersham Ch. DAR** 3 vols. (1910; rep. ed., Easley, S.C.: Southern Historical Press, 1968). [Vol. 3, pp. 92-5, includes list of wills, 1790-1835.]

John M. Sheftall, **Sunbury on the Medway, A Selective History of the Town, Inhabitants, & Fortifications** (Atlanta: State Printing Off., 1977).

James Stacy, **History of the Midway Congregational Church, Liberty Co., Ga.** (1903; Newnan: S.W. Murray Press, 1951).

Caroline P. Wilson, **Annals of Ga.: Important Early Records of the State** 2 vols. (1928-1933; rep. ed., Easley, S.C.: Southern Historical Press, 1969). [Almost all of Vol. 1 is devoted to Liberty Co. records.]

Caroline P. Wilson, **Annals of Ga.: Important Early Records of the State** 3 vols. (Savannah: Braid & Hutton, 1928-1933). [Vol. 3, pp. 277-85, has cemetery records.]

Bird & Paul Yarborough, **Taylors Creek: Story of the Community & Her People Through 200 Years** (Pearson: Atkinson Co. Citizen, 1963).

An unpublished history of Liberty Co. by James A. LeConte is in the possession of the LeConte heirs. See Sheftall, **Sunbury on the Medway** (above), p. 250.

Lincoln

Ga. Chapters DAR, **Historical Collection** 4 vols. (1926; rep. ed., Easley, S.C.: Southern Historical Press, 1968). [Vol. 1, pp. 61-9, has lists of wills, estates, and marriages.]

Clinton J. Perryman, **History of Lincoln Co., Ga.** (1933; Ann Arbor, Mich.: University Microfilms International, 1979). [Ga. Archives has a typescript of this unpublished manuscript.]

Sarah Q. Smith, **Early Ga. Wills — Lincoln Co.** (Washington, Ga.: author, 1960).

Lowndes

R.L. Cox, **History of the 1st Methodist Church of Valdosta, Ga., 1859-1951** (Valdosta: the author, 1951).

Leota M. Feagan, **History of Lee St. Baptist Church, 1907-1957** (Valdosta: the author, 1957).

First Baptist Church of Valdosta, Historical Sketch of the First Baptist Church of Valdosta, Ga. (Valdosta: the author, 1940).

Gen. James Jackson Chapter DAR, **History of Lowndes Co., Ga., 1825-1941** (1942; rep. ed., Spartanburg, S.C.: The Reprint Co., 1978).

Alton J. Murray, **S. Ga. Rebels: the True Wartime Experiences of the 26th Regiment, Ga. Vol. Inf.** (St. Mary's: the author, 1976).

Jane T. Shelton, **Pines & Pioneers: A History of Lowndes Co., Ga., 1825-1900** (Atlanta: Cherokee Pub. Co., 1976).

Lumpkin

Andrew W. Cain, **History of Lumpkin Co. for the 1st 100 Years, 1832-1932** (1932; rep. ed., Spartanburg, S.C.: The Reprint Co., 1978).

E. Merton Coulter, **Auraria, the Story of a Ga. Gold Mining Town** (Athens: Univ. of Ga. Press, 1956).

Sybil McRay, **Sesquicentennial History of the Chattahoochee Baptist Assoc. & Its Affiliated Churches** (n.p.).

Macon

Louise F. Hays, **History of Macon Co., Ga.** (1933; rep. ed., Spartanburg, S.C.: The Reprint Co., 1979).

John D. Wade, **Marshallville Methodist Church From Its Beginning to 1950** (Marshallville: the author, 1952).

Madison

Grover H. Cartledge, **Historical Sketches: Presbyterian Churches & Early Settlers in NE Ga.** (Athens: Univ. of Ga. Press, 1960).

Grover H. Cartledge, **Sketches of the Early History of Madison Co., Ga.** (Danielsville, 1967).

Colbert Museum Committee, **Memories of Our Home Town, Colbert, Ga.** (Colbert: the authors, 1976).

Ga. Chapters DAR, **Historical Collections** 5 vols. (1926; rep. ed., Easley, S.C.: Southern Historical Press, 1968). [Vol. 1, pp. 69-78, has lists of wills & marriages.]

William C. Stewart, **Gone to Ga.: Jackson & Gwinnett Cos. & Their Neighbors in the Western Migration** (Washington, D.C.: Nat'l. Genealogical Society, 1965).

Paul Tabor, **History of Madison Co., Ga.** (n.p., 1974).

Marion

Norman Munro Unit, American Legion, **Service Record Book of Men & Women of Marion Co., Ga., WWI & Registry of WWI** (n.p., 1 May 1949).

Nettie Powell, **History of Marion Co., Ga.** (Columbia: Historical Pub. Co., 1931).

McDuffie

Pearl Baker, **A Handbook of History: McDuffie Co., Ga., 1870-1970** (Thomson: Progress-News Pub. Co., 1971).

Pearl Baker, **Story of Wrightsboro, 1768-1964** (Warrenton: Warrenton Clipper, 1965). [Avail. from Wrightsboro Foundation, 633 Hemlock Dr., 30824].

• Ga. Archives has an unpublished, typescript history of McDuffie Co. by Mrs. W.C. McCommons & Miss Clara Stovall in 2 vols. It is on the oversize shelf in the co. histories sec. of the Central Research Library.

McIntosh

Bessie Lewis, **They Called Their Town Darien: Being a Short History of Darien & McIntosh Co., Ga.** (Darien: Darien News, 1975).

Alton J. Murray, **S. Ga. Rebels: True Wartime Experiences of the 26th Reg., Ga. Vol. Inf.** (St. Mary's: the author, 1976).

Caroline Wilson, **Annals of Ga.: Important Early Records of the State** 3 vols. (Savannah: Braid & Hutton, 1928-1933). [Vol. III, pp. 266-77 has cemetery records.]

Virginia S. Wood, **McIntosh Co. Academy, McIntosh Co., Ga., Minutes of Commissioners, 1820-1875; Acct. Book of Students, 1821-1834** (author, 1973).

Meriwether

William H. Davidson, **Brooks of Honey & Butter: Plantations & People of Meriwether Co.** (Alexander City, Ala.: Outlook Pub. Co., 1971), 2 vols.

Regina P. Pinkston, **Historical Account of Meriwether Co., 1824-1974** (Greenville: Meriwether Historical Society, 1974).

Charles S. Reid, **Brief Historical Sketch of the Town of Woodbury, Meriwether Co., Ga.** (n.p.).

Miller

Nellie C. Davis, **The History of Miller Co., Ga.** (Colquitt: Citizens Bank, 1980).

Mitchell

Mildred J. Cole, **From Stage Coaches to Train Whistles: History of Gum Pond, Mt. Enon & Baconton in Mitchell Co., Ga., 1856-1976** (Baconton, 1977).

Marion D. Rogers, **Building of a Town: a Partial History of Pelham, Ga. & Surrounding Areas, 1881-1974** (Pelham: the author, 1976).

Margaret Spence & Anna M. Fleming, **History of Mitchell Co., 1857-1976** (n.p.).

Monroe

Jack K. Fletcher, **Methodism in Monroe Co., 1823-1973** (n.p.).

James Monroe Chapter DAR, **Monroe Co. Marriage Records, 1824-1872** (Forsyth, 1949).

Monroe Co. Historical Society, Inc., **Monroe Co., Ga., a History** (Forsyth: W.H. Wolf Ass., 1979).

Silas E. Lucas, Jr., **Some Ga. Co. Records** 3 vols. (Easley, S.C.: Southern Historical Press, 1978). [Vol. 3, pp. 227-61, has the first deed and marriage books.]

Thomas M. Norwood, **The Story of Culloden** (Savannah: Braid & Hutton, 1909).

Eugenia W. Stone, **Yesterday at Tift** (Doraville: Foote & Davies, 1969).

Nanie M. Worsham, **History of Stroud Community in Monroe Co.** (n.p., 1958).

Montgomery

James E. Dorsey, **Montgomery Co.: A Collection of Newspaper Sources, 1873-1885** (Swainsboro: Emanuel Co. Jr. College Library, 1980).

Mrs. William L. Peel, **Historical Collections of the Joseph Habersham Ch., DAR** 3 vols. (1910; rep. ed., Easley, S.C.: Southern Historical Press, 1968). [Vol. 3, pp. 95-106, has lists of jurors, 1816; wills, 1809-1850; & marriages, 1810-1850.]

Morgan

Etta S. Few, **The Story of Apalachee** (Apalachee: Apal. Improve. Club, 1926).

Ga. Chapters DAR, **Historical Collections** 5 vols. (1926; rep. ed., Easley, S.C.: Southern Historical Press, 1968). [Vol. 1, pp. 78-83, has lists of wills & marriages.]

Louise M. Hicky, **Rambles Through Morgan Co.** (Madison: Morgan Co. Historical Society, 1971).

Silas E. Lucas, Jr., **Some Ga. Co. Records** 3 vols. (Easley, S.C.: Southern Historical Press, 1977). [Vol. 2, pp. 83-101, has Marriage Book A, 1807-1818.]

• The Georgia Department of Archives and History has a typescript of Morgan County records by the Georgia Chapter, USD War of 1812.

Murray

Charles H. Skinner, **History of Murray Co.** (Dalton: A.J. Showalter Co., 1911).

Mrs. Raymond H. Whitehead, **Genealogical History of Original Murray Co., Ga.** 2 vols. (Atlanta: the author, 1972).

Muscogee

Frank J. Dudley, **100 Years History of St. Luke M.E. Church, S. Columbus, Ga., 1828-1929** (Columbus, 1930).

James J. Gilbert, **A History of the 1st Presbyterian Church of Columbus, Ga. During 1st 100 Years of Its Existence** (Columbus: Gilbert Print. Co., 1930).

Historical Records Survey, **Inventory of the Co. Archives of Ga., #106: Muscogee Co. (Columbus)** (Atlanta: the author, 1941).

Frank Holder, **Records of the Town of Columbus & the Coweta Falls Reserve** (Atlanta: State Print. Off., 1971). [Inventory of records in the Ga. Surveyor Gen. Dept. relating to Columbus & Muscogee Co. in the 1820s.]

John S. Lupold, **Columbus, Ga., 1828-1978** (Columbus: Columbus Sesquicentennial, Inc., 1978).

John H. Martin, **Columbus, Ga., From Its Selection as a "Trading Town" in 1827 to Its Partial Destruction by Wilson's Raid in 1865** (1874; rep. ed., Easley, S.C.: Southern Historical Press, 1972). [Ga. Archives has typescript index to this history.]

Nancy Telfair, **History of Columbus, Ga., 1828-1928** (Columbus: Columbus Office Sply., 1951).

Margaret L. Whitehead & Barbara Bogart, **City of Progress: A History of Columbus, Ga.** (Columbus: Columbus Off. Sply., 1978).

W.C. Woodall, **Home Town & Other Sketches** (Columbus: Col. Off. Sply., 1935).

Etta Worsley, **Columbus on the Chattahoochee** (Columbus: Col. Off. Sply., 1951).

Buster W. Wright, **Abstracts of Marriages Reported in the Columbus Enquirer, 1832-1852** (Columbus: author, 1980).

Buster W. Wright, **Abstracts of Deaths Reported in the Columbus Enquirer, 1832-1852** (Columbus: author, 1980).

• Ga. Archives has a typescript of Muscogee Co. marriages, 1838-1845. Abstracts of genealogical information from the **Columbus Enquirer** has been published in back issues of **Ga. Genealogist.**

Newton

Sara A. & Mary Jane Dixon, **Newton Co., Ga., Cemeteries** 3 vols. (Starrsville: the authors, 1968).

Genealogical Enterprises, **The Ga. Enterprise & Covington Star, 1865-1904** (Morrow: the author, 1969). [Genealogical data from a Newton Co. newspaper.]

Sara L. Gray, **Baptist Heritage: Bethlehem Baptist Church of Christ, 1823; 1st Baptist Church, 1973, Covington, Newton Co., Ga.** (Covington: 1st Baptist Church, 1973).

Mrs. Abram L. Loyd, **Newton Co., Ga., Marriages, 1822-1914** (n.p., 1976).

Silas E. Lucas, Jr., **Some Ga. Co. Records** 3 vols. (Easley, S.C.: Southern Historical Press, 1978). [Vol. 3, pp. 211-26, has Will Book 1, 1823-1851.]

William B. Williford, **Glory of Covington** (Atlanta: Cherokee Pub. Co., 1973).

Oconee

Frances W. Reid & Mary B. Warren, **Mars Hill Baptist Church (constituted 1799) Clarke Co., Oconee Co., Ga.** (Athens: Heritage Papers, 1966).

• Ga. Archives has a short manuscript history of Oconee Co. by Mrs. R.R. Burger.

Oglethorpe

Ga. Chapters DAR, **Historical Collections** 5 vols. (Atlanta & Athens: various printers, 1926-). [Vol. 5, pp. 149-210, has marriage records, 1795-1852.]

J.E. Hill, "Orphans of Oglethorpe Co., Ga., 1794-1806," **Nat'l. Genealogical Society Quarterly** 41 (1953), pp. 74-78. [Taken from inferior ct. min.]

Martha L. Houston, **Land Lottery List of Oglethorpe Co., 1804, & Hancock Co., 1806** (1928; rep. ed., Danielsville: Heritage Papers, 1968).

Silas E. Lucas, Jr., **Some Ga. Co. Records** 3 vols. (Easley, S.C.: Southern Historical Press, 1977). [Vol. 2, pp. 143-61, has wills, 1793-1826.]

Clarence Mohr, "Oglethorpe Co., Ga., During the Formative Period, 1773-1830," (Masters Thesis, Univ. of Ga., 1970).

Mrs. William L. Peel, **Historical Collections of Joseph Habersham Chapter DAR** 3 vols. (1926; rep. ed., Easley, S.C., Southern Historical Press, 1968). [Vol. 3, pp. 106-19, has lists of jurors, 1794; wills, 1794-1866; headrights, 1794-1800; & marriages, 1794-1798.]

Florrie C. Smith, **History of Oglethorpe Co., Ga.** (Washington, Ga.: Wilkes Pub. Co., 1970). [Supplement pub. 1972.]

Gussie Reese, **This They Remembered** (Washington, Ga.: Wilkes Pub. Co., 1965).

Sarah Q. Smith, **Oglethorpe Co., Wills** (Washington, Ga.: the author, 1962).

William C. Stewart, **Gone to Ga.: Jackson & Gwinnett Cos. & Their Neighbors in the Western Migration** (Washington, D.C.: Nat'l. Genealogical Society, 1965).

Lena Smith Wise, **A History of Oglethorpe Co.** (Athens: Univ. of Ga., 1953). [This dissertation has been reprinted as **The Story of Oglethorpe Co.** by Historic Oglethorpe Co., Inc., P.O. Box 1793, Lexington, Ga. 30648.]

• Ga. Archives has a typescript, "Abstracts of Oglethorpe Co., Ga., 1793-1834," (1956).

Paulding

Hubert G. Holland, **Brief History of Pegmore Creek, Raccoon Creek, the Old Log House and Pokey Hole [and Other Papers About Paulding Co.]** (Marietta: the author, 1975-1977). [Order from author at 7 Atlanta St., Suite A, Marietta, Ga. 30060. Holland has written more than 30 pamphlets on Paulding Co. churches, schools, & other sites. These are on file at the Ga. Archives & at several libraries in N. Ga. Contact author for complete list.]

• Ga. Archives has typescript copy of L.E. Roberts, "A History of Paulding Co., Dallas, Ga.," (1933). New history of Paulding Co. being prepared for publication by Taylor Pub. Co.

Peach

Gov. Treutlen Chapter DAR, **History of Peach Co.** (Atlanta: Cherokee Pub. Co., 1972).

Pickens

Lucius Eugene Tate, **History of Pickens Co.** (1935; rep. ed., Spartanburg, S.C.: The Reprint Co., 1978).

Charles O. Walker, **Through the Years — 1848-1963. A History of the 1st Baptist Church of Jasper, Ga.** (Jasper: the author, 1963). [Walker is currently preparing an updated ed. Both have info. on other Pickens churches.]

• Vol. of Pickens Co. cemetery records is currently being prepared for pub.

Pierce

Dean Broome, **History of Pierce Co., Ga.** (Blackshear: Broome Print. & Off. Sply., 1973)., vol. 1.

Alton J. Murray, **S. Ga. Rebels: True Wartime Expe. of 26th Reg., Ga. Vol. Inf.** (St. Mary's: author, 1976).

Nellie Stewart, **Recollections of Blackshear From 1857-1914** (Tampa: W.W. Edwards & Co., 1915).

Pike

Joyce H. Gossett, **Abstracts of Pike Co. Will Books A & B, 1826-1846** (E. Point: author, 1980). [Order from author at 2453 Constance St., E. Point, Ga. 30344.]

Historical Committee, **Sesquicentennial, 1822-1972, Pike Co., Ga.** (Zebulon: author, 1972).

Lizzie R. Mitchell, **History of Pike Co., Ga., 1822-1932** (1932; rep. ed., Easley: Southern Historical Press, 1980).

R.W. Rogers, **History of Pike Co. From 1822-1922** (Zebulon: author, 1972).

Barbara J. Smith, **Pike Co. Marriage Records, 1822-1836** (Hapeville: author, 1980). [Order from author at 3209 Forest Hills, Hapeville, Ga. 30354. Smith is preparing other books on Pike Co. for pub.]

Pulaski

Ga. Chapters DAR, **Historical Collections** 4 vols. (1926; rep. ed., Easley, S.C.: Southern Historical Press, 1968). [Vol. 1, pp. 83-4, has list of wills.]

Hawkinsville Chapter DAR, **History of Pulaski & Bleckley Cos., Ga., 1808-1956** (Macon: J.W. Burke Co., 1957-58). [Updated ed. of 1935 history, updated to incl. Bleckley Co.]

Putnam

Ga. Chapters DAR, **Historical Collections** 5 vols. (1926; rep. ed., Easley, S.C.: Southern Historical Press, 1968). [Vol. 1, pp. 84-96, has lists of wills & marriages.]

Edward F. Hull, **Early Records of Putnam Co., Ga., 1807-1860** (Ashland, Ala.: author, 1975). [Marriage, wills, & cemetery records.]

Silas E. Lucas, Jr., **Some Ga. Co. Records** 3 vols. (Easley, S.C.: Southern Historical Press, 1977). [Vol. 2, pp. 102-42, has wills, 1808-1857.]

Frances Wynd, **Putnam Co., Ga., Records** (Albany: author, 1966).

• Ga. Archives has W. Dennis Reid Collection of materials for Putnam Co. history (Microfilm Library).

Rabun

Andrew J. Ritchie, **Sketches of Rabun Co. History, 1819-1948** (1948; rep. ed., Clayton: author, 1959).

Randolph

Ga. Chapters DAR, **Historical Collections** 5 vols. (1926; rep. ed., Easley, S.C.: Southern Historical Press, 1968). [Vol. 1, pp. 35-43, has lists of wills & appraisements, jurors, & marriages.]

Iva P. Goolsby et al., **Randolph Co., Ga., a Compilation of Facts, Recollections, & Family Histories** (Columbus: Randolph Co. His. Society, 1977).

• The shortest official co. history for Ga. is a Randolph history, only 63 words long, found on microfilm reel 142-8 at Ga. Archives.

Richmond

Pat Bryant, **English Crown Grants for Islands in Ga., 1755-1775** (Atlanta: State Print. Off., 1972).

Edward J. Cashin, Jr., **The Story of Augusta** (Augusta: Richmond Co. Bd. of Ed., 1980). [Order from College Bookstore, Augusta College, Augusta, Ga. 30904. This book supersedes Cashin's **An Informal History of Augusta** (1978).]

Walter A. Clark, **A Lost Arcadia, or the Story of My Old Community** (Augusta: Chronicle, 1909).

Crawford Ave. Baptist Church, **A Progress Report . . . 85 Years of Crawford Ave. Bap. Church, Augusta, Ga.** (Augusta: author, 1955).

Grace G. Davidson, **Historical Collections of Ga. Chs. DAR** 4 vols. (1926; rep. ed., Southern Historical Press, 1968). [All of vol. 2 devoted to Richmond Co. records. Vol. 1, pp. 115-36, has list of marriages from St. Paul Church in Augusta.]

1st Presbyterian Church, **1st Presbyt. Church, Augusta, Ga., Birthplace of Sou. Presbyt. Assembly** (Augusta: author, n.d.).

Marion R. Hemperley, **English Crown Grants in St. Paul Parish in Ga., 1755-1775** (Atlanta: State Print. Off., 1974).

Hill Baptist Church, **1st Quarter Century Service for God, an Historical of Hill Baptist Church** (Augusta: Walton Print. Co., 1955).

Historical Records Survey, **Inventory of Co. Archives of Ga., #121, Richmond Co. (Augusta)** (Atlanta: author, 1939).

Charles C. Jones, Jr., & Salem Dutcher, **Memorial History of Augusta, Ga.** (1890; rep. ed., Spartanburg, S.C.: Reprint Co., 1980).

Lutheran Church of the Resurrection, **100 Years of Lutheranism in Augusta, Ga., 1856-1967** (Augusta: author, 1959).

Mrs. William L. Peel, **Historical Collections of Joseph Habersham Ch. DAR**, 3 vols. (1910; rep. ed., Southern Historical Press, 1968). [Vol. 3, pp. 119-26 has lists of: wills, 1777-1840; justices, jurors & constables, 1790; & marriages, 1806-1812.]

Lillian L. Powell et al., **Grave Markers in Burke Co., Ga., With 39 Cemeteries in 4 Adjoining Cos.** (Waynesboro: Chalker Pub. Co., 1974).

Richmond Co. His. Soc., **Historical Markers in Richmond Co., Ga.** (Augusta: Richmond Co. His. Soc., 1971).

Arthur R. Rowland, **Guide to the Study of Augusta & Richmond Co.** (Augusta: Richmond Co. His. Soc., 1967).

St. James Methodist Church, **A Chronicle of Christian Stewardship, St. James Meth. Church, 1856-1967** (Augusta: author, 1967).

St. Mary's on the Hill Church, **A History of St. Mary's on the Hill School & Church** (Augusta: Tidwell Print, 1961).

St. Paul's Episcopal Church, **History of St. Paul's Parish Episcopal Church** (Augusta: Tidwell Print., 1945).

Ada R. Walden, "History of Richmond Co.," (1936; rep. ed., Ann Arbor, Mich.: Univ. Microfilm Internat'l., 1975). [Copy of unpublished manuscript.]

Rockdale

Margaret G. Barksdale, **History of Rockdale Co.** (Conyers: Tom Hays Print. Co., 1978).

Robert W. Bevis, **History of the Conyers Presbyterian Church** (n.p., 1960?).

The Rockdale Citizen; Rockdale Co. Centennial Ed., 1871-1971 (Conyers: Citizen Pub. Co., 1971).

Schley

Steve Gurr, **Ellaville & Schley Co., an Historical Sketch for All Schley Countians, Yesterday, Today, Tomorrow** (Ellaville: Schley Co. Bicentennial Com., 1976).

Mrs. H.J. Williams, **History of Schley Co.** (n.p., 1933).

Screven

Clyde Hollingsworth, **Pioneer Days: a History of Early Years in Screven Co.** (Sylvania: author, 1947).

Mrs. William L. Peel, **Historical Collections of Joseph Habersham Ch. DAR**, 3 vols. (1926; rep. ed., Easley, S.C.: Southern Historical Press, 1968). [Vol. 3 has lists of: wills, 1806-1877; & marriages, 1837-1851.]

Lillian L. Powell et al., **Grave Markers in Burke Co., Ga., With 39 Cemeteries in 4 Adjoining Counties** (Waynesboro: Chalker Pub. Co., 1974).

Caroline P. Wilson, **Annals of Ga.: Important Early Records of the State** 2 vols. (1928-1933; rep. ed., Easley, S.C.: Southern Historical Press, 1969). [Vol. 2, pp. 134-59, has marriages, 1835-1860, & early wills.]

• A new history of Screven Co. by Dixon Hollingsworth will soon be in print.

Seminole

Lewis W. Rigsby, **Historic Ga. Families** (1925-1928; rep. ed., Baltimore: Genealogical Pub. Co., 1969).

• Seminole Co. history is now being prepared for pub.

Spalding

John H. Goddard, Jr., **History of 1st Baptist Church of Griffin, Ga., 1841-1977** (Atlanta: Cherokee Pub. Co., 1978).

Silas E. Lucas, Jr., **Some Early Ga. Records** 3 vols. (Easley, S.C.: Southern Historical Press, 1978). [Vol. 3, pp. 288-93, has 1845-1846 tax digests of Griffin, Ga.]

Quimby Melton, **History of Griffin** (Griffin: Griffin Daily News, 1959).

Stephens

Kathryn Curtis Trogdon, **History of Stephens Co., Ga. (1715-1972)** (Toccoa: Toccoa Womans Club, 1973).

Stewart

Helen E. Terrill & Sara R. Dixon, **History of Stewart Co., Ga.** 2 vols. (Vol. 1, Columbus: Columbus Off. Sply., 1958; vol. 2, Waycross: A.H. Clark, 1975).

• The Manuscript Section, Georgia Department of Archives and History, has the Sara R. (Mrs. Harry M.) Dixon Collection of papers relating to the History of Stewart County.

Sumter

Jacquelyn Cook, **From Violence to Love: History of DeSoto, Ga.** (DeSoto: author, 1969).

Mr. & Mrs. William D. Harvey, **Sumter Co., Ga., Cemetery Records** (Americus: M.M. Harvey, 1972).

William B. Williford, **Americus Through the Years: 1st 125 Years of a Ga. Town & Its People, 1831-1956** (Atlanta: author, 1975).

Talbot

Robert H. Jordan, **There Was a Land: a Story of Talbot Co., Ga., & Its People** (Columbus: Columbus Off. Sply., 1971).

Taliaferro

Alvin M. Lunceford, **Early Records of Taliaferro Co., Ga.** (Crawfordville: author, 1956).

Tattnall

Ga. Chapters DAR, **Historical Collections** 5 vols. (1926; rep. ed., Southern Historical Press, 1968). [Vol. 1, pp. 96-103, has lists of early deeds, wills, & marriages.]

Joseph T. Grice, **Sketches of Bygone Days: Historical Facts of Tattnall Co. & Her People as Gathered Together & Written by a Citizen Proud of His Heritage** (Glennville: author, 1958).

Joseph T. Grice, **History of 1st Baptist Church, Glennville, Ga., 1857-1951** (Glennville: author, 1958).

Telfair

Ga. Chapters DAR, **Historical Collections** 5 vols. (1926; rep. ed., Southern Historical Press, 1968). [Vol. 1, pp. 109-15, has list of marriages.]

Floris P. Mann, **History of Telfair Co. From 1812-1949** (1949; rep. ed., Spartanburg, S.C.: Reprint Co., 1978).

Terrell

Mrs. B.H. Hood, **Records & Reminiscences of Confederate Soldiers in Terrell Co.** (Dawson: News Print Co., 1914).

Stone Castle Chapter DAR, **History of Terrell Co.** (Dawson: n.d.).

Terrell Co.'s Centennial Panorama, 1856-1956, Dawson, Ga. (n.p., 1956).

• New Terrell Co. history now being prepared for pub.

• Ga. Archives has photostatic copy of typescript "History of Terrell Co.," by Mrs. Ivey C. Melton (1933); also Ella C. Melton & Augusta G. Raines "History of Terrell Co." (1970) on microfilm reel 227-54.

Thomas

Robert C. Balfour, **This Land I Have Loved** (Tallahassee: Rose Print. Co., 1975).

Lillian B. Heinaohn, **Saints & Sinners: the History of the 1st Presbyterian Church of Thomasville, Ga.** (author, 1967).

William I. MacIntyre, **History of Thomas Co., Ga., From the Time of DeSoto to the Civil War** (Thomasville: Times Enterprise, 1923).

Mary P. Robison, **1st Methodist Church, 1815-1951** (Thomasville: 1st Methodist Church, 1961).

William W. Rogers, **Ante-Bellum Thomas Co., 1825-1861** (Tallahassee: Fla. State Univ. Press, 1963).

William W. Rogers, **Thomas Co. During the Civil War** (Tallahassee: Fla. State Univ. Press, 1964).

William W. Rogers, **Thomas Co., 1865-1900** (Tallahassee: Fla. State Univ. Press, 1973).

Thomas Co. Public Schools, **Thomas Co. Folklore & Historical Data** (Thomas Co. Schools, 1951).

John Triplett, **Thomasville (Among the Pines) & Thomas Co., Ga.** (1891; rep. ed., Thomasville: Thomasville-Thomas Co. Ch. of Comm., 1967).

Vashti Blasingame Home & School for Girls, **A Narrative History of Vashti School, 1903-1959** (Thomasville: the school, 1959?).

• Ga. Archives has on microfilm the Elizabeth F. Hopkins Collection of materials for a Thomas Co. history.

Tift

Ida Belle Williams, **History of Tift Co.** (Macon: J.W. Burke Co., 1948).

Toombs

Amos M. Teasby, "The History of Toombs Co.," (Masters Thesis, Univ. of Ga., 1940).

Towns

Jerry A. Taylor, **Marriage Records, 1856-1900, Towns Co., Ga.** (Hiawassee: author, 1976?).

• Ga. Archives has the Jerry Taylor Collection of materials on Towns Co. history (microfilm reel 62-66).

Treutlen

J. Clayton Stephens, Jr., **Treutlen Co. Necrology** (Soperton: author, 1977). [Tombstone inscriptions.]

Troup

Chattahoochee Valley His. Soc., **Pioneer Members & History of Temple Beth-El & Diary of Private Louis Merz, CSA of W. Point Guards, 1862** (W. Point: author, 1959).

Chattahoochee Valley His. Soc., **W. Point on the Chattahoochee** (W. Point: author, 1957).

William H. Davidson, **Pine Log & Greek Revival: Houses & People of Three Cos. in Ga. & Ala.** (Alexander City, Ala.); [Outlook Publishing Co., 1964.]

William H. Davidson, **Proudest Inheritance, a Bicentennial Tribute** (W. Point: Chattahoochee Val. His. Soc., 1975).

William H. Davidson, **This Was Our Valley: Photogravures of 1901** (W. Point: Chatt. Val. His Soc., 1973).

William H. Davidson, **Valley Historical Scrapbook** (W. Point: Chatt. Val. His. Soc., 1970).

1st Baptist Church of LaGrange, **150 Years of History, 1st Baptist Church of LaGrange, Ga., 1828-1978** (LaGrange: Troup Co. Baptist Assoc., 1980). [Includes list of church members, 1828-1843.]

John H. Jones, **Americanism: World War History of Troup Co., Ga.** (Atlanta: Webb & Vary, 1919).

Clifford L. Smith, **History of Troup Co.** (Atlanta: Foote & Davies, 1935).

• Ga. Archives has Fred D. Cooper, "Hogansville Scrapbook."

Turner

John B. Pate, **History of Turner Co.** (1933; rep. ed., Spartanburg, S.C.: Reprint Co., 1970).

Twiggs

Kathleen J. Carswell, **Collections of Twiggs Countians Here & There** (n.p., 1973).

Lanette O. Faulk, **Historical Collections of Richland Baptist Church** (Macon: J.W. Burke Co., 1950).

Lanette O. Faulk & Billy W. Jones, **History of Twiggs Co., Ga.: Sesquicentennial, 1809-1959** (1960; rep. ed. Easley: Southern Historical Press, 1969).

Billy W. Jones et al., **History of Ebenezer Missionary Baptist Church Assoc. (of Ga.), 1814-1964** (Dry Branch: authors, 1965).

Billy W. Jones, **History of Stone Creek Baptist Church, Twiggs Co., Ga., 1808-1958** (Columbus: author, 1961).

J.L. Lawson, **History of Twiggs Co., Ga.** (Columbus: Major Gen. John Twiggs Chapter DAR, 1960).

Eleanor D. McSwain, **Abstracts of Some Documents of Twiggs Co., Ga.** (Macon: Nat'l. Print. Co., 1972).

Alton J. Murray, **S. Ga. Rebels: True Wartime Experiences of 26th Reg., Ga. Vol. Inf., Lawton-Gordon-Evans Brigade Confed. States Army, 1861-1865** (St. Mary's: author, 1976).

Union

Ken Akins et al., **Mountain Relic** 2 vols. to date (Blairsville: authors, 1980-).

Ernst V. Brender & Elliott Merrick, "Early Settlement & Land Use in the Present Toccoa Experimental Forest," **Scientific American** 71 (1950), pp. 318-25. [On the Mulkey Creek community.]

C.R. Collins et al., **Sketches of Union Co., a Pictorial History of Union Co.** 2 vols. (Blairsville: Union Co. His. Soc., 1976).

Edward L. Shuler, **Blood Mountain: an Historical Story About Choestoe & Choestoeans** (Jacksonville, Fla.: Convention Press, 1953).

• Ga. Archives has Lassie A.C. Brackett, "Scrapbook of Obituaries & Births, Fannin & Union Cos., Ga." compiled from now-lost newspapers. (G 975.8 Fannin). Univ. of Ga. libraries has on microfilm Preston Turner, "History of Union Co., Ga.," (1959).

Upson

Jack Morgan, **Upson Co., Ga. Cemeteries** (Danielsville: Heritage Papers, 1969).

Caroline W. Nottingham & Evelyn Hannah, **History of Upson Co., Ga.** (1930; rep. ed., Easley, S.C.: Southern Historical Press, 1969).

Walker

Flora Mae Patterson et al., **Index for History of Walker Co.** (LaFayette: Cherokee Regional Library, 1978).

James A. Sartain, **History of Walker Co., Ga.** (Dalton: A.J. Showalter Co., 1932).

Walton

John L. McKinnon, **History of Walton Co.** (Atlanta: Byrd Printing Co., 1911).

Anita B. Smith, **Wayfarers in Walton: a History of Walton Co., Ga., 1818-1967** (Monroe: General Charitable Found. of Monroe, 1967). [Ga. Archives' copy is footnoted.]

Celebrating Walton's Sesquicentennial. Supplement to the Walton Tribune (Monroe: Walton Tribune, Dec. 11, 1968).

Ware

Alton J. Murray, **S. Ga. Rebels: True Wartime Experiences of 26th Ga. Reg., Ga. Vol. Inf., Lawton-Gordon-Evans Brigade, Confed. States Army, 1861-1865** (St. Mary's: author, 1976).

Laura S. Walker, **History of Ware Co., Ga.** (1934; rep. ed., Easley, S.C.: Southern Historical Press, 1974).

Warren

Mary Carter, **A Century of Warren Co., Ga., Wills, 1790-1890** (1968) & Warren Co., Ga.: **Early Marriage Records** (1966) (Albany: Ga. Pioneers).

Silas E. Lucas, Jr., **Some Ga. Co. Records** 3 vols. (Easley, S.C.: Southern Historical Press, 1971). [Vol. 1, pp. 184-391, has deeds, 1794-1808; marr., 1794-1814, & wills, 1794-1852.]

Mrs. William L. Peel, **Historical Collections of Joseph Habersham Chapter DAR** 3 vols. (1910; rep. ed., Easley: Sou. Historical Press, 1967). [Vol. 3, pp. 135-50, has list of wills & marr.]

Virginia H. Wilhoit, **History of Warren Co., Ga., 1793-1974** (Washington, Ga.: Wilkes Pub. Co., 1976).

• Ga. Archives has 7 vols. of typescripts of Warren Co. records by Virginia Hill Wilhoit.

Washington

James E. Dorsey, **Emanuel Co. Legal Notices: Pre-1860 Notices Appearing in Selected Ga. Newspapers** (Swainsboro: Emanuel Historic Preservation Soc., 1978), pp. 1-2, 4-5.

Ella Mitchell, **History of Washington Co.** (Atlanta: Byrd Print. Co., 1924).

Elizabeth P. Newsome, **Washington Co., Ga., 1825 Tax Digest** (Sandersville: author, 1968).

Elizabeth P. Newsom, **Washington Co., Ga., Tombstone Inscriptions** (Sandersville: author, 1967).

John W. Wilkins, **The Central Georgian: Abstracts of Death Notices & Obits. From 1852-1855** (Lufkin, Tex.: n.d.) [Washington Co. obituaries.]

Frances Wynd, **Washington Co., Ga., Records** (Albany: author, 1966).

• Manuscripts Sec., Ga. Archives, has the Annie Louise Irwin Collection, incl. "Georgia Bicentennial, 1733-1933: Contributions of Washington Co.

Wayne

Folks Huxford, **Pioneers of Wiregrass Ga.: a Biographical Account of Some of the Original Counties of Irwin, Appling, Wayne, Camden, & Glynn** 7 vols. (Adel: Patten Pub. Co., 1951-1967).

Margaret C. Jordan, **Wayne Miscellany** (Jesup: The Jesup Sentinel, 1976).

Alton J. Murray, **S. Ga. Rebels: True Wartime Experiences of 26th Reg., Ga. Vol. Inf., Lawton-Gordon-Evans Brigade, Confed. States Army, 1861-1865** (St. Mary's: author, 1976).

Webster

• A Webster Co. history is being prepared for publication through W.H. Wolf Associates.

Whitfield

Mrs. R.M. Herron et al., **Official History of Whitfield Co., Ga.** (Dalton: A.J. Showalter, 1936).

Wilkes

Alden Associates, **"Ceded Lands": Records of St. Paul Parish & Early Wilkes Co., Ga.** (Albany: authors, 1964).

Lundie W. Barlow, "Some Va. Settlers of Ga., 1773-1798," **The Va. Genealogist** 2 (1958), pp. 19-27.

Bartram Trail Regional Library, **Washington-Wilkes History & Genealogy, a Bibliography** (Washington, Ga.: authors, 1978).

Grace G. Davidson, **Early Records of Ga., Wilkes Co.** 2 vols. (1932; rep. ed., Easley, S.C.: Southern Historical Press, 1968). [Includes Ceded Lands journal (1773-1775; provides the state from which each family came), 1779 court minutes, and abstracts of estate, deed, & marriage records.]

Robert S. Davis, Jr., **Kettle Creek Battle & Battlefield** (Washington, Ga.: Wilkes Pub. Co., 1978). [Includes lists of all known soldiers.]

Robert S. Davis, Jr., **Wilkes Co. Papers, 1773-1833** (Easley, S.C.: Southern Historical Press, 1979). [Abstracts of loose Wilkes Co. records.]

George R. Gilmer, **Sketches of the 1st Settlers of Upper Ga.** (1855; rep. ed. Genealogical Pub. Co., 1965).

Marion R. Hemperley, **English Crown Grants in St. Paul Parish in Ga., 1755-1775** (Atlanta: State Print. Off., 1974).

Alex M. Hitz, "Earliest Settlements in Wilkes Co.," **Ga. Historical Quarterly** 40 (1956), pp. 260-80.

F.M. & Nell H. Newsome, **Wilkes Co. Cemeteries & a Few From Adjoining Cos.** (Washington, Ga.: Wilkes Pub. Co., 1970).

Mrs. William L. Peel, **Historical Collections of Joseph Habersham Chapter DAR** 3 vols. (1910-; rep. ed., Southern Historical Press, 1967). [Vol. 3, pp. 150-72, includes lists of: justices & jurors, 1779; traitors to be hanged, 1779; wills and mixed records, 1777-1783; wills, 1801-1836; administrators records, 1800-1819; guardians bonds, 1822-1828; early marriages; & deed rec.]

Jo Randall, **Wilkes County Churches** (Washington, Ga.: Wilkes Pub. Co., 1970).

Sarah Q. Smith, **Early Ga. Wills & Settlements of Estates, Wilkes Co.** (1959); rep. ed., Danielsville: Heritage Papers, 1971.

Janet H. Standard, **Wilkes Co. Scrapbook** 2 vols. (Washington: Wilkes Pub. Co., 1970-1972).

Mary B. Warren, **Chronicles of Wilkes Co. Ga., From Washington Newspapers, 1889-1899** (Danielsville: Heritage Papers, 1978). [Articles by Eliza Bowen, Rev. F.T. Simpson, S.A. Wooten, & others. Includes contents of Eliza Bowen, **Story of Wilkes Co., Ga.**]

Robert M. Willingham, Jr., **No Jubilee: the Story of Confederate Wilkes** (Washington, Ga.: Wilkes Pub. Co., 1976).

Robert M. Willingham, Jr., **We Have This Heritage: the History of Wilkes Co., Ga., Beginning to 1860** (Washington: Wilkes Pub. Co., 1969).

• Ga. Archives has C. Willis Lindsay, "A History of Washington, Wilkes Co., Ga." (1922) on microfilm reel 45-22.

Wilkinson

Victor Davidson, **History of Wilkinson Co.** (1930; rep. ed., Spartanburg, S.C.: Reprint Co., 1978).

Billy W. Jones et al., **History of Ebenezer Missionary Baptist Assoc. of Ga., 1814-1964** (Dry Branch: author, 1965).

Joseph T. Maddox, **Wilkinson Co., Ga., Historical Collections** (Irwinton: author, 1973). [Was updated in 1978.]

Joseph T. Maddox, **Wills & Cemeteries, Wilkinson Co., Ga., 1817-1920** (Irwinton: author, 1977).

Worth

Barnard Trail Chapter DAR, **History of Worth Co., Ga., vol. II for the 3rd 40 Years, 1934-1974** (Ann Arbor, Mich.: Edwards Brothers, 1975).

Lillie M. Grubbs, **History of Worth Co., Ga., for the 1st 80 Years, 1854-1934** (Macon: J.W. Burke Co., 1934).

12
GLOSSARY OF TERMS

The following lists of terms used in Georgia county records have been compiled by Archives personnel over the years and is reproduced here through the courtesy of Sally Moseley, JoAnne Smalley, and Jane Adams of the Microfilm Library. Other very valuable sources for definitions of legal terms encountered in Georgia search are Mary Warren, "Obscure Phrases, Abbreviations, and Legal Terms," **Family Puzzlers** (August 19-26, 1971). nos. 200-1; Shelby Myrick, Jr., **Glossary of Legal Terminology: An Aid to Genealogists** (American Association for State and Local History Technical Leaflet no. 55), which can be ordered from the association at 1400 Eighth Avenue, South, Nashville, Tn. 37203; and Henry Campbell Black, **Black's Law Directory**, which should be available in one of its several editions at almost any public or college library.

LEGAL TERMINOLOGY APPEARING IN ESTATE RECORDS

Administration cum testamento annexo
Administration with the will annexed. Administration granted in cases where the testator makes a will without naming an executor or where the executor named is incompetent to act or refuses to act; or in the case of the death of the executor named.

Administration de bonis non
Administration of the goods not administered by the former administrator or executor.

Administration de bonis non cum testamento annexo
A type of administration which is granted when an executor dies leaving a part of the estate unadministered.

Administration of estates
The management and settlement and distribution of estates by either an executor or administrator. The administration is performed under the supervision of the court by a person duly qualified and legally appointed and usually involved: (1) collection of decedent's assets, (2) payment of debts and claims against the estate and expenses, and (3) distributing the remainder of the estate among those entitled thereto.

Administration pendite lite
Administration during suit. Administration granted during the pendency of a suit concerning the validity of a will.

Annual returns
A yearly report on the disposition of a deceased person's goods or property made to the court by an administrator or executor.

Appraisements
An estimated or actual valuation of articles of property of a deceased person.

Bequest
Testamentary disposition of the testator's personalty (synonymous with legacy).

Codicil
An addition or supplement to a will to alter the provisions of a will. It must be executed with the same formality as a will; and when admitted to probate, it forms a part of the will.

Collateral consanguinity
That which subsists between the same persons who have the same ancestors but who do not descend (or ascend) one from the other. Uncle and nephew are related by collateral consanguinity.

Consanguinity
Kinship or blood relationship. The connection or relation of persons descended from the same stock (as opposed to affinity, which is the connection existing in consequence of marriage).

Coparcerners
Persons to whom an estate of inheritance descends jointly. The right of possession is in common, though the respective shares may be unequal.

Decedent
A deceased person, testate or intestate.

Devise
A testamentary disposition of land or realty.

Dismission
Discharge by the court of an executor or administrator who has completed his duties in regard to an estate's administration.

Division
Apportionment among heirs of an estate.

Dower
The right of a wife to an estate for life in one-third of the lands, according to valuation, including the dwelling house (which is not to be valued unless in a town or city), of which the husband was seized and possessed at the time of his death, or to which the husband obtained title in right of his wife. (See Ga. Code Annotated 31:101.)

Emblements
Growing crops regarded as personal property which pass to executor or administrator of the occupier of land (i.e., one who grew them). The term is synonymous with vegetable chattels.

Heir
A person who succeeds by the operation of the laws of descent and distribution of an estate in lands, tenements or hereditaments on the death of his ancestor by descent or rights of relationship.

Holographic Will
Will written entirely in the handwriting of the testator (no longer legal in Georgia).

Inheritance
Property obtained through laws of descent and distribution from the estate of a deceased person.

Intestate
Without making a will. The word is often used to identify the person himself, the one who died without making a will.

Inventory
A detailed list or schedule of the articles of property of a deceased person.

Legacy
Testamentary disposition of property (synonymous with bequest).

Letters of Administration
The instrument of appointment issued by a court by which an administrator is authorized to take charge and administer the goods and property of an intestate.

Letters of Testamentary
An instrument granted by a court to an executor empowering him to enter upon the discharge of his duties as executor of an estate.

Lineal Consanguinity
That which subsists between persons of whom one is descended in a direct line from the other, as between son, father, grandfather, great-grandfather and so up in the direct ascending line; or between son, grandson, great-grandson and so downwards in the direct descending line.

Mutual Will
A will made jointly or separately by two persons, the revocation of one is the destruction of the other. Such a will implies reciprocal action.

Nuncupative Will
Oral will declared by a testator in extremis, or under circumstances considered equivalent thereto, before witnesses and afterwards reduced to writing.

Partition of a succession
A division of the effects of which a succession is composed among all the co-heirs according to their respective rights. A partition may be voluntary or judicial. If voluntary, then by mutual consent. If judicial, then made with the authority of the court according to formalities prescribed by law.

Per capita
By the head; i.e., according to the number of individuals, share alike.

Per stirpes

By root or stock, by representation. That method of dividing an intestate estate where a class or group of distributees take the share which their deceased ancestor would have been entitled to taking thus by their right of representing such ancestors and not as so many individuals.

Probate

Proof of a will; i.e., act or process of proving a will in a court of law having jurisdiction over estate matters. The residence of the testator at death usually determines where the will shall be offered for probate. Probate may be in solemn or common form. The principle difference between probate in common and solemn form is that while probate in either form will prove and admit a will to record, probate in common form is not conclusive on all the parties until after a statutory period elapses; probate in solemn form is conclusive of the will's validity. The application to probate a will concludes with a prayer for issuance of letters testamentary.

Residuary devisee

Person named in a will who is to take all the real property remaining after other devisees have been satisfied.

Residuary legatee

The person to whom the testator bequeaths the remainder of his personal property after the payment of such other legacies as are specifically mentioned in the will.

Residue

Surplus of a testator's estate remaining after all debts and particular legacies and devises have been discharged.

Rules of Inheritance (See page 260.)

Sale

A transfer of title and right of possession of property for a consideration.

Temporary letters of administration

May be granted by the court upon any unrepresented estate for the purpose of collecting and taking care of the effects of the deceased and such letters are to continue and give effect until permanent letters are granted. From orders granting temporary letters there is usually no appeal.

Tax Digests

A list of taxable landowners in a county and the amount of tax paid or owing and the location of the land.

Tenements

Franchises, rents and several other interests arising out of land.

Venue

Place at which the action is tried. A county of geographical division in which an action or prosecution is brought for trial. (A change of venue is a transfer of a cause to another jurisdiction.)
Divorce: county of defendant's residence if a resident of this state.
Land Titles: county where land lies.
Equity: Defendant's county of residence.

Joint Obligors or Co-partners: county of residence of either.

Maker or Endorser: county where the maker or the acceptor resides.

Other Civil Cases: county where the defendant resides.

Criminal Cases: county where crime is committed — subject to change of
venue in a non-impartial jury situation.

Warranty Deed

One which contains a covenant of warranty, of title and right of possession.
It is given contemporaneously with a contract or deed.

Wild Lands

Land in a state of nature or wilderness state as opposed to improved or
cultivated land.

Writ

An order or direction of the court of justice in writing commanding performance of a certain act either by the sheriff or an individual.

LEGAL TERMINOLOGY APPEARING IN COURT RECORDS OTHER THAN ESTATE

Abstract of Title

In an abstract of title, each link in the chain of title is given in chronological order; and every written instrument, decree, or other conveyance that
shows an interest or lien on the property is given. Such liens are commonly:
deeds to secure debt, security deed, loan deed, mortgages, mechanics liens,
judgments, judicial sales, attachment proceedings, taxes, tax sales and
charges. An abstract also shows how property is acquired; and if by descent, whether the probate proceedings have been had in order to transfer
the title properly, and that all claims against the estate have been settled
according to law. An abstractor also checks on marriage records, divorce
records, year's support records, local paving, etc., assessments and bank-
ruptcies.

Appellant

The party who takes an appeal from one court or jurisdiction to another.

Appellee

The party against whom an appeal is taken; i.e., party answering to or op-
posing an appeal.

Apprenticeship

A contract by which one person, usually a minor, called an apprentice is
bound to another person, called a master, to serve him during a prescribed
term of years in his art, trade or business; in consideration of being in-
structed by the master in such art, trade or business, and of receiving support and maintenance from the master during such a term.

Banns of Matrimony

Public notice or proclamation of a matrimonial contract and the intended
celebration of the marriage of the parties in pursuance of such a contract.

Chain of Title

Series of successive conveyances from the original grantor to present owner
(each instrument included is a "link" in the "chain" of title).

Chancery
A court of equity or the system of jurisprudence administered in courts of equity.

Choses in Action
A right to personal things which the owner has not the possession thereof but merely a right of action for their possession.

Declarations
Pleadings; i.e., statement of a cause of action.

Deed
A conveyance passing a present interest (as opposed to a will which passes no interest until after the death of the maker).

Deed of Gift
A voluntary conveyance or assignment of land or transfer of goods made without a consideration; i.e., gratuitously.

Deponent
One who deposes (that is, testifies or makes an oath, in writing) to the truth of certain facts.

Docket
A list or calendar of causes set for trial at a specified term of court.

Easement
A right in the owner of one parcel of land by reasons of such ownership to use the land of another for special purposes not inconsistent with the general property of the owner; i.e., right of way.

Equity
A body of jurisprudence or field of jurisdiction differing in its origin, theory and method from the common law.

Emoluments
Profit arising from office or employment; i.e., compensation for services.

Estrays
Wandering or strayed cattle or animals whose owner is unknown to the person who takes it up.

Fee Simple Estate
The largest estate and most extensive interest in land, being the entire property therein, and it confers an unlimited power of alienation (synonymous with: Absolute Estate, Fee Simple).

Grantee
The person to whom a grant is made.

Grantor
The person by whom a grant is made.

Guardian
One who legally has the care and management of the person or estate or both of a child during its minority, or of another adult who for some peculiarity of status, or defect of age, self-control or understanding, is considered incapable of administering his own affairs.

Heriditaments

Things capable of being inherited be it corporeal or incorporeal, real, personal or mixed, including land and everything thereon. (The term includes a few rights unconnected with land, but it is generally used as the widest expression for real property of all kinds and is therefore employed in conveyances after the words "lands and tenements" to include everything of the nature of realty which they do not cover.)

Homestead

A house and land designated by the head of a family as subject to tax exemption of a certain amount allowed by law.

Inferior Court

A constitutional tribunal abolished by the 1868 Constitution of Georgia. (Its functions were assumed by the Ordinary of each county.)

Indenture

A deed to which two or more persons are parties and in which these enter into reciprocal and corresponding grants or obligations toward each other.

Land Court

A court composed of three Inferior Court Justices sitting as a court to issue warrants for survey of land.

Marks and Brands

A character made as a substitute for purposes of identification.

Minor

A person under the age of legal competence, one less than 21 years of age.

Minutes

Memoranda of a court's proceedings.

Moiety

The half of everything.

Mortgage

Under the Common Law was a conditional sale of property designed as a security for the payment of a debt or performance of some other obligation subject to the condition that upon performance, title revests in the mortgagor. Under the modern view, a mortgage is a mere lien and does not create title or estate though it is cast in the form of a conveyance.

Personalty

Personal property or chattels; i.e., things which are movable in point of law as opposed to realty or real property.

Petition

An application in writing made to a court praying for the exercise of judicial power of the court in relation to some matter.

Plat

A map or representation on paper of a piece of land which may be subdivided into small lots or parcels of land and is usually drawn to scale.

Pleadings

Formal allegations by the parties of their respective claims and defenses for the judgment of the court.

Pony Homestead
Personal property designated by the head of the household for purposes of tax exemption.

Power of Attorney
An instrument authorizing another to act as one's agent.

Quitclaim Deed
A deed of conveyance operating by way of release intending to pass title, interest or claim of grantor. It does not warrant or profess that title is valid.

Register of Charters
A register of charters is a listing of corporations authorized to do business within a state. In Georgia, the charter must be registered with the secretary of state. The superior court of each county contains a register of each corporation incorporated in such county.

Sale
Absolute transfer of property or goods in which title passes to the buyer.

Voucher
A receipt or release which may serve as evidence of payment or discharge of a debt or certify to the correctness of an account.

Will
The legal declaration of a person's intention as to the disposition of his property after his death. Usually names the wife, children, and sometimes other family members. Sometimes children are not named or even mentioned.

Year's Support
Land or property of the deceased husband set aside out of his estate for widow for the support of herself and minor children for twelve months. Title to property set aside as year's support vests in the widow — and on her death, to her minor children — and is not subject to sale for her debts or her husband's; i.e., this estate set aside is not administered as the estate of the deceased husband or father or widow. (Note: The right of widow to year's support did not exist at common law.) (See Ga. Code Annotated Title 113:1002.)

RULES OF INHERITANCE (Ga. Code Annotated 113:903)

The following rules shall determine who are the heirs at law of a deceased person: (1) Upon the death of the husband without lineal descendants, the wife is his sole heir; and upon the payment of his debts, if any, may take possession of his estate without administration; (2) Whenever the husband or widow of a deceased person shall be under the age of 21 years and entitled to a share in the estate of such deceased husband or wife, he or she shall be entitled to take and hold such share without the intervention of a guardian or other trustee; (3) If upon the death of the husband, there are children — or representatives of deceased children — the wife shall have a child's part unless the shares exceed five in number, in which case the wife shall have one-fifth part of the estate. If the wife shall elect to take her dower, she shall have no further interest in the realty; (4) Children shall stand in the first degree from the intestate and inherit equally all property of every description, accounting for advancements as hereinafter provided. Posthumous children shall stand upon the same footing with children in being upon all questions of inheritance. The lineal descendants of children shall stand in the place of their deceased parents; but in all cases of inheritance from a lineal ancestor, the distribution is per stirpes and not per capita; (5) Brothers and sisters of the intestate shall stand in the second degree and shall inherit if there is no widow, child, or representative of a child. The half-blood, both on the paternal and maternal side, shall inherit equally with the whole blood. The children and grandchildren of brothers and sisters deceased shall represent and stand in the place of their deceased parents, but there shall be no representation further than this among collaterals. If all the brothers and sisters be dead at the death of the intestate, then the distribution is between the nephews and nieces, per capita; and if any of the nephews and nieces be dead, leaving children, distribution is to be made as though the nephews and nieces were all alive — the children of the deceased nephew or niece standing in place of the parent; (6) The father and mother inherit equally with brothers and sisters and stand in the same degree; (7) In all degrees more remote than the foregoing, the paternal and maternal next of kin shall stand on equal footing; (8) First cousins stand in next degree; uncles and aunts inherit equally with cousins; (9) The more remote degrees shall be determined by the rules of the canon law as adopted and enforced in the English courts prior to the fourth day of July, A.D. 1776.

GENERAL SUBJECT AND COUNTY INDEX

Jasper (created 1807 as Randolph County;name changed to Jasper County in 1812), 24, 43, 116, 117, 158, 178, 234

Jeff Davis (created 1905 from Appling and Coffee Counties), 117, 204

Jefferson (created 1796 from Burke and Warren Counties), 29, 117, 158, 159, 178, 204, 234, 235

Jenkins (created 1905 from Bulloch, Burke, Emanuel, and Screven Counties), 117, 205, 235

Johnson (created 1858 from Washington, Emanuel, and Laurens Counties), 118, 159, 178, 209, 235

Jones (created 1807 from Baldwin County), 43, 118, 159, 178, 209, 235

Kinchafoonee (see Webster)

Lamar (created 1920 from Monroe and Pike Counties), 119, 235

Lanier (created 1920 from Berrien, Clinch, and Lowndes Counties), 119, 235

Laurens (created 1807 from Wilkinson County), 44, 119, 159, 178, 209, 235, 236

Lee (created 1825 from Indian lands), 43, 119, 159, 178, 236

Liberty (created 1777 from Colonial Georgia), 119, 120, 159, 178, 205, 209, 236, 237

Lincoln (created 1796 from Wilkes County), 43, 120, 121, 159, 178, 204, 209, 237

Long (created 1920 from Liberty County), 121

Lowndes (created 1825 from Irwin County), 40, 121, 160, 178, 204, 237

Lumpkin (created 1832 from Cherokee County), 121, 160, 178, 209, 237

Macon (created 1837 from Houston and Marion Counties), 122, 160, 179, 209, 237

Madison (created 1811 from Oglethorpe, Clarke, Jackson, Franklin, and Elbert Counties), 43, 122, 160, 179, 209, 238

Marion (created 1827 from Lee and Muscogee Counties), 122, 123, 160, 179, 209, 238

McDuffie (created 1870 from Warren and Columbia Counties), 123, 179, 204, 238

McIntosh (created 1793 from Liberty County), 28, 43, 123, 160, 179, 204, 238

Meriwether (created 1827 from Troup County), 123, 124, 161, 179, 238, 239

Miller (created 1856 from Baker and Early Counties), 124, 161, 179, 204, 239

Milton (created 1857 from Cherokee, Cobb, and Forsyth Counties; abolished and merged with Fulton County in 1932), 124, 125, 161, 179

Mitchell (created 1857 from Baker County), 125, 161, 204, 239

Monroe (created 1821 from Indian lands), 43, 125, 161, 179, 209, 239

Montgomery. (created 1793 from Washington County), 24, 126, 161, 173, 179, 209, 239

Morgan (created 1807 from Baldwin County), 24, 43, 126, 161, 162, 179, 209, 239, 240

Murray (created 1832 from Cherokee County), 63, 127, 162, 179, 209, 240

Muscogee (created 1825 from Indian lands), 28, 43, 51, 127, 162, 179, 209, 240, 241

Newton (created 1821 from Jasper, Walton, and Henry Counties), 44, 127, 128, 162, 179, 209, 241

Oconee (created 1875 from Clarke County), 128, 241

266